Information Science

Information Science

Edited by
Fabrice Papy

ISTE

WILEY

First published 2008 in France by Hermes Science/Lavoisier entitled: *Problématiques émergentes dans les sciences de l'information* © LAVOISIER, 2008
First published 2010 in Great Britain and the United States by ISTE Ltd and John Wiley & Sons, Inc.

ISTE Ltd
27-37 St George's Road
London SW19 4EU
UK

www.iste.co.uk

John Wiley & Sons, Inc.
111 River Street
Hoboken, NJ 07030
USA

www.wiley.com

Library of Congress Cataloging-in-Publication Data

Problématiques émergentes dans les sciences de l'information. English.
Information science / edited by Fabrice Papy.
p. cm.
Includes bibliographical references and index.
ISBN 978-1-84821-168-1
1. Information science. 2. Information technology. I. Papy, Fabrice. II. Title.
Z665.P94313 2009
020--dc22

2009038815

British Library Cataloguing-in-Publication Data
A CIP record for this book is available from the British Library
ISBN 978-1-84821-168-1

Printed and bound in Great Britain by CPI Antony Rowe, Chippenham and Eastbourne.

FSC
Mixed Sources
Product group from well-managed forests and other controlled sources
Cert no. SGS-COC-2953
www.fsc.org
© 1996 Forest Stewardship Council

Table of Contents

Preface

Writing the preface for a collective scientific work is a particularly demanding exercise as it announces – such is its vocation – the purpose of a book that has just been completed and which has long kept the secret of its coherence. It is only once the last chapter is added that the scientific coordinator, the thematic initiator, better grasps through a vision that is now whole the strong points, weak points, points of strong stability and weak equilibrium of this work which he/she has accompanied over several months.

In spite of a directing strategy and a starting pulse determined with the editorial vision of the scientific coordinator, that which he/she was given to perceive as the collective piece was developed for each chapter, with each author. That which was the object of exchanges, adjustments and clarifications unveiled neither the global structure of the work nor the articulation points and routes which each author is capable of having. Each author preserves this, in spite of him/herself, up until the moment he/she hands in the version of his contribution that he/she feels is the most successfully completed.

Finally, it is when the deadline for handing in the collective typescript is near that the fluidity and articulation of the different scientific contributions must be decided. Finally, among numerous possibilities, the sequencing of chapters is accomplished. A journey across the parts and chapters is therefore brought to light through the *raison d'être* of this preface explaining the circumstantial outlook through which the work managed to be organized, and therefore be offered for reading.

Let us stop for a moment on the title of the work as it will remain, implicitly or explicitly, the leading thread of different scientific contributions gathered around the thematic approach.

The great majority of authors participating in *Information Science* are professors in information and communication sciences. This scientific discipline, which gathers a few hundred members, concerns the study of information and communication processes.

Institutional stakeholders – essentially professors – within the information and communication sciences section, working towards their missions of public service in higher learning establishments, are wholly linked to this intimate information and communication union. Yet grass-roots university reality, scientific as well as educational, shows that some fields of research are mainly harvested by information science researchers while others remain the domain of scientific efforts of communication science researchers.

Although places for meeting and exchanging ideas exist, like the unavoidable mix of information and communication in institutional research teams, members of information and communication science are like two sides of the same coin. They share the material but remain on sides that, often, outshine each other. The presence in universities of training and research departments dedicated to "information-documentation", "art and culture" or even "culture and communication" proves the preponderance of information science on the one hand, and communication science on the other.

The creation in 2007 of the Communication Sciences Institute of the CNRS[1] (ISCC)[2] stresses that communication science represents, for itself only, an interdisciplinary theoretical object and a theory of knowledge. On another side, the French National School of Library and Information Sciences (ENSSIB[3]) has a mission to develop research in information sciences, library science, and history of the book. This is despite it remaining the place for training library and information executives (curators, librarians, masters). The Information Society for Knowledge Organization[4] (ISKO), which has French[5], Indian, German, Italian, etc. chapters, and favors research and exchanges, is in the domain of knowledge organization in information sciences and all related disciplines.

---

1. The CNRS is the French National Center for Scientific Research, a science and technology agency operating under the auspices of the French Ministry of Research. It operates through its own laboratories, as well as others run jointly with universities, fellow research organizations, and industry.
2. http://www.iscc.cnrs.fr.
3. http://www.enssib.fr.
4. http://www.isko.org.
5. http://www.isko-france.asso.fr/.

(All websites accessed October 5, 2009.)

From this point of view, the research activities I have been leading for several years on thematics linked to:

– the hypertext (considered as concept, technology, system, method, etc);

– the accessibility of information and knowledge;

– the technological mediation carried by information and communication technology in organized documentary environments of hybrid libraries;

– the impacts on issues related to use, users and appropriation of these new digital environments;

are fields of research that are more or less embraced by information science.

In spite of the lurking political and economic discourse that accompanies the techno-informational abundance from which the information society monolithically emerges, novel situations appear, questions become clear, complexities are revealed. All this at the level of individuals who are supposed to maintain a satisfying activity in this changing society as well as at the level of the societal macrostructure which must find (once again) a new stability.

We can easily illustrate our aim through the conclusions taken in 2007 by the European Union Council concerning access, distribution and conservation of scientific and technical information in the digital era[6]. With regards to the problematics identified by many researchers, problematics related to archiving of structured or un-structured data, accessibility and sharing, intellectual property, digital documentation, information retrieval, methods of interaction with technical systems, information literacy, information qualification and relevance, information profiles, etc. the invitations addressed by the European Union Council to Member States in order that an intra-state plan of these conclusions is quickly initiated, can only arouse circumspection, even embarrassment, from a scientific point of view.

Indeed, the most recent scientific approaches are always convened and tested on fields that are supposed to be fully identified, whose implementation order in Europe now seems to be inevitable. Furthermore, this collective work, made up of 12 original chapters from information and communication science researchers, attests the sensitive character of some scientific problematics. These problematics exhaustively presented in this volume, which are old for some areas and more recently formulated for others, were brought to light by the new digital era.

---

6. Council Conclusions on Scientific Information in the Digital Age: Access, Dissemination and Preservation, 2832nd session of the COMPETITIVENESS Council (Internal Market, Industry and Research), Brussels, 22nd and 23rd November 2007.

The conclusions of the recent European Council here constitute, as has already been explained, only an illustration, though a major one, of the proximity of scientific problematics formulated today in the domain of information sciences with current transformations of our post-modern societies.

This work also responds, first and foremost, to the approach for finding the founding, structural, organizational and epistemological canvas thanks to which different pieces of research have led to the emergence of information and communication sciences. The intradisciplinary mesh ensures a solidity for the whole, and through this solidity offers to each one the bases and points of support necessary for building a work of methodologically valid research, and participation in the coherence of the developing discipline. Each researcher uses the mesh – by sometimes testing its solidity – to launch constructive scientific breakaways. He/she does this in the research he/she conducts and which leads him/her, in the best cases, to open original paths, or to modestly reconsider a problematic in the light of new phenomena or new factors.

This approach, desirable as it may be, is too often carried out by single researchers and too rarely in groups. Because it is inscribed in the reality of university research practice, it leads to a form of isolation of scientific stakeholders. There is tension between the temptation to always further prolong promising and demanding works, and the requirements of scientific communications, so research is often reduced to the state of witnesses of the path already traveled.

A scientific compilation of this type therefore represents a situation privileged with communications between disciplinary research colleagues. It is not only a place of high-level scientific exchanges and sharing, but is a particular opportunity for comparing the most in-depth research strategies, thus procuring for each contributor, the chance to relate his/her own research to that of other contributors.

I express my sincerest thanks to the information and communication science authors and colleagues who have offered, through their written participation, the fruits of their scientific expertise to the readers. I myself have benefited from the experience of some authors and/or coordinators of scientific works, who have had to oversee the rigors of editing and coordinating works.

The scientific contributions, which have their roots in university research that has been led for several years, beyond the specialties that are expressed in this collective work are revealed to be synthetic, dense, methodical and well-argued. They make this volume a precious guide for all students engaged in studies of the vast domain of human science, more specifically circumscribed, considering the theme of the work, to that of information and communication science.

The authors of *Information Science*, by participating in this collective edition have given the gift – in the noblest meaning – of a long-term endeavor.

They invite us to share here the results of difficult and demanding intellectual journeys of reflections and exchanges with the stakeholders of research, in and outside of the discipline of reference. They offer the results of incessant methodological as well as epistemological comings and goings, without which scientific thought would be only popular thought. Finally, they provide the results of a certain fluid and determined writing, designed by the recurrent practice of scientific communication.

For each author, such a publication represents a test. Their duty is to respond to a double demand. First to accept being presented to the critical eye of their peers and members of the community to which they belong. Second, to communicate in the most didactic way possible, and without too much harshness, the subjects and notions approached, to readers, with the prerequisites and the profiles that are difficult to appreciate.

Editing such chapters, because it responds to an exceptional appeal originating from the scientific coordinator of the book, is always inscribed over and above time-consuming and urgent daily activities and projects whose conclusion – the due dates of which are set by greater authorities – cannot be pushed back. Therefore, for the authors, it is not only a matter of finding the time for this demanding editing but also of conducting the preliminary analyses. It is always tricky to accurately grasp the time and means they will require so my greatest thanks go to them.

Fabrice PAPY
December 2009

Chapter 1

Some Revisions of the Concept of Information

1.1. Introduction

Since the Second World War, information has become a major preoccupation for everyone. It is found in the scientific work of many disciplines, but it has also invaded the personal space of individuals. It has saturated social space to the point where an "information society" has been spoken about – moreover, without knowing exactly what this name encompasses, aside from a few million computers connected on a network of worldwide coverage.

However, despite this central place, we hardly take time to give a precise definition to the term. Often enough it is used without any sort of liminal precaution, as if its meaning were obvious.

Nevertheless, it is clear that common references need to be specified when we mention a computer scientist, a biologist or a journalist, all three of which deal with information. The list is limited to three illustrations but the examples could multiply in a variety of ways. Therefore, the concept is not as "trivial" as it seems – to echo the idea of "trivial culture", as defined by Yves Jenneret [JEA 08].

Compared to the "disorder linked with digital technology", researchers are therefore once again beginning to seriously study the very concept of information. This chapter is a study of some revisions put forward in recent literature, notably literature written in the

---

Chapter written by Sylvie LELEU-MERVIEL and Philippe USEILLE.

English Language. We will be able to refer to Philippe Useille's thesis [USE 08] for a finer, more complete and detailed analysis.

1.2. A double-sided concept: Capurro and Hjorland [CAP 03]

By its protean and polysemic nature, information is a concept that has been taken over by several disciplines. Rafael Capurro and Birger Hjorland's article [CAP 03] is a detailed study of this key concept[1]. But it highlights quite a few difficulties. This is because it shows that a slightly refined study of the concept of information covers disparate entities, such as:

– a physical measure;

– a pattern of communication between a sender and a receiver;

– a form of control or feedback;

– the probability of a message being transmitted over a communication channel;

– the content of a cognitive state;

– the meaning of a linguistic form; or

– the reduction of an uncertainty;

as many meanings as are legitimate in their theory of origin[2].

How can we equip ourselves with a theoretical concept of information that is well-founded and operational for a given piece of research in accordance with our framework of reference?

1.2.1. *Towards an operational concept*

According to Rafael Capurro and Birger Hjorland, "In scientific discourses, theoretical concepts are not true or false elements or pictures of some part of reality, but are constructions designed to do a job the best way possible" [CAP 03]. This means that conceptual work must find an opening that is not only theoretical (a concept playing a role in a given theory), but also methodological, that is to say giving a clear direction to the "job to do". First, information will be described, to a certain extent, as a human phenomenon: a production of the mind.

---

1. Luciano Floridi states the problem in the following way: "Information seems to have become a key concept to unlock several philosophical problems... The problem is that we still have to agree about what information is exactly." in [FLO 05].

2. [CAP 03, p. 11].

The question of information can therefore be formulated in the following way: what makes something informative for one person in a given context? Under what conditions does this information favor the construction of meaning? This formulation puts the focus on the semantics of information and its reception on the activity of the person (the cause of subjectivization processes) of elaborating information in order to do something based on some end. The attention accorded to the history of science will explain the entire extent of the stakes surrounding the concept of information, its impact from a human sciences point of view (which is ours) and its difficult relationship with the question of meaning.

1.2.2. *An etymological explanation*

As a component of a theory in the process of being elaborated, information is actually defined in direct relation to other closely-related concepts: sign, signification and sense, learning and knowledge, mediation, document, device, which enables us to relate with, data, trace, etc.

Etymology helps to clarify that which fundamentally connects information to the construction of knowledge. Capurro and Hjorland's article provides useful markers in this matter. Studying the Latin etymology of the term information (from the verb *informare*: the action of giving form to, of shaping), they highlight its various uses. Two key contexts stand out: first, information corresponds to "the act of modelling the mind and the act of communicating knowledge"[3], two things that are closely linked. Second, they note that the term is used in classical Latin to designate either something intangible or something tangible; one is linked to the semantic field of morals and pedagogy (in order to evolve towards the spiritual when Christianity appears), the other, coming from Greek, is linked to the primitive context of pottery (to shape) and to that which is perceived by the senses.

This legacy undoubtedly explains why in the Middle Ages in a notion of man that unites body and soul, Thomas Aquinas, Aristotle's disciple, used the concept of information to affirm the unity of the education process as a double movement of abstraction. This concept aimed at bringing out the form of things and a return, both sensorial and intellectual, to things in order to recognize their form. Therefore, intellectual knowledge crosses physical experience.

Whereas the Classical Age conserved information like an activity or a process consisting of giving form to a tangible entity, the Renaissance Period[4] contested the

3. [CAP 03, p. 11].

4. The Renaissance Period was a cultural movement in Europe that ran from the 1400s to the 1600s, approximately.

medieval conception according to which the universe is organized into forms, because only the mind causes this information process. The transition from the Middle Ages to modern times in the use of the concept of information is achieved through Descartes, according to whom, ideas give form to thought. No longer are we dealing with images of reality but more with something that informs the mind. Hence, the doctrine of ideas, initially developed by the French philosopher, played a central role in modern philosophy, with as much rationalist inspiration as empiricist: the mind does not communicate directly with nature without ideas intervening like a problematic relationship with what we call reality. One of the roots of constructivism is recognized there. From then on, information, thus understood, no longer took a seat in the world, but in the mind and the senses. Empiricism closely unites the two dimensions (intangible and tangible) in describing sensation. The objects of the world *in-form* the senses, but the sensation is distinguished from form: whereas one is sensual and subjective, the other is intellectual and objective.

1.2.3. *Oppositions and relations, division and complexity*

The extent to which the notions of information and knowledge are linked and mutually clarify each other is noted. Nevertheless, we must stress the need to make a distinction between interpersonal public learning and idiosyncratic knowledge. Supposedly, information is the bridge we cross to go from one order to another, from a (trans)formative perspective. The etymology of the concept, all too briefly outlined, also helps to seize the main themes that run through the theorizations of information. Rafael Capurro and Birger Hjorland maintain some of them[5] (from the works of Mickael K. Buckland [BUC 91]), reproduced in the table below.

	Intangible	*Tangible*
Entity	Information as knowledge/ knowledge	Information as thing, data, document, recorded knowledge
Process	Information as process/ becoming informed	Information, data processing, document processes Knowledge engineering

Table 1.1. *Four aspects of information according to [CAP 03]*

5. Their reflections are rooted in the field of information science.

Mickael K. Buckland has actually studied the different uses of the term in information science. One is in relation to a thing or an entity, the other to a process. Both are divided according to the categories tangible/intangible, a division that is open to dispute. Indeed, this classification undoubtedly has the advantage of clarifying the concept of information but the disadvantage of splitting up interlinked dimensions.

Entity/process and tangible/intangible: a dialogic conception of information can hardly be satisfied by these oppositions. According to Edgar Morin[6] [MOR 94], "the dialogic principle involves taking notions which, taken absolutely, are antagonistic and dismiss each other, and making them play together in a complementary way". A complex approach to information will therefore consist of placing a hyphen between these dimensions separated by the analysis.

1.2.4. *Carrying on… between measurable signal and meaningful emergence*

Let us recall immediately that using the concept of information is problematic in terms of its relationship with knowledge, meaning and sense. Capurro and Hjorland point out that information naturalization is accompanied by the elimination of "psychological factors" so that it can be measured in terms of physical quantity.

This was clearly stated by Warren Weaver; therefore, information does not mean anything. Or, in other cases, information ends up being confused with the double concept of meaning/sense. Bernard Floris [FLO 04] shows this feature by examining the common use made of information, which therefore "indistinctly" designates "perceptions, impressions, knowledge, opinions, teaching, reinforcements or events"[7].

Are we condemned to sink into the polysemy of a chameleon-concept, changing with theoretical needs? This confusion is due to the fact that information comes from two opposing sources: on one hand, the physico-mathematical theory of information as a signal; on the other hand, the social space of relational, exchanged and circulating information, like journalistic information.

It is time to explore the field, history and contours of information so that later we will have a better understanding of the recent studies reviewed here.

---

6. Their reflections are rooted in the field of information science.

7. Edgar Morin is a French philosopher and sociologist who began his career at the CNRS of which he is also the president.

1.3. The mathematical theory of information (MTI): Segal [SEG 03]

Taking on the issue of information forces us to consider the legacy of the mathematical theory of information (MTI), or signalling theory. This was imposed in the 20th century as a matrix to reflection on information.

Science historian Jerome Segal, in his top-notch book *Le Zéro et le un. Histoire de la Notion Scientifique d'Information au 20e Siècle* (*The Zero and the One. History of the Scientific Notion of Information in the 20th Century*) [SEG 03], explains the historical dynamics of this emergence.

1.3.1. *Mathematics rejoining human sciences?*

MTI leads to the hope of a fruitful dialog between different disciplines. This hope was entertained by a certain scientific community in the middle of the last century. This theory dreamed of seeing mathematics rejoin the human sciences by confronting the delicate issue of sense. Jérôme Segal's work [SEG 03] traces the relationship between science and the notion of information. This ambition was expressed from the very beginning of Claude Elwood Shannon's[8] MTI. For this reason, Jérôme Segal refers to the postscript given by Warren Weaver[9] in the new edition of Sahnnon's work [SHA 49]. Therein he explains what presided when the theory was being developed.

1.3.2. *A senseless measure of information*

Tackling the problems linked to this notion, Warren Weaver in his postscript distinguishes three levels that show all the difficulty with unifying the approaches. He uses the division model (of disciplines with language as the object) established by the semiotician Charles Morris[10]. The first level is syntax and technique, the second is related to semantics and the last to pragmatics. The first case deals with

---

8. Claude Elwood Shannon (1916–2001), engineer in the Bell laboratory, is one of the fathers of the theory of information. The article [SHA 48] is one of his masterpieces.

9. Warren Weaver (1894–1978) is an American mathematician and co-author with Claude Shannon of *The Mathematical Theory of Communications* [SHA 49], in which they establish the mathematical foundations of information. While Shannon emphasizes the consequences of engineering the mathematical model, Weaver develops the philosophical implications.

10. Charles W. Morris (1901–1979), American semiotician and philosopher, separates different disciplines that deal with language: syntax (i.e. the grammar that studies the relationship between signs), semantics (which is devoted to the meaning understood as the relation between signs and what they designate) and finally pragmatics (the relationship between signs and their users).

taking into consideration the quantity of information, the second case stops at the meaning of information, while the last is formulated in these terms: "with what efficacy does the meaning received affect being lead in the desired direction?"[11].

Whereas Claude Shannon [SHA 48] considers semantic problems to be irrelevant[12], for Warren Weaver they deserve to be tackled for future development of the theory. If not, the concept of information developed in TMI would fall short[13]. Moreover, the MTI excelled especially in a quantitative approach to information in order to respond to two fundamental problems: determining the maximum level of data compression and the maximum rate of data transmission.

As stated by Luciano Floridi [FLO 05], quoting the same Warren Weaver, the term information is not linked that much to what you say but more so to what you could say. MTI is concerned with the carrier of information, the symbols and signals, not information by itself in its semantic dimension. "That is, information is your measure of freedom of choice when you select a message"[14]. Information is defined as the operation through which a signal is selected from a possible set of symbols, a way of quantifying information consisting of counting the number of binary questions (with yes or no answers) necessary to determine what the source is communicating.

For Luciano Floridi, MTI is not a theory of information in the popular sense of the term. Information is considered in its technical dimension. Thus, "yes" the word contains the same quantity of information, whether it answers the question "have the lights of your car been left switched on for too long without recharging the battery?" or "would you marry me?"[15]. Thus, to the extent that MTI is a theory of information that is not seeking to clarify the meaning of the message, it will be more correctly perceived as a branch of the probabilities.

---

11. [SEG 03, p. 704].

12. Shannon writes "The fundamental problem of communication is that of reproducing at one point either exactly or approximately a message selected at another point. Messages often have meaning; that is they refer to or are correlated according to some system with certain physical or conceptual entities. These semantic aspects of communication are irrelevant to the engineering problem".

13. [SHA 48, p. 139].

14. Luciano Floridi is quoting directly from Warren Weaver's article in *Scientific American*, entitled "The mathematics of communication" (p. 11-15). These words are translated into French by the present author as "*ce par quoi se mesure la liberté de choix quand on sélectionne un message*". They have also been translated by other authors as "*la mesure statistique de la liberté de choix lors de la sélection d'un message*".

15. [FLO 05].

MTI does not deal with information itself, but the data that constitute it, messages comprising strings of uninterpreted symbols; therefore it remains at the syntactic level of information as it is implemented in information and communication technology, with the efficacy and success that we know.

1.3.3. *A plan for unification that stumbles over semantics*

MTI was so successful, however that it caused the initial plan to be forgotten. Warren Weaver therefore turned his hopes towards cybernetics, which was only just beginning in the works of the MACY Conferences[16] (1946–1953) and those of Norbert Wiener[17]. The notion of information, mathematized by MTI, occupied a central position in the debates and was placed at the heart of the cybernetics, defended and illustrated by Norbert Wiener in his work [WIE 48].

According to Jérôme Segal, Norbert Weiner's work clearly contained a plan to unify the sciences[18]. In particular, it touched on the notion of information[19], contrary to Shannon's mathematical theory which lacked this ambition. It was becoming possible to connect the human sciences and mathematics "without taking sense from the sensitive, mechanizing the organic and killing the living by doing so"[20]. The sciences would be unified under the aegis of cybernetics provided that it integrated "psychological factors" for some and "semantic aspects" for others.

This plan to unify the sciences was finally aborted during the last conference dedicated to the semantic aspects of information. Actually, in August 1953, shortly after the final MACY conference, the 9th International Summer Psychological Linguistics Conference, held in Amersfoort in the Netherlands, was devoted to the semantic aspects of modern communication theories. It therefore tackled head-on what was preoccupying many mathematicians, philosophers or logicians who were seeking to construct a model for the meaning of information. Jérôme Segal notes

16. The MACY conferences were mainly organized in New York from 1946–1953 under the aegis of the MACY foundation. They gathered scientists from very diverse horizons, but united by a similar interest in the budding field of cybernetics.

17. Norbert Wiener (1894–1964), American mathematician considered as the founder of cybernetics, the principles of which he exposed in [WIE 48].

18. Jérôme Segal shows that the theme of unity of sciences recurs throughout his history; an initial attempt took place at the turn of the 19th century around the notion of energy [SEG 03, p. 694-699].

19. [SEG 03, p. 699].

20. This is the way Schmidt, cited by Jérôme Segal as representative of the ambition to combine languages and mathematics, expresses himself [SEG 03, p. 705].

that none of the papers presented at this conference dared to envisage a theory of information that covered all the senses of the word information[21].

Roman Jakobson[22] (who participated in the MACY conferences) is a renowned linguist who was also attracted to the MTI at that time. Even he was prepared to renounce the meaning of the object of his field so that he would consider only the "mathematical sense", which is the only thing taken into account by the formalism of the mathematical theory. The conference was undoubtedly a victim of the mentality of the time, manifested in some researchers as a type of reductionism, or even scientism, pushing them to want to quantify "something that is by nature qualitative"[23], like the doublet signification/sense of information.

1.3.4. *The irruption of information in the human sciences*

Although the plan set in motion by the MACY conferences was unsuccessful, it paved the way for other researchers who helped the human sciences to integrate this concept of information in their field of study. As stated by Weaver, some of them stopped at the effects of information, its pragmatic dimension. This strategy is illustrated, for example, with the works of MacKay [MCK 69], for whom the meaning of a message is defined in relation to "its selective function among all possible reactions"[24] of the receiver. The pragmatic dimension of information no longer refers directly to the effective reaction of the receiver, but to "the way he [or she] can react"[25] in a finite set of possibilities determined by a form that ensures this function of selectivity.

The success of Shannon's theory is undoubtedly linked to the fact that it suggested the unit – the bit – making it possible to measure information and around which different disciplines are rallied. But finally, theories focusing on the semantic, even pragmatic dimension of information, and the generalization of the MTI to domains distant from telecommunication techniques, would not have answered all the hopes it aroused[26].

---

21. [SEG 03, p. 723].
22. Roman Osipovitch Jakobson (1896–1982) was a Russian linguist and an anthropologist. His very vast work embraces language sciences, from phonology to communication science and semiotics. He is considered as one of the founders of the structuralist movement.
23. [SEG 03, p. 724].
24. [SEG 03, p. 728].
25. [SEG 03, p. 728].
26. See [SEG 03], in particular, Chapter 11 devoted to "The notion of information in the emergence of the unit of knowledge" (p. 693–748).

This craze provoked by the notion of information is perhaps due to the fact that it concerns a physical grandeur and a malleable notion at the same time. In fact, are the attempts to get out of a mathematical conception of information struck by individuality because they make use of a polysemic concept? What is the heuristic power of the notion[27]? Jérôme Segal concludes by affirming that the history of the theory of information lead to "a deception on the epistemological plane"[28] but "a success on the scientific and technical plane"[29].

This severe finding does not, however, hide the fact that the works of engineers and mathematicians on self-correcting mechanisms contributed to the birth of cybernetics. This, by generalizing the approach system to biology and social organization, constituted a crucible and a zone of intense exchanges between remote disciplines, which gave rise to very fruitful works (for example, French structuralism derives from them).

1.3.5. *Beyond MTI*

In conclusion, a theory of information unified, backed up by the rigorous MTI, finally turned out to be impossible. However, the MTI is generally thought of as a matrix – the cardinal meeting place of diverse disciplines – which continues to feed, sometimes implicitly, the different concepts of information. But without being able to ignore it, and without definitively ruling it out, other paths were to be explored from then on. Jérôme Segal's study shows how much the works of MTI irrigated, even in a "metaphorical"[30] way, several scientific fields.

Therefore, today, it is still useful to reflect on the status of the term "information" as a founding component of theoretical discourse. Is it a notion? How is it turned into a concept? Beyond their synonymy, the two words, notion and concept, are distinguished in the following way. A notion expresses an immediate, intuitive knowledge of something. It is a way of conceiving, showing a certain point of view. It is why Jérôme Segal speaks of a scientific notion of information from a certain point of view – that of MTI (the zero and the one) – and taking on its developments in the most diverse fields. A concept, on the other hand, is an epistemological element giving coherence to discourse.

---

27. Jérôme Segal is seeking to return "informational discourse" to historian, as it was post-war: it is accompanied by a social and political dimension, the words of discourse also implying things and practices [SEG 03, p. 778].

28. [SEG 03, p. 779].

29. [SEG 03, p. 779].

30. [SEG 03, p. 780].

It turns out that information is far from being a "clear and distinct" entity. Even more, it appears as a "multi-dimensional macro concept"[31] as defined by Edgar Morin [MOR 94], "combining normally separate, even antagonistic notions in them, structured around other macro-concepts that are complementary and opposing at the same time"[32]. Therefore, how are these different semantic molecules of information-for-someone-in-a-given-context, information-for-doing-something, information as an entity, information as process, linked together, themselves in an "organic junction"[33] with the objective pursued? It is this very question that must guide the conceptualization of information useful for a contemporary scientific approach.

1.4. The diaphoric definition of data: Floridi [FLO 05]

The reflection lead in parallel with the generalization of recourse to computer science has weaved the concept of information directly with that of data.

The works of the information philosopher Luciano Floridi, from Oxford University, bring an essential contribution in this sense.

1.4.1. *Information, data, meaning*

The founding hypothesis on which the approach presented in this part is constructed in the following: information has a permanent stake in shaping the construction of experience from undifferentiated personal experience. To begin with, it is difficult to analytically define information as the term designates that which is communicated ("what") and the way in which it is communicated ("how") at the same time.

In a socio-constructive view, experience does not enable direct access to "reality in itself" (Kantian *noumenon*[34]). Actually, constructivism radically calls into question the ontological hypothesis that postulates a reality that can be dissociated from an observer. Knowledge of the world passes through experience. According to Jean-Louis Le Moigne, "the subject does not know 'things in themselves' (ontological hypothesis) but he knows the act through which it perceives interaction between things" [LEM 95]. Therefore, in this hypothesis nothing can be said on the

31. [MOR 94, p. 326] (extract taken from *La Méthode* I [The Method I], p. 371-373).

32. [MOR 94, p. 326].

33. [MOR 94, p. 326].

34. According to Kant, noumena designates the thing in itself absolute reality, which remains out of reach when the phenomenon refers to what is seized by the senses.

subject of "reality in itself" from experience. According to George Kelly: "An analysis of experience, then, becomes a study of the field of fact, which one has segmented into meaningful events; the way those events, in turn, are construed; the kinds of evidence against which one has checked the validity of his predictions"[35]. For Edgar Morin [MOR 94], our only immediate reality is reduced to our representation of reality. Furthermore, information plays a crucial role in it.

Let us remember that according to François Rastier [RAS 03], *sense* is a "contextual phenomenon"[36]. Sense is "taken" following an "action of interpretation". François Rastier establishes a reversal of sense and signification. Sense is not signification altered by context but it is actually more signification that is similar to "standardized sense"[37] detached from its context. As for significations, they are "data"; they are acquired or transmitted and marked by a certain stability. Therefore they come under *nomos*. This is why they have a social dimension. Significations imply the presence of public signs. The entire difficulty consists of restoring sense as an act of interpretation, situated in its context and in tension with signification as the product of standardization. For now, questioning is done in an abstract and conceptual way in order to define the place of information in this act of interpretation that presides over the construction of experience from undifferentiated personal experience, term of a process of meaning.

To avoid all confusion, we resort to the term "meaning" (*significance*) forged in this use in [LEL 04]. It enables us to support that the production of sense is not reduced to signification, as signification causes components exceeding rational aspects of decoding (for example, emotional intelligence) to intervene. Meaning is therefore "the fact of signifying in one register and/or in another"[38], or it is more the name granted to the process of dialog tension between signification and sense.

How can information be defined in relation to data and signifying in such a way that this dynamic, this process of meaning, is understood? The works of Luciano Floridi in the domain of philosophy of information[39] enable us to respond, in part, to this question.

35. [KEL 55, p. 172].

36. [RAS 03, p. 9].

37. [RAS 03, p. 9].

38. [LEL 04, p. 128].

39. Recall that he is a member of the Philosophy Department and the Computing Laboratory of Oxford University. His research focuses on the philosophy of computer science and information: http://www.philosophyofinformation.net/ (last consulted 23 September 2009).

1.4.2. *A definition of information based on data*

Luciano Floridi studies the possibility of "a data-based definition of information" [FLO 05]. However, it is notable that the concept of data seems imprecise at first sight, risking displacement of the difficulty instead of lifting it. Yet Luciano Floridi considers it to be less rich and slippery than that of information, and therefore easier to manipulate. Also, a definition based on data is a good starting point.

For 30 years, what Luciano Floridi calls a "general definition of information", or GDI, has been adopted by information science, information systems theory, decision theory, etc[40]. This definition was imposed in fields that treated data and information as entities. It is transcribed as "data + meaning", with meaning being translated into French as *significance.* GDI considers σ to be an example of information, equipped with semantic content if and only if:

– GDI 1: σ consists of one or more datum;

– GDI 2: the data in σ are well-formed;

– GDI 3: the well-formed data in σ are meaningful.

According to this definition data are the "stuff" of which information is made. Later, we will return to their nature. "Well-formed" means that the data are clustered in accordance with the syntactic rules that govern a given code or language. Syntax must be understood as that which determines the form, construction or structure of something. In these two steps, the grammatization implied by data digitization is recognized[41]. GDI 3 causes the semantic dimension to intervene. "Meaningful data" means that the data are executed according to semantic rules of a given system (code or language), making them belong to the sole interpretation that also generates sense.

1.4.3. *Diaphoric definitions of data on three levels*

How are data defined? We know that they are necessary for information, without being sufficient. Luciano Floridi states, "Now a datum is reducible to just a lack of

40. The author gives a more exhaustive list: [FLO 05].

41. It is "grammatization" that materializes the substance of an expression in discrete elements that can be manipulated by a computer. The advantage of such an operation consists of formalizing significations that have become data, which are submitted to different operations (sorting, comparison, classification on a scale), as observed when resorting to computer science to evaluate individual performances", *Le Texte en Jeu. Permanence et Transformations du Document.* Available online at the following address: http://rtp-doc.enssib.fr/article.php3?id_article=209, p. 6, (last accessed 23 September 2009).

uniformity (*diaphora* is the Greek word for "difference")"[42]. He therefore suggests a diaphoric definition of data (DDD): "A datum is a putative fact regarding some difference or lack of uniformity within some context."

Luciano Floridi's DDD has three different levels of application, one making the next possible:

– DDD1: data are *diaphora de re,* i.e. revealing lacks of uniformity in the "real world out there". They are pure data, above all, seized by an observing consciousness, "proto-epistemic" data that show "fractures in the fabric of being"[43]. They are comparable with Kant's *noumena.* They can be directly known but simply inferred from experience;

– DDD2: data are *diaphora de signo*, i.e. revealing lacks of uniformity in the perception of two physical states (for example, a variation in the electric signal during a telephone conversation);

– DDD3: data are *diaphora de dicto*, i.e. revealing a lack of uniformity between two symbols, for example, the letters of the Latin alphabet.

DDD1	*diaphora de re*	Proto-epistemic data	Inferred by experience
DDD2	*diaphora de signo*	Absence of uniformity between two physical states	Variations of an electric signal during a telephone conversation
DDD3	*diaphora de dicto*	Absence of uniformity between two symbols	A is different to B in the Latin alphabet

Table 1.2. *Three levels of application of DDD [FLO 05]*

42. [FLO 05]. The Greek *diaphora* means "différence", "diversity" according to A. Bailly's *Abridged Ancient Greek Dictionary*, available online at the following address: http://www.lexilogos.com/grec_ancien_dictionnaire.htm (last accessed 23 September 2009). In such cases, the French form "diaphorie" is used with reference to Luciano Floridi's works.

43. [MUG 97].

1.4.4. *Diaphora and saliences*

The DDD formulated by Luciano Floridi reminds us of what some cognition researchers call "salience", the noun derived from the adjective "salient" (that which stands out, is put forward, is raised).

For Frédéric Landragin [LAN 04], the notion of salience is linked to the emergence of a shape on a background. This background is called "context" by Luciano Floridi. The fact that data lack uniformity therefore makes them salient.

Alain Cardon[44] specifies that, for him, salience is the transfer of one form of the environment in the individual's receiving system, the reception having a sudden and local character which sensitively modifies the current state of this receiving system. To what extent? This modification touches the "individual's system of representation of the world"[45], eventually causing him or her to act. He or she gives the example of a noise heard when everything is quiet. This perceived form (what stands out from a background) can therefore be semiotized and, through that, coded, even in a summary way: the noise signals, for example, a danger for the individual in a given context. The wailing of sirens signifies priority passage of a vehicle on the public route.

The perception of a salience (or its data) is the act through which some form that is dependent on the "reception system"[46] stands out from a background. This system, itself, is linked to the "system of representation of the world"[47], through which the individual constructs his/her environment of the moment.

This conception of salience supposes that of the unlimited semiosis of Umberto Eco, Peirce's commentator. Some interpretants that are not signs but an action or a behavior must therefore be included in this: it is what Umberto Eco calls "energetic or emotional interpretant"[48]. Without forming part of the message, salience also makes it possible[49]. In other words, salience belongs to the principle of meaning.

---

44. [CAR 01, p. 50].

45. [CAR 01, p. 49].

46. [CAR 01, p. 49].

47. "A salient form is the recognition of a discontinuity in some space. The current representation of the world for the individual is some space that represents the environment and the irruption of the salient form introduces a more or less strong discontinuity in it. But the individual who perceives this salient form is under the engagement of his tendencies of the moment, wich tend to make him notice some forms more than others", [CAR 01, p. 49].

48. [ECO 79, p. 52].

49. "Salience does not explicitly form part of the message communicated, but the entire message is based on it, is structured as a function of it, and is explained by it", [ECO 79].

Whereas Luciano Floridi does not evoke it, it seems nevertheless that this notion links up with what he calls *diaphora*.

1.4.5. *Of data as relational entity*

According to Luciano Floridi, the three diaphoric levels of data supposedly correspond: each level makes the next possible[50]. But how do we go from one level to the next? This question is asked in quite a precise perspective: the one that consists of studying how information helps to construct experience from an undifferentiated personal experience.

DDD1 (*diaphora de re,* i.e. noumenal differences) "makes possible" DDD2-type signals (*diaphora de signo,* i.e. differences perceived between physical states in the semiosos).

DDD2 signals therefore enable the coding of these differences in the form of DDD3 symbols (*diaphora de dicto,* i.e. differences perceived between symbols.

DDD3 refers to an explicit system of symbols). At this stage, the datum becomes a symbolic entity that codes a difference.

This version is of course linked with Gregory Bateson's very famous formula [BAT 77]:

> "A unit of information can be defined as a difference that produces another difference. Such a difference that shifts and undergoes successive modifications in a circuit constitutes an elementary idea".

Here, information is seen as a difference circulating in a "group considered as a totality."[51] The difference therefore proceeds from a comparison, MacKay would say a distinction, a *diaphora* according to Luciano Floridi. It will therefore be held that the information process is identified as a process of differentiation. Producing information is nothing other than producing difference.

In order to grasp what this difference is, one of the possible routes is to understand the "map" that expresses such a process. In one of his conferences entitled *Form, Substance and Difference*, Gregory Bateson states that what we report on a map is difference. A uniform territory would be difficult to plot on a map:

---

50. "Dedomena in (1) may be either identical with, or what makes possible signals in (2), and signals in (2) are what make possible the coding of symbols in (3)".
51. [BAT 77, p. 272].

"(...) that which appears on the map is in fact the difference, whether it is a matter of a difference in altitude, vegetation, demographic structure, surface area, etc. These are the differences carried on the map."

Gregory Bateson shows, for example, that a piece of chalk is not knowable in itself. An infinite number of differences exist in and around this piece of chalk: furthermore, the person selects a limited number of differences that become information. He specifies in a clarifying note: "We can still express the problem in another way and say that at each stage – i.e. each time a difference is transformed and transmitted along the network – the incarnation of difference before the stage is a "territory", of which the incarnation after a stage is a "map". In such a way that the "map-territory" relation exists at each stage".

It is therefore clear that data are not imposed themselves: they are understood from an act of reading on the part of the acting subject. It will therefore be said that "one is never faced with raw (or crude) data", as stated by Gregory Bateson [BAT 77][52]. Data are always selected, transformed, as the totality of past, present, future data can not be accessed. Data proceed from a difference or a lack of uniformity in a context and emerge from the fact of some composition (which does not happen by accident and always names an acting subject). The comprehension of data as being a form of perceptive salience, emergence of a shape on a background, furthermore confirms this feature.

In the DDD framework, it is advisable to question what makes difference. For Luciano Floridi, a datum (that which is salient) is classified as a specific entity when it stands out from a background. However, it is a matter of binary and symmetric relational inequality. A sheet of paper is not simply the background on which a black dot appears as a datum. Luciano Floridi specifies that it is constitutive of the group "black-dot-on-white-sheet", a group that constitutes the datum itself. Therefore, considering that there is no datum in itself, Luciano Floridi is joined with Gregory Bateson when he states: "a datum is a relational entity"[53].

Finally, Luciano Floridi underlines all the difficulty with attributing a signification to data in a semiotic system, the issue being to know whether data, information material, acquire a semantic dimension independently or not of the receiver of information. He assumes that there is also "*environmental information*" (italics from original): the growth marks visible on a tree stump are a good example of it. This information coming from the environment does not necessarily

52. [BAT 77, p. 17].

53. The term "entity" does not refer to a being or an object here, but more to something that is defined in a system of relations, in the same way as the linguistic entity is only understandable through the association of a signifier and a signified.

imply meaning. It can be a matter of a group of data forming a coherent whole, which is similar to affordances[54]. Plants, animals, even machines are capable of making use of this information, even in the absence of data signifying something for someone. This hypothesis deserves to be discussed. *A contrario*, we could actually limit ourselves to the radical affirmation of Heinz von Foester, according to whom, "the world does not contain information. The world is as it is" [AND 06][55]. Even if Heinz von Foester voluntarily admits that "the environment presents some structure" (order), the entire issue is defining the meaning potential carried by information.

1.4.6. *Beyond DDD*

In conclusion, GDI causes information to depend on well-formed data, according to some syntax that favors meaning. Information depends on the way in which data are well-formed according to a definite syntax; *data* themselves depend on their physical implementation.

Information intervenes in the action of a subject as a component of reasoning that produces anticipations. Therefore, the information subject (taken in a diaphoric dynamic) cannot be detached from is action plans when a systemic point of view is adopted. As stressed by Miora Mugur-Schächter [MUG 97]: "'Systemic' thought reveals the decisive importance, for all beings as well as for these meta-beings that are social organizations, pragmatic modellings, 'conceptions' induced by subjective goals, which are placed in the future but which shape present actions. These goals,

54. Affordances were studied by the American perception psychologist J. J. Gibson. This neologism was formed from the verb "to afford". Affordances designate the possibilities that an actor has of interacting with his environment. Affordances that come from things are what they enable for an observer. They are the properties of interaction between the world and an actor. Affordances are of relational order. They are ecological in the sense that they are properties of the environment relative to an organism. They exist even if they are not perceived by someone. "The hypothesis that things have affordances, and that we perceive or learn to perceive them, is very promising, radical, but not yet elaborated." (*Perceptual Systems,* p. 285). "Roughly, the affordances of things are what they furnish, for good or ill, that is, what they afford the observer. (...) I assume that affordances are not simply phenomenal qualities of subjective experience (tertiary qualities, dynamic and physiognomic properties, etc.). I also assume that they are not simply the physical properties of things as now conceived by physical science. Instead, they are ecological, in the sense that they are properties of the environment relative to an animal", [GIB 71] In Chapter 4.9, Part II. p. 403–406, 1982, accessible online at the following address: http://www.huwi.org/gibson/prelim.php (last accessed 30 January 2007).

55. [AND 06, p. 77].

linked to beliefs and anticipations, relate back to the action as it gets closer or further away, however, action, by developing, modifies goals".

Thinking in a systemic way, information leads us to adopt a point of view that increases the value of the pragmatic dimension of information as retrieval of something that gives form to experience, that can fit. Only the consideration of this pragmatic dimension can enable us to understand how the different diaphoric levels are linked up.

1.5. A patterns approach: Bates [BAT 05]

The pragmatic dimension is very readable, notably across information science in its American version. This is because American researchers are federated in an association – the American Society for Information Science and Technology, ASIS&T – which gathers stakeholders working in diverse fields: documentation, information science, communication technology, computer science and digital information services[56].

Despite, or because of, its diversity, this community developed a detailed theoretical reflection in which the concept of information is questioned across the notions of behavior, need for information and information retrieval, without ever losing sight of the practical applications that can come out of it[57].

In this framework, Marcia J. Bates' effort at a summary brings a fundamental contribution to the clarification of concepts, not only of information and meaning but also knowledge, notably in their reciprocal relationships.

1.5.1. *A definition of information based on patterns*

This section is a study of the work of Marcia Bates relying on two central publications: "Information and knowledge: an evolutionary framework for

---

56. The association's website is: http://www.asis.org/index.html (last accessed 23 September 2009).

57. Harold Borko [BOR 68] defines information science as "that discipline that investigates the properties and behavior of information, the forces governing the flow of information, and the means of processing information for optimum accessibility and usability. It is concerned with the body of knowledge relating to the collection, organization, storage, retrieval, interpretation, transmission, and utilization of information". These assumptions are presented on the Information Science conference website: http://icisc.neasist.org/about.html#is (last accessed 23 September 2009).

information science" [BAT 05] and "Fundamental forms of information" [BAT 06]. The following paragraph will be reserved for discussion.

Her intention is to summarize the different acceptances of the concept of information in such a way that they can be used in physics, biology, human and social sciences. Her quest is to supply a solid conceptual socle capable of supporting some intention formulated by the question "under what conditions are we in the presence of information?"

Marcia J. Bates is trying to gain a "subjective" perspective (belonging to human sciences) and an "objective" perspective that is the heir of positive sciences. Completing the review of literature in the domain, she notes that most definitions consider information in three ways: either as knowledge, or a process of "in-formation" (of the mind), or as an entity. In a knowledge approach, other works considered information to be linked to changes in a mental map. Finally, more recently, information has been defined as a stimulus that conforms or informs the world view of the one who is informed.

To begin with, she differentiates between three categories – information 1, information 2 and knowledge:

– "information 1 is defined as a pattern of organization of matter and energy;

– information 2 is defined as some pattern of organization of matter and energy that has been given meaning by a living being;

– knowledge is defined as information given meaning and integrated with other contents of understanding" [58].

1.5.2. *Discussion*

In the first place, Marcia Bates relies on Edwin Parker's definition [PAR 74] to formulate her definition of information 1: "Information 1: pattern of organization of matter and energy". She sticks to the double meaning of pattern. She explains first, that the word designates the marking, configuration or design, like that left by frost on a window. Luciano Floridi evoked the rings that indicate the growth of the tree. In addition, it concerns a combination of quantities, acts, tendencies, forming a consistent and characteristic group. Pattern in information 1 refers to something that is not chaotic and is not the equivalent of a system.

Information 2, on the other hand, implies that some features are gathered to form a coherent whole for a living being above and beyond the visible traces of frost on

58. [BAT 05, p. 11].

the window. In both cases, pattern is characterized as a grouping that exceeds the sum of its parts, something qualitatively new and distinctive. We therefore notice that pattern partially recaps the concept of order, architecture and organization.

Information 1	Pattern of organization of matter and energy	A hand signal
Information 2	Pattern of organization of matter and energy + signification	A hand signal meaning "come here"
Knowledge	Information 2 + relation with pre-existing knowledge	This gesture is strange for itself. Something unusual is happening

Table 1.3. *From information to knowledge*

Finally, a pattern of organization designates something that escapes entropy. This notion has to be integrated with a "moderate" constructivism defended by Marcia Bates so that there is something that exits beyond consciousness. The universe is not pure disorder: it includes some structure independent of the experience of living beings. But she rejects that idea that there is only one "true" form. There exist as many patterns of organization as beings with nervous and sensorial systems. It is to this extent that information is "objective" and "subjective" at the same time, she notes in her own terms.

The question we want to know, according to Marcia J. Bates, is why is information experienced? Why not be happy with each item or bit of information? Undoubtedly because it is infinitely more efficient to implement and stick to a pattern of organization than to detect and conserve each item taken in isolation. For the author, the product of a long evolution of our species is perceived in it, language use, hundreds of capacities of abstraction and categorization intervene in it. Marcia Bates is therefore defending a constructivist, evolutionist and emergent[59] approach to information, where humans are conceived as beings capable of elaborating and remembering global patterns. Not being mixed up with matter, "the information is this pattern of organization of the material, not the material itself'[60]. Such a concept

59. "Information principally exists for organisms at many emergent levels", [BAT 05, p. 18].
60. [BAT 05, p. 18].

connects with that of the GDI, which assumes that a datum is a relational entity. Consciousness has to do with organized patterns of stimuli received by our senses. According to Marcia Bates, information has to do with something ordered, even structured. In the first definition put forward (information 1), information therefore does not signify anything. It is a pattern of organization of matter and energy, nothing more.

On the other hand, when we are said to be informed, something else is happening. In ordinary use as well as in studies focusing on information, she notes[61], this means the following: after receiving information about someone or something, we consider ourselves to be informed. For example, I learn that France won against Ireland in the Six Nations Rugby Tournament[62]. This means that I am receiving patterns of organization of matter and energy in the form of vibrating waves or written words (information 1). And I attribute meaning to what is communicated to me: the defeat of Ireland is a surprise, as they were the favorites. It is necessary to suggest a second definition of information taking in charge, in a pragmatic point of view, meaning instantiated here in the form of signifying and structuring contribution. "Information 2: some pattern of organization of matter and energy that has been given meaning by a living being".

Marcia Bates specifies that meaning accompanies, even precedes, the cognitive act of pattern understanding. For a human being, the chair that I am walking towards is associated with the concept of chair before being perceived as a distinctive silhouette[63]. This seems to be similar to an affordance (see section 1.4.5). In fact, different types of information are understood according to the data implicated. Marcia Bates therefore identifies data corresponding to DDD1 (noumenal differences, according to Luciano Floridi) with information created by the environment as perceived by the organism[64]. As for DDD2 type data (*diaphora de signo*, i.e. revealing lacks of uniformity in the perception of two physical states), they are incorporated in information selected and generated by humans in pursuit of social goals. To this category belong, for example, scientific data produced by researchers scrutinizing the sky with a telescope or observing a group of people and recording the observations according to a defined protocol. Human beings are therefore capable of manipulating, thanks to scientific methods, portions of the world in such a way as to enrich the information available, which enables them to learn more. DDD1 type data become DDD2 type data when they signify something,

61. [BAT 05, p. 12].

62. Six Nations Rugby is Europe's premier international rugby tournament. The countries taking part are England, France, Ireland, Italy, Scotland and Wales.

63. [BAT 05, p. 12].

64. "Data 1 may be seen as that portion of the entire information environment available to a sensing organism that is taken in, or processed, by that organism" [BAT 05, p. 13].

so that they change into knowledge when they are based on other pre-existing knowledge in the mind.

1.5.3. *Evaluation in the form of attempts to reconcile the different points of view*

What relations exist between information and knowledge? Knowledge is information that signifies something and is linked to other elements of understanding (because what makes sense refers to experience). Let us reproduce the examples, often more telling than definitions, to properly understand Marcia Bates' thoughts. She states that a book sitting in a closed library over the holidays contains information 1. Once read by a reader, information 1 transforms into information 2. The text of the book therefore signifies something for someone and the reader finds him- or herself informed by it. Information is related to and comes to be inserted among the reader's pre-existing knowledge, thus generating new knowledge for the individual.

Birger Hjorland's reading of Marcia Bates' work is indispensable for a first attempt at a summary. It opposes two conceptions of information: one presupposes that information has an "objective" existence in the universe independently of the situation and the observer (Bates' information 1: all difference is some information, there are patterns of organization and energy in the universe); the other posits that information is understood in relation to a subject in a given situation ("information is a difference that produces another difference" – see Bates on: information 2). It is, in his own terms, a "subjective" and "situational" conception of information. Luciano Floridi's GDI conforms to this second view to the extent that it relies on a relational definition of data. According to Birger Hjorland, "this view of information as a noun is related to becoming informed (informing as a verb). Something is information if it is informative (or rather: something is information when it is informative". The central question of such an approach is therefore: how and when does something become informative for someone in a given situation "in-the-process-of-being-informed-in-order-to-do-something", and is not so for someone else or for the same person in another situation[65]?

Therefore, Birger Hjorland adopts Marcia Bates' example of frost on a window. This fragile group of crystals corresponds to the idea that it becomes a pattern presenting some apparent regularity. Furthermore, Birger Hjorland notes that a pattern (information 1) becomes informative (information 2) for someone precisely and relatively to the interpretive context that animates it. Information will differ depending on whether an artist, a physician or a meteorologist is concerned. Each

65. Birger Hjorland's original question is as follows: "What is information for one person in one situation need not be information for another person or in another situation", [CAP 03].

one maps out information in a different way, based on what he/she knows, what he/she does, his/her culture, his/her experience.

Information translates a singular point of view determined notably by knowledge, shared public meanings, its own perspective governed by a questioning that reveals and makes some differences, and not others, relevant. Therefore, the geologist will examine a stone following a protocol that will not be that of the archaeologist, attentive to the biface flakes. Whereas the domain concerned is heterogenous and is not the object of a consensus, that which becomes informative is therefore negotiated and emerges in an inter-subjective way. An informational approach therefore serves to understand the singular outlook of a subject and what makes him change and orientate himself differently.

Bates' analysis, reinterpreted by Birger Hjorland, reinforces a conception of information as vector of a process of meaning through which meaning (*significations*) becomes sense (sense-making), knowing that this remains subjective (even if the process that leads to it can be inter-subjective in a socio-constructive perspective). Therefore, Birger Hjorland suggests that "[to] consider something information is thus always to consider it as informative in relation to some possible questions"[66]: information relates something with some question. The general conception of information defended here is therefore (inter-)subjective, situated in pragmatics.

1.6. The general method of relativized conceptualization: Mugur-Schächter [MUG 06]

Mioara Mugur-Schächter's work, already cited several times, completes and adds the finishing touches to the review carried out here, by dealing notably with a relation between the process of conceptualization, data and information.

1.6.1. *Constructing reality*

In her book *Sur le Tissage des Connaissances* [MUG 06], Mioara Mugur-Schächter works at analyzing the processes by which we conceptualize from an a-conceptual reality. She methodologizes, with an absolute rigour, the operation of object generation, then the formation of an outlook composed of a group of views corresponding to some qualifying properties (aspects) of the generated object.

66. [CAP 03].

She calls back into question the existence of entity-objects-in-themselves that pre-exist the descriptions we are elaborating of them, qualified in advance by properties they possess in their raw state, in reality and independently of all examination by human consciousness. It is therefore no longer a matter of simply detecting, almost passively, a pre-existing property that is just waiting to be discovered on a pre-existing entity-object. In this view, knowledge is no longer only a construct whose relationship with what is real in all its complexity (which remains definitively inaccessible to us) can only be defined by specifying the processes of elaboration of constructs, in essence, fundamentally subjective and subservient to a given project.

As she shows, indeed, that quantum mechanics in its own way postulates "microsystem states" that are similar to the constructed form that takes the real-world-out-there with what is reconstructed by man during his observation.

In [MUG 97], she states:

> "quantum mechanics studies 'states of microsystems'. These words designate entities whose existence we affirm but which are not directly accessible to man. (...) How, firstly, can an unknown state, of a microscopic object, be fixed as an object of study[67]?"

She adds that:

> "we must not forget that an observable quantum is not a property of a microstate, it is an operation of interaction of a microstate with a microscopic apparatus, therefore the proper perceptible value created qualifies the interaction"[68]... "It is the cognitive situation and the descriptional goal – not the internal structure of the object of study – which delimit the domain of relevance of quantum descriptions in the face of a domain of relevance of 'classical' descriptions"[69].

1.6.2. *Constituting each outlook on reality*

Edgar Morin [MOR 99] showed that reality is infinitely complex, built up with facts and events in interaction that infinitely influence each other, interact, interfere and modify one another. It is in the way we grasp this immeasurable complexity,

---

67. [MUG 97, p. 5].
68. [MUG 97, p. 9].
69. [MUG 97, p. 16].

impossible to embrace in all its completeness, that our relationship with reality is constructed.

Therefore, it is a matter of defining how we circumscribe reality, keeping in mind that we can only, at best, build partial, biased, discrete representations, gross, imprecise and empty approximations of the underlying infinite complexity.

While we are here, let us fully recognize the total relativity of these constructions, showing that neither the poet, nor the physician, nor the meteorologist, nor the sick child will look at the crystals of frost with which the window was adorned in the night, in the same way. Each outlook is therefore made up relatively to a singular point of view that, in addition, is variable and moving.

1.6.3. *Representing reality*

Without going deep into the general method of relativized conceptualization (MRC) that Mioara Mugur-Schächter details in her book[70], it can be summarized succinctly by the following few steps:

– the first phase is generation, through a consciousness-functioning, of the "entity-object", i.e. capturing purely factual, still a-conceptual, fragments of substance, obtained through a voluntary cut in the density of reality and which, as a result, are treated like a primary material for progressive semantizations;

– then emerge aspects or dimensions of qualification, across which aspect-views of the entity-object are elaborated;

– then, a grid for qualification which consists of an arbitrarily large but finite number of aspect-views, is called an outlook or a view, which defines a representation (among infinite possibilities) of the entity-object in the volume of the thing conceptualized, indicated in the diagram below.

We can note that the grid for qualifying properties can result from an objective and quantified measure generated by one or more recording devices and/or apparatus, or from a qualitative appreciation that comes under the subjective, emotional and/or physical sphere.

Figure 1.1 shows that a similar plane of observable reality can generate, via diverse choices of qualifying properties, differing outlooks. This is although all are receivable in terms of valid representation, with regard to a similar reality.

70. [MUG 06, p. 29-146].

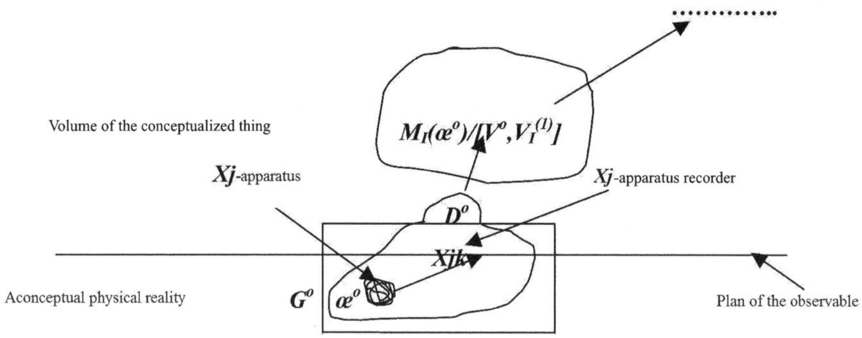

Figure 1.1. *Process of conceptualization according to [MUG 06]*

1.6.4. *Data versus information*

The group of parameters recorded in the grid for qualification, which Mioara Mugur-Schächter designates by aspects, are indifferently assimilated in data. These data, selected relative to a goal, translate the inter-subjective, pragmatic and well-situated dimension of the informational process. In addition, they can be of qualitative or quantitative nature. This terminological adoption is in coherence with Jacques Melese's ancient definition [MEL 79]:

DEFINITION.– A datum is a recording, in a code agreed by a social group, of some attributes of an object or an event.

Melese's attributes correspond to aspects or dimensions of qualification shown by Mugur-Schächter, and indifferently become data by consignment and/or recording. This procedure of agreement and/or recording corresponds exactly to the passage of DDD1 *diaphora de re*, a-conceptual discontinuities or differences, to DDD2 *diaphora de signo*, translations in variations in the perception of two physical signals in Luciano Floridi's theory.

Let us simply emphasize that a datum is in principle an objective fact, most often quantifiable. Still, for a social group, we must specify who established a consensus on the attributes chosen, on the method of measure, on the code used, and who has confidence in the honesty of the process, or who can control it. Outside of these conditions, a datum is not a "given", but can be suspected of being neither neutral nor objective. Since it is most often quantifiable, a piece of data is quantified as often as possible. But not always. And most of all not in essence itself.

Information is distinct from the data that make up its primary matter.

A clarifying example being worth more than a long speech, we can adopt this extract from Jean-Paul Delahaye's book [DEL 94] as an illustration:

> "it can be said that the stock page of a newspaper is a group of data. Its informational content is null for all individuals who are not aware of what the stock exchange is, and it is different for diverse speculators as the same data can have as an effect on one, to sell such a share, on the other to buy, on the third to commit suicide".

The process of meaning therefore produces, from these data, distinct information by action/interaction with different structures of reception. This shows all the importance of the structure of reception in the process of transformation of data into information.

1.6.5. *Liction reliances and mechanisms of meaning*

Producing knowledge and dealing with sense remains a specificity that belongs to human intelligence. Intelligence isolates attributes considered as qualifying aspects for the a-conceptual entity-object generated by the consciousness functioning at work. But it is also intelligence that creates, in a second time, information on the basis of relations between these data [LEL 08].

Meaning designates the active relational process of construction of sense. The mechanisms of it are the following, successively:

– the individual is dynamically inscribed in the data he consults and filters;

– by relation, by juxtaposition or by comparison, data held come into tension with each other;

– attractive or repulsive forces (links, echoes, relations etc.), called lictions, are installed among them;

– it is these lictional reliances that create semantic resonance (or dissonance [FES 57]), sense, emotion etc.

The hypothesis supported here relies on a construction of signifying, structuring and organizing comprehension schemes, elaborated by intelligence from discrete qualifying aspects connected by links. The liction of different aspects enables us to combine an elaborated representation that carries innovative comprehension indexes. To give a trivial example, the notion of speed, which is manifest sensorially by an effect of "wind of the course", through the vision of a landscape moving to a superior rhythm. This intuitively (and spontaneously enough) causes it to appear that the faster we go, the longer the distance traveled at the same time, hence liction of the superior order:

$$s = d/t$$

The three concepts (distance, speed and time) and the liction that connects them structure the representation of a movement in one go. This vision of the process of meaning translates in terms of liaison or links, the structural and/or organizing dimension that Marcia Bates designates as a pattern (simplistic enough in the example suggested here).

Nevertheless, general reasoning remains very evasive on the nature of links. The nature of liaison therefore remains the central point of elucidation. In [LEL 04] a notion of proximity of neighboring was proposed. This notion was based on a topological apprehension of the imaginary space of knowledge, the distance between fragments therefore being a semantic distance relying on some aspects whose similarity generates resonances between fragments. Two close or neighboring fragments are therefore not two fragments situated in contiguous information units in the space of data, but fragments that can be compared to the outlook of some qualifying properties they share or which enter in resonance.

Mioara Mugur-Schächter [MUG 05], in her *Method of Relativized Conceptualization*, evokes "neighboring coherences", "semantic attractions by continuity on the edges of elementary events" on the basis of aspects that compose the qualificational structure of communicable knowledge. Let us suppose that the term liction designates precisely this space of attraction qualified by the relation of some aspects.

Future works will be focused on deepening these notions to attempt to better define the human process of conceptualization, only in a position to enable the operationalization of what we no longer call link, nor liaison, but liction. Whatever it may be, whereas digital devices enable the evidence to juxtapose data everywhere, they have the capacity to identify by themselves signifying schemes of superior level. And whereas they show them, it is by pure accident and without "knowing" it.

1.7. Conclusion

According to this journey, the facts seem to show that the concept of information is currently found at the heart of a true scientific revision.

In view of the quantity of ongoing work, it is probable that the updating of elements supplied in this chapter risk being rapidly outdated. By outlining some necessarily simplifying markers, we nevertheless wanted to show the dynamics of reflection at work in order that each person can take part in it or appropriate it more easily.

1.8. Bibliography

[AND 06] E. ANDREEWSKY, R.DELORME, *Seconde Cybernétique et Complexité, Rencontres avec Heinz H. von FOESTER*, L'Harmattan, Paris, 2006.

[BAT 77] G. BATESON, *Vers une Ecologie de l'Esprit* (volume 1), Le Seuil, Paris, 1977.

[BAT 91] G. BATESON, *Une Unité Sacrée. Quelques Pas de plus vers une Ecologie de l'Esprit*, , La couleur des idées, Le Seuil, Paris, 1991, 1996.

[BAT 05] M.J. BATES, "Information and knowledge: an evolutionary framework for information science", *Information Research,* vol. 10, no. 4, paper 239, p. 1-24, 2005. Available online at: http://informationr.net/ir/10-4/paper239.html#goo91 (last accessed September 24, 2009).

[BAT 06] M.J. BATES, "Fundamental forms of information", *Journal of the American Society for Information Science and Technology*, vol. 57, no. 8, p. 1033-1045, 2006.

[BOR 68] H. BORKO, "What is information science", *American Documentation*, vol. 19, no. 1, 1968.

[BUC 91] M.K. BUCKLAND, "Information as thing", *Journal of the American Society for Information Science*, vol. 42, p351-360, 1991.

[CAP 03] R. CAPURRO, B. HJORLAND, "The concept of information", *Annual Review of Information Science and Technology*, B. CRONIN (ed), vol. 37, no. 8, p. 343-411, 2003. Available online at: http://www.capurro.de/infoconcept.html (last accessed September 24, 2009.

[CAR 01] A. CARDON, "Modeles et systems", in : *L'information dans un Système*, p. 50. Available online at: http://www.automatesintelligents.com/biblionet/2001/images/CH1.pdf (last accessed September 24, 2009).

[DEL 94] J.P. DELAHAYE, *Information, Complexité et Hasard*, Hermès, Paris, 1994.

[ECO 79] U. ECO, *Lector in Fabula. Le Rôle du Lecteur ou la Coopération Interprétative dans les Textes Narratifs*, Grasset, Paris, 1979, 1985.

[FES 57] U. FESTINGER, *A Theory of Cognitive Dissonance*, Stanford University, Stanford California, 1957.

[FLO 05] L. FLORIDI, "Semantic conceptions of information", *Stanford Encyclopeadia of Philosophy*, Stanford University, Stanford, 2005. Available online at: http://plato.stanford.edu/entries/information-semantic/ (last accessed September 24, 2009).

[FLO 04] B. FLORIS, "L'information a-elle du sens?", *Systèmes d'Information Organisationnels?*, in C. LE MOENNE (ed.), *Revue des Sciences de la Société*, vol. 63, p. 75-92, 2004.

[GIB 71] J.J. GIBSON, "A preliminary description and classification of affordances", in: *Reasons for Realism*, Lawrence Erlbaum Associates, Hillsdale N.J., Chapter 4.9, Part II. pp. 403-406, 1982.

[GLAS 81] E. GLASERFELD, "Introduction à un constructivisme radical", in: P. WATZLAWICK P. (ed.), *L'Invention de la Réalité. Comment Savons-Nous ce que Nous Croyons Savoir? Contributions au Constructivisme*, Le Seuil, Paris, 1988, p. 19-43.

[JEA 08] Y. JEANNERET, *La Vie Triviale des Etres Culturels*, Hermès, Paris, 2008.

[KEL 55] G. KELLY, *The Psychology of Personal Constructs*, Norton, New York, 1955.

[LAN 04] F. LANDRAGIN, "Saillance physique et saillance cognitive", *Corela*, vol. 2, no. 2, 2004. Available online at: http://edel.univ-poitiers.fr/corela/document.php?id=142 (last accessed September 24, 2009).

[LE M 95] J.L. LE MOIGNE, *Les Epistémologies Constructivistes*, PUF, Paris, 1995.

[LEL 04] S. LELEU-MERVIEL, "Effets de la numérisation et de la mise en réseau sur le concept de document", in: *Information, Interaction, Intelligence*, J.M. SALAÜN, J. CHARLET (eds), *Le Document Numérique* (numéro thématique), vol. 4, no. 1, p. 121-140, 2004.

[LEL 08] S. LELEU-MERVIEL, "L'information crée-t-elle de l'intelligence ou l'inverse?", *SIIE'08 Systèmes d'Information et Intelligence Economique*, vol. 1, no. 2, p. 710-730, 2008.

[McK 69] D. MACKAY, *Information, Mechanism and Meaning*, MIT Press, Cambridge (Ma), 1969.

[MEL 79] J. MELESE, *Approches Systémiques des Organisations*, Hommes et Techniques Editions, Suresnes, 1979.

[MOR 94] E. MORIN, *La Complexité Humaine*, Champs-l'Esssentiel, Flammarion, Paris, 2005.

[MOR 99] E. MORIN, J.L LE MOIGNE, *L'Intelligence de la Complexité*, L'Harmattan, Paris, 1999.

[MUG 97] M. MUGUR-SCHÄCHTER, "Les leçons de la mécanique quantique: vers une épistémologie formalisée", 1997. Available online at: http://www.cesef.net/index.html (last accessed October 5, 2007).

[MUG 05] M. MUGUR-SCHÄCHTER, "Représentation et mesures des complexités sans amputation du sens", in: J.L. LE MOIGNE, E. MORIN (ed), *Intelligence de la Complexité. Epistémologie et pragmatique* , de l'Aube Editions, 2007, p. 85-130.

[MUG 06] M. MUGUR-SCHÄCHTER, *Sur le Tissage des Connaissances*, Hermès, Paris, 2006.

[PAR 74] E. B. PARKER, "Information and society", in: C.A. Cuadra, M.J. Bates (eds), *Library and Information Service Needs of the Nation: Proceedings of a Conference on the Needs of Occupational, Ethnic and Other Groups in the United States*, U.S.G.P.O., Washington DC, 1974, p. 9-50.

[RAS 03] F. RASTIER, "De la signification au sens. Pour une sémiotique sans ontologie", *Texto!*, 2003. Available online at: http://www.revue-texto.net/Inedits/Rastier/Rastier_Semiotique-ontologie.html. (last accessed September 24, 2009).

[SEG 03] J. SEGAL, *Le Zéro et le Un. Histoire de la notion scientifique d'information au 20e siècle,* Syllepse Editions, Paris, 2003.

[SHA 48] C.E. SHANNON, "A mathematical theory of communication", *The Bell System Technical Journal,* vol. 27, p. 379-423, 623-656, 1948.

[SHA 49] C.E. SHANNON, W. WEAVER, *The Mathematical Theory of Communication,* University of Illinois Press, Urbana (Illinois), 1949.

[USE 08] P. USEILLE, Une approche informationnelle du document: vers l'émergence du sens formatif, Univerisity of Valenciennes and Hainaut-Cambrésis thesis, December 2008.

[WIE 48] N. WIENER, *Cybernetics or Control and Communication in the Animal and the Machine*, John Wiley & Sons, New York, 1948.

Chapter 2

From Scientific Communication to Specialized Mediation: Communication of Knowledge and Forms of Hybridizations

2.1. Introduction

The position, which we consider to be central in information sciences, of this concrete object, which is the document, leads us to question it. It is actually the mould in which information, the contents, takes shape on the communication plane. At the same time it is the support that allows it to circulate. It has its place in this branch which is interested in the uses of information. A branch that is also, but in a different way, taken on by information science and communication science. In this way we can cause a set of ramifications, ranging from the organization of knowledge to its distribution and its appropriation, and passing through diverse domains of knowledge, to ensue from this.

At the risk of seeming reactionary, we are therefore moving towards a document science, a documentology, some basics of which had been laid down by its founders at the beginning of the 20th century. But is it not the role of research to reinvest in the past? By returning the document to its place as container and contents, this documentology indeed presents the advantage of situating what we can call "scientific and technical information" (STI), in the group made up of information and communication sciences (ICS) in France.

Chapter written by Viviane COUZINET.

This point of view led to an outlook focused on another branch that studies the construction of knowledge. This branch is less frequently approached than those expressed before but is focused, like them, on the document as a convergence point of research in the domain. It combines analyzing the social context of emergence and analyzing the media that convey knowledge, the content it distributes, and the forms of writing it uses in order to enable its unusual appropriation.

This comfortable split, in diverse branches, to situate epistemological positionings does not exclude partial overlapping, nor does it exclude interweaving of its own branches. It is therefore a matter of understanding the complexity of the construction and distribution of knowledge by inscribing it in a progression of research carried out in ICS.

Inserted in the domain of sciences and techniques, and favored by research in information science, the study of scientific information, its social stakes and the way it presents itself will progressively move from scientific communication to the emergent analysis of a few forms of hybridization with different worlds.

This route enables us to understand the mediations at work in research communication. Each step will be approached from its social, followed by its media-related, and finally discursive angles. However, the order in which works will be presented will not be chronological. The division of themes in time indeed remains artificial as it is linked to an object that is invested, in the long run, by different researchers.

Beyond revealing new problematics, the plan here is to prepare the ground for collective reflection and attempt to show how the preoccupations of informatologists and the preoccupations of communicologists are connected in order to construct a domain of common knowledge in the discipline.

2.2. Scientific communication and communication between researchers

Taking on scientific communication supposes, first, an interest in the works that contributed to positioning it as a strong research thematic in ICS. A new outlook, compared to that of sociologists, but not ignoring them, introduced the journal as an essential medium of communication for science.

2.2.1. *The researcher, sole stakeholder*

The ICS encyclopedia, *Dictionnaire Encyclopédique des Sciences de l'Information et de la Communication*, written in 1997 by Bernard Lamizet and Ahmed Silem, suggests the following definition for scientific communication:

> "This expression designates a) the transmission, between researchers, of knowledge produced and information produced during research activities [...]; b) the activity displayed by each researcher to shape his work, make it known to his peers, keep up to date with the research of others [...]; c) the scientific debate, in other words, the competing positions defended by researchers, at the same time"[1] [LAM 97].

The researcher needs to publicize the results of his or her research for several reasons. First and foremost, because the results ensure an informative function, they enable him/her to make his/her colleagues aware of breakthroughs. Therefore, colleagues will, in turn, be able to rely on this work, criticize it, and check it against other corpora, on other grounds or with other methods, in order to participate in making conclusions more general. Next, when the results are published they are accepted by a group of peers who give credibility to the work. At the same time, through the exchanges they suppose in the laboratory as well as with editorial committees, and the return to hypotheses, methods, results and rewriting, they ensure a training function. Finally, in this way they date and give a priority over other inventions or discoveries [LAT 91].

As a system of relationships between acquired positions, the scientific field is defined by Pierre Bourdieu as the "place (i.e. the game space) of a competition struggle whose specific stake is the monopoly of scientific authority jointly defined as technical capacity and social power" [BOU 75]. In this place, producing research results is the means to accumulate scientific capital. This capital is acquired through contributions, recognized by peers, to progress discoveries and inventions. Authority is constructed through publications, particularly in the most selective media, that are also often the most prestigious [BOU 97]. This "authority capital" plays a role in promoting researchers, as shown by Marcel Fournier, Yves Gingras and Creutzer Mathurin for education sciences [FOU 88] in the context of a Quebec university.

---

1. "*Cette expression désigne à la fois a) la transmission, entre chercheurs, des connaissances produites et des informations produites au cours des activités de recherche [...] ; b) l'activité que déploie chaque chercheur pour mettre en forme ses travaux, les faire connaître à ses pairs, se tenir au courant des recherches d'autrui [...] ; c) le débat scientifique, autrement dit les positions concurrentes défendues par les chercheurs*".

Research activity, including in human and social sciences, can no longer be viewed without being incorporated into a group that is well identified for its part in the breakthrough of knowledge. Teams or laboratories are evaluated by peers and experts, most often originating in the same discipline. In the contracts framework this is done in the framework of quadrennials contracts for France's Minister of Higher Education and of temporary contracts for requests for proposals of diverse minsters or specifically dedicated agencies, such as the French National Research Agency, which attribute the financial means necessary for carrying out investigations.

These evaluations are based on the scientific quality of propositions and the publications of respondents. The researcher is therefore directly linked to his/her laboratory. It is why he/she participates in improving works by organizing events whose publication of acts he/she ensures with external financial aids. These works can be inscribed in more or less recurrent collections to have a more or less wide distribution. Some labs possess the necessary energy and university funding to go into producing journals on a regular basis. Whereas the editor is renowned in the breakthrough of the researcher's career, the medium's notoriety is linked to the scientific community's reception of it. It is most often linked to the reception of its founder or founders, the scientific committee in which it works hard and the laboratory that gave birth to it.

Scientific communication therefore belongs only to the direct research world. Produced by it, it is reserved for it. Author and reader are merged, as stated by Eliseo Verón, through communication that is endogenous, i.e. "whose starting point is within the scientific institutions", and interdisciplinary, i.e. during which the researcher addresses his peers [VER 97].

2.2.2. *Spaces for research distribution*

Whereas there are a relatively large number of media for communication between researchers, the importance given to each one of them varies according to the discipline. In technical and health sciences (THS), journals are largely predominant. They are followed by proceedings from big international symposiums with a scientific community whose manner of evaluating and choosing communication proposals is very strict.

Nevertheless, quite a few variations exist from one domain of knowledge to the next, with symposiums being highly valued or not considered, according to the case. In human and social sciences (HSS), the importance given to books, published by a scientific editor and in a collection whose scientific committee is recognized in the community to which it belongs, still remains the main medium. Proceedings from international symposiums occupy a diverse place, which is always linked to the notoriety of the scientific committee and to the modes of selection that have been made public and respected.

Successive attempts by authorities in charge of research and researcher evaluation to make the identifiers of scientific activity uniform, however, contribute to giving journals a preponderant place. In fact, journals are therefore the main research distribution medium, and each discipline is devoted to establishing the list of the research it thinks is being used in its domain. Some therefore suggest a classification system, and provide the most demanding attribute, on each account, a coded value that enables the productivity of a laboratory or a researcher to be calculated[2].

Journals are indeed the space where research takes shape and in which it is observable while it is being updated and progressing. The symposium, as the place where ongoing research is exhibited, is valued less highly than the article. As for the book, and its chapters, it is the medium preferred by research that is mostly complete, due to the sum of works it represents.

The HSS scientific journal was the object of the first works of a research seminar entitled *Communication et Information Scientifiques entre Spécialistes* hosted, at the beginning of the 1990s, in the LERASS (Social Sciences Study and Applied Research Laboratory – University of Toulouse 3, University Institutes of Technology), by Robert Boure. He put forward a definition from a series of criteria that enable journals to be qualified as scientific, the degree of scientificity being proportional to the number of criteria present. It isolated:

– *The function*: it is in charge of the distribution of research results and the conditions under which they were obtained.

– *The content*: it is made up of scientific works, i.e. work expressing a "cognitive or interpretive ambition of reality by referring to a validated theoretical and methodological apparatus". It is where "the logic of investigation always prevails over that of exposition" and which "is inscribed in the scientific and institutional field of one or more academic disciplines". The journal, "publishing opportunity" and "source of information" [BOU 93] at the same time, is to a certain extent the prerequisite for being a researcher. It is the place of scientific debate, i.e. for us, the place of discussion aimed at causing progress, the proof of sustained research activity and source of information in ongoing or recent investigations.

– *The specificity of its production and distribution*: this is taken over by researchers who are not qualified in jobs related to books or publishing. The activity

2. Other criteria are added for one and the other, notably the number of newly trained doctors.

of production and distribution cannot be developed without the financial support of large research establishments such as the French National Center for Scientific Research, or administrative organizations like the French National Book Center[3] [BOU 93]. However, it seems that this criterion can be adjusted as some publishing houses produce and distribute journals, including in HSS. Armand Colin, for example, or other similar University Presses (for example the Oxford University Press and MIT Press) can be cited.

– Finally, the process of acceptance of articles for publication makes them a reliable source of information. Submitted to critical reading by researchers renowned in their scientific field, they are modified or amended and appear in their definitive form, in a thus validated version [BOU 93].

These criteria set up for HSS journals could easily be transposed to THS. To our knowledge, it was not set up in ICS using the same definitions as those of these last disciplines.

Another criterion, that of being regularly indexed in large national or foreign scientific databases, can also be added. For example, in Library and Information Science Abstracts (UK) and Information Science Abstracts (US), which gives a journal national visibility for the "scientific community". The need for the researcher to emphasize the priority of his/her work, to exchange it with his/her colleagues, to take into account previous results produced in his/her domain and to be inscribed in a relationship network makes this "visibilizing" particularly important. With the generalization of internet use, the largest possible distribution, geographically speaking, was from then on essential for research [COU 99].

Indexation is also an opening to other disciplines. In large institutes dedicated to scientific and technical information distribution, information retrieval can be carried out simultaneously in several disciplinary bases. This means that visibility is no longer only intradisciplinary. Therefore, we understand why a discipline may be interested in rubbing shoulders, using the media to which it is attached, with those from which it wants to differentiate itself or, on the contrary, with which it wants to show its complementarity.

The recent example of installation of the "information science" database in Francis, while continuing to be maintained in Pascal, is a "compliance" with HSS, the academic discipline it belongs to. It is an affirmation of its entry in an

---

3. The French National Book Center (*Centre National du Livre*) is a public establishment of the French Ministry of Culture and Education. Its mission is to encourage the creation and distribution of quality works across diverse support devices for stakeholders of the chain of books.

interdisciplinarity, and its uniqueness compared to computer science, all at the same time.

2.2.3. *Research writing*

Within the medium, social distribution of research passes through discourse. According to Dominique Maingueneau, the media is actually part of a communication device that shapes the discourse genre [MAI 98]. Under the influence of pragmatics, this notion of discourse is a product of a certain way of understanding verbal communication [MAI 91]. The wording of texts, governed by rules of organization belonging to a particular social group [ESC 73], enables "participants' mutual recognition of their roles and their communication framework"[4] [MAI 98]. These rules can be implicit or "formalized" by specific literary works, such as formal standards produced by particular organizations.

Regarding scientific discourse, UNESCO in 1962 and at the request of information professionals wanting to facilitate and improve document processing, produced a Code of Good Practice for Scientific Publications[5] which was widely distributed in several different languages. Suggestions and commentaries brought by users of this code and notably by the International Union of Pure and Applied Physics[6] (IUPAP) to produce the publishing of a Guide for the Preparation of Scientific Papers for Publication[7]. This guide sets global standards for types and forms of presentation, and specifies that there are three categories of scientific articles:

– *The "original scientific paper"*, "describing new research, techniques or apparatus", it "constitutes a significant extension of knowledge or understanding" and it "is written in such a way that a qualified research worker is able, on the basis of the information given, (i) to reproduce the experiment and secure the results described with equal accuracy or within the limits of experimental error specified by the author, or (ii) to repeat the author's observations, calculations or theoretical derivations and judge his findings".

---

4. "*La reconnaissance mutuelle des participants de leurs rôles et du cadre de leur communication*".

5. The UNESCO/NS/177 document, 1962. The explanatory statement reveals "the lack of freely accepted discipline in drafting and publishing scientific information".

6. The IUPAP was established in 1922 in Brussels. It is made up of members representing identified physics communities and its slogan is: "To stimulate and facilitate international co-operation in physics and the worldwide development of science". The Union's website is http://www.iupap.org.

7. It was fully published in *Documentaliste* [*Documentalist*], vol. 6, no. 1, 1969. Subscribers were invited to distribute it widely.

– *The "provisional communication" or "preliminary note"*, a text that contains "one or more novel items of scientific information, but is insufficiently detailed to allow readers to check the said information in the ways described above. Another type of short note, generally in letter form, gives brief comments on work already published" also belong to this category.

– *The "subject review article",* which is a "survey of one particular subject, in which information already published is assembled, analyzed and discussed".

Many elements of this guide are adopted by several French norms arising from the *Association Française de Normalisation* Standards Service (AFNOR)[8]. The article is mostly concerned with three of them in particular, which deal, respectively, with:

– its summary (NF Z 44-004);

– bibliographic references (NF Z 44-005); and

– presentation (NF Z 41-003).

The latter applies to "original, theory- or experiment-based scientific or technical articles" and can be extended, as far as editing is concerned, to "overviews" or "progress reports on the state of an issue". Compared to the UNESCO guide, the provisional publication is missing.

It is therefore the "original paper" or "original article" and the "overview" or "progress report" which, at least in the formal plan, represent the scientific article or primary article. The latter is therefore a literary work that includes elements of the authorial paratext:

– an author's name accompanied by site of practice and address,

– an abstract,

– key words or descriptors, depending on the case,

– footnotes,

– bibliographic references.

8. NF Z 41-003. Presentation of contributions to periodicals. Approved French standard, January 1974.
NF Z 44-004. Recommendations to authors of scientific and technical articles for the wording of abstracts. Approved French standard, December 1984.
NF Z 44-005. Bibliographic references: content, form and structure. International standard ISO 690-1987, December 1987.

The original article has an introduction, a description of materials and methods used, a presentation of results (in the form of tables, diagrams, graphs, appendices, etc), followed by commentary and a conclusion. Each part is the object of developments that we will retain. This will be done in order to further specify the meaning attributed to "original article", whether the latter gives the origin, object and aim of the work in its introduction, or situates it in relation to work carried out in the same domain and specifies the hypotheses retained. It is therefore the vector of scientific communication, whose object, according to Jean Meyriat, is:

> "to transmit knowledge that is useful on a long-term basis to those who receive it by increasing their ability to solve problems thanks to a piece of knowledge made up for that purpose" [MEY 81].

Furthermore, scientific articles rely on a set of other articles cited in the argumentation. All scientific articles include a list of references [CAL 93], "*citations preuves*" or "*citations-authorité*" [MAI 91], that mark the movements in which the researcher is inscribed, the debates he/she opens with his/her peers, the field in which he/she is located. Manuals presenting the scientific research method base the method on this outline.

Whereas this basic definition may seem more similar to THS, journal editing protocol recommends that we conform to it. Although it is less apparent, the construction of HSS articles enables us to find each of the elements cited. This is because it is expressed in a less abrupt way than in "hard" sciences, where the plan of HSS articles adopts the designation of parts as stated in the standard. The results and their interpretation can be combined, with interview excerpts or document analyses replacing the numerical results and those in graph form. Nevertheless this formalization necessary for understanding distributed research proves neither the many returns, which are often necessary, to one or more of the previous steps, nor the readjustments, difficulties encountered or obstacles overcome in empirical work. It does not prove the annotations of data sheets or all the literary work that precedes the final text either [LAT 79].

The make-up of the article – notes, tables, graphs, bibliographies – to name only the most common elements, is added to this. But here again, the tendency varies according to the discipline. For example, Muriel Lefebvre revealed that in mathematics, whereas some researchers emphasize the heuristic value of what she generically calls "image", they forbid each other from using it in their publications [LEF 03]. On the contrary it is highly used in scientific popularization.

This diverse research is centered around communication in a closed world – that of research – with its operation standards, its relational modes and their production in time, which Bourdieu called *scientific habitus* [BOU 75]. Furthermore whereas the researcher's mission is essentially to advance the sciences, it is also his/her mission to make his discoveries known to a wider public. Respecting statutory obligations and moral obligations, some follow the path of popularization.

2.3. Popularization

We saw that scientific publication is necessary for advancing research and researchers on the scientific and academic front. Why do some researchers also risk popularizing science? Works lead in ICS from the 1980s renew scientific communication problematics by postulating a continuum between research and popularization.

2.3.1. *Journalists and researchers*

Going back to the ICS encyclopedia, *Dictionnaire Encyclopédique des Sciences de l'Information et de la Communication*, the definition of the French counterpart of "popularization" (*vulgarization*) refers to "scientific communication". It is defined in opposition to the latter, which it specifies:

> "must not be confused with what some people call 'public scientific communication' or 'popularization', which takes its name from the necessity, which appeared in the 18th century – at that time scholars exposed their discoveries themselves in salons – to distribute science to the *vulgare plebis*"[9] [LAM 97].

Science popularization therefore seems to belong to a world other than that of research. Further, still by opposition, it is specified that it is addressed to the "wider public" or the "cultivated public". We are therefore in the midst of multiple addressees, having levels and cultural practices that are different from those of researchers. In order to enable the appropriation of knowledge by the largest number of people, an intra-lingusitics of literary research is necessary. These styles are revealed to be esoteric, in the original sense of "reserved for the adept", for most unspecialized readers. In this process of rewriting,

> "those who polularize science see themselves as natural and essential intermediaries in charge of bridging the gap between scientists and the wider public in order to re-establish broken communication" [JAC 88].

9. "*Ne doit pas être confondue avec ce que certains appellent "la communication scientifique publique" ou "vulgarisation", laquelle tire son nom de la nécessité, apparue au XVIII*e *siècle – les savants exposaient alors eux-mêmes leurs découvertes dans les salons – de diffuser la science à la vulgare plebis*".

Authors of productions that can be popularized are always mediators. The expression "third man", a paradigm in which Moles and Oulif are entered and that designates "professionals of communication or the conception of educational products"[10] goes back to this [LAM 97].

However, popularization is rarely associated with teaching in the school context [CAR 90]. It is a matter of installing "elsewhere than in habitual places for education, a communication between specialists and non-specialists, which focuses on scientific and technical issues"[11] [AIT 85]. This role of intermediary is held by the so-called "scientific" journalist whose expertise is based on disciplinary education of a high level (masters) and on a knowledge of operations of the sciences doubled with that of public expectations. This is supported by a capacity to translate, in the written or audiovisual form, in order to explain discoveries and breakthroughs in science.

The objective pursued is indeed to awaken the public's interest and critical mind, to grab its attention, as highlighted by Martine Barrère, journalist for the *Recherche* journal in 1985 [BAR 85]. The importance of popularization can be recalled in a broad outline: to arouse curiosity, to initiate us into an approach for questioning phenomena, and to help to take a stand on personal or public issues.

Its social role is stated in "Manifeste pour une Vulgarisation Créatrice" [Manifesto for Creative Popularization], which appeared in the French newspaper, *Figaro*, on 21 June 1995, and was written by three researchers – Yves Jeanneret, Pierre Lazslo and Lionel Salem:

> "Knowledge needs to be shared so that culture can be spread and renewed. This sharing of knowledge is also a condition for the maintenance and breakthrough of knowledge itself, and for research to continue. Today, all important decisions in economic, political or social domains necessitates the active sharing of knowledge; school and university achievement is no longer sufficient"[12].

---

10. "*professionnels de la communication ou de la conception de produits éducatifs*".

11. "*ailleurs que dans les lieux habituels de la formation, une communication entre spécialistes et non-spécialistes, portant sur les questions scientifiques et techniques*".

12. "*Partager les savoirs est indispensable à l'élargissement et au renouveau de la culture. C'est aussi une condition du maintien et de l'avancée des savoirs eux-mêmes, et de la pérennité de la recherche. Aujourd'hui, toute décision importante dans les domaines économique, politique ou social nécessite le partage actif de la connaissance ; l'acquis scolaire et universitaire ne suffit plus*".

It is a matter of publicizing research – through researchers and labs – the great trends of scientific thought, and of informing others about discoveries and their applications.

Nevertheless, journalist/researcher relationships are not obvious. Whereas the former claim to have made the separation between knowledge "manufacturing" and distribution, they criticize the latter for having an elitist and corporatist conception of science that alienates them from the public [BAR 85]. As for researchers, they find it difficult to trust journalist intermediation, as they accuse the journalists of too great a simplification. Therefore some of them take charge of translating their own work themselves and think that "popularization is particularly efficient when it is done by the scientist himself"[13] but "it is criticized by scientific colleagues as being a detour for gaining recognition"[14] [CAR 90].

In fact, the *Law on Technological Research and Development Policy and Programming* in France, 1982, stipulates that participating in wide distribution of science is part of the missions of researchers. A report on activity, in terms of popularization, of workers at the French National Center for Scientific Research (CNRS) in 1989 reveals that only 22% participated in at least one act in this domain [KUN 92]. This is mainly because of researchers who are well advanced in their career and "who can more easily overcome risks of criticism"[15] [JAC 88]. The main obstacle for slow development of this activity is due to its non-recognition by authorities in charge of evaluation [KUN 92].

Research from the 1980s lead by Daniel Jacobi shows that, in the unfolding of a researcher's career, whereas poor recognition is an obstacle in their participation or interest in popularization, another form of acknowledgment can be brought to light. By considering its content and cognitive dimension, comparing the reformulation to the source, situating everything in the mode of functioning of the scientific community and categorizing groups of addressees, his/her work leads us to distinguish levels of reception, use and forms of accumulation of symbolic capital [JAC 88]. Eliseo Verón generalized, in part, this communication diagram which he called "trans-scientific endogenous communication". Its characteristics are the following:

> "the speaker is self-defined as scientific, as producer of knowledge. The starting point of the communication act is therefore in scientific institutions,

---

13. "*la vulgarisation est particulièrement efficace quand elle est faite par les scientifiques eux-mêmes*".

14. "*elle est critiquée par les collègues scientifiques comme détour pour accumuler de la reconnaissance*".

15. "*qui peuvent plus facilement surmonter les risques de critique*".

hence the qualification, endogenous"; "the receiver is defined by difference: it is because he is not a scientist that the speaker addresses him"; "it is this difference which founds the justification and legitimacy of the act of the speaker, it is because he has a certain expertise in a scientific domain, and because the addressee does not have it, because he speaks"[16] [VER 97].

This research and its stands reveal the multiplicity of participants, authors as well as addressees. By positing the hypothesis of the continuity of socio-distribution practices and by integrating content, they place popularization in scientific communication, and by extent ICS. Until this point popularization had been taken on essentially by cultural sociologists. A synthesis of diverse work, from the question of knowledge sharing, was suggested by Yves Jeanneret in 2003 [JEA 04].

2.3.2. *Places of distribution of popularized knowledge: France as an example*

Since the appearance in 1834 of the French newspaper *L'Écho du Monde Savant* [*The Echo of the Scholar's World*], which was considered as the first French popularized periodical, science distribution media has continued to diversify. *L'Illustration* [*The Illustration*], a general newspaper, or the *Gazette de Santé* [*Health Gazette*] and the *Bon Jardinier* [*Good Gardener*], which are specialized, are more well-known. Print relay is ensured, by researchers, with the use of film, and the founding of the *Institut Cinématographique Scientifique* [Scientific Film Institute] in 1930 by Jean Painlevé. This was than followed with the radio, from 1936, and the broadcasting of Paul Langevin's conferences at the *Collège de France*. Followers, however, remain relatively few.

The creation of science museums, the *Palais de la Découverte* [Palace of Discovery] in 1937, and more recently the *Cité des Sciences et de l'Industrie* [City of Science and Industry] in la Villette, in 1986, shows the desire for public authorities in France to favor the seizing of innovations by supplying a showcase for science and technology. The regional opening of scientific, technical and industrial cultural centers, and the annual organization of the event entitled the "National Science Festival" is inscribed in the preoccupation with informing as many people as possible about progress in the field.

---

16. "*l'énonciateur s'autodéfinit comme scientifique, comme producteur de connaissances. L'acte de communication a donc son point d'origine à l'intérieur des institutions scientifiques, d'où la qualification d'endogène*"; "*le destinataire est défini par différence: c'est parce qu'il n'est pas un scientifique que l'énonciateur s'adresse à lui*"; "*c'est cette différence qui fonde la justification et la légitimité de l'acte de l'énonciateur, c'est parce qu'il a une certaine compétence dans un domaine scientifique, et que le destinataire ne l'a pas, qu'il prend la parole*".

It is this path that was opened on research, from the 17th century, by what would become France's Museum of Natural History, which is also borrowed by Interpretation Centers as places for information, education and exhibition. Those devoted more particularly to architecture and heritage served, in part, as a terrain for analyzing the mediation of monuments [FRA 06]. The role of the science exhibition can indeed be studied as a composite media aimed at collecting knowledge and facilitating its appropriation by the wider public [DAV 99].

Other analyses are centered on interpretation aids for texts displayed, followed by images and illustrations reproduced and associated to the texts. By applying enunciation theories, interferences between text and image are revealed, as well as the role of indexation and referencing as interpretation aids by diverse publics and as a point of view imposed by the "creator" [JAC 05].

From then on, whereas the exhibition has more and more recourse to multimedia and robots, publishing production continues to develop. French magazines specializing in popularization, such as *Science et Vie* [*Science and Life*], *Science et Avenir* [*Science and Future*] and *Historia*, occupy a large commercial niche [CAR 90]. Some are also available in collections destined more particularly to young people. Sociologists have studied the cultural role of these media in particular social groups. There also exists what Paul Caro qualifies as a "secondary form of scientific literature" presenting "summaries on topical news matters, brief articles that report the latest great ideas across all scientific sectors, commentaries on scientific policy in institutions or States and those which become the echo of the problems that science poses for the Organization"[17] [CAR 90]. The journals *Nature* (UK) and *Science* (United States), that are well known in higher education belong to this group. This is notably since the classification, called "Shanghai classification", which lead university presidents to recommend soliciting them for publication.

Carlos Elías, professor at the Carlos III University of Madrid, studied *Science* and *Nature* journals, in their printed and online versions, as an essential source used by scientific journalists. Through the intermediary of press agencies, they announce the summary of their next issue – some 4,000 contacts across the world for *Nature* – which ensures them coverage in newspapers, radio and television. *Science*, published by the American Association for the Advancement of Science, benefits from the support of this scientific lobby, the most powerful in the world [ELI 08]. Despite the impact of publication in these journals on obtaining financing for research projects and on researchers' careers, here it is a matter of advertising

---

17. *"des synthèses sur des sujets d'actualité, de brefs articles qui rapportent les dernières trouvailles à travers tous les secteurs scientifiques, des commentaires sur la politique scientifique des institutions ou des Etats et qui se font l'écho des problèmes que la science pose à la Société*".

scientific events [SCH 85]. Furthermore "these journals are submitted to strong competition to be the most influential in the domain of scientific communication" [SEM 99]. Publication, popularization and communication of science can therefore be joined together.

This recourse to media, whose notoriety is different to those of the world of research, can be considered complementary and useful, not only because the law leads researchers to it, but also because it recognizes scientific expertise and authority. By assuming a continuum of practices of socio-distribution of knowledge in the scientific field, Daniel Jacobi renewed the outlook focused on the communication link, or lack thereof, between scientific communication and science popularization. In other words, he adopted the outline suggested by Eliso Verón between "intradisciplinary endogenous communication" and "trans-scientific endogenous communication".

2.3.3. *Forms of writing*

If scientific popularization works hard to re-establish the link between common knowledge and scientific knowledge [JAC 88], it therefore supposes the use of a simplified vocabulary and a particular shaping. Although, "whatever the context – radio or television program, conference, exhibition, book, specialized journal, company visit, etc – (...)"[18] we can determine "neither a specific technique, nor a homogenous discourse"[19] [AIT 85].

Journalists defend the qualities of their writing style and oppose school methods. These methods seem to be incapable of mobilizing interest. They do not facilitate the learning of sciences. On the contrary, the journalists consider their articles to be "more apt for furthering the analytical mind, a reasoning, an opening to general ideas, whereas traditional teaching favors knowledge and the accumulation of details"[20] [JAC 88]. They advocate the need for an account of science constructed:

> "around an action told by a witness [...]. It is a matter of situating a beginning in time and space. This action must be adventurous, breaking with

---

18. "*quel que soit le contexte – émission radiophonique, télévisuelle, conférence, exposition, livre, revue spécialisée, visite d'entreprise, etc – (...)*".

19. "*ni une technique spécifique, ni un discours homogène*".

20. "*plus aptes à favoriser l'esprit de synthèse, une démarche de l'esprit, une ouverture aux idées générales, alors que l'enseignement traditionnel privilégie les connaissances et l'accumulation de détails*".

daily ordinariness. Finally, actors must be put in place so that the action, and notably the hero or heroes, unfold"[21] [BAR 85].

The introduction of the direct form, of animation sequences and the systematic recourse to schematization and illustration make it a "pluri-graphic message" [JAC 84].

Dramatization, simplification, but also the spectacular and the entertaining are used to grab the receiver's attention to the point that it was possible to say "science seems to work miracles and its success are an amplifying factor of wonder at the same time as a reducing factor in a stage of 'magic' mentality"[22] [CAR 90]. Between the desire to be attractive, pleasing to read – as a newspaper is made to be sold [BAR 85] – and the need to replace in a group, to select, to simplify, the risk of sacrificing rigor and exactitude is great.

Vladimir de Sémir, teacher at the University of Barcelona, also a scientific journalist, accused his colleagues of participating in social exclusion during a symposium dedicated to this thematic. Referring to Pierre Bourdieu's paper on television (1996)[23], he denounced the production of fast thinking "which, like fast food, prevents us from thinking, reflecting and choosing [...] with the fast thinking that we, journalists, impose, the capacity of cultural election and development of a social critical mind diminishes more and more"[24] [SEM 99].

Science, mainly technology and health are studied by researchers as thematics approached by popularization. Generally, the interest is focused on their history, impact, language and rhetoric, the place they occupy and relations they entertain with the media [JEA 94]. On a more precise thematic, a recent piece of research analyzed fear in the presentation of an invention. It analyzed the case of information on the laser given by the journal *Science et Vie*, between 1960 and 1994. The ambiguity of discourse, the passage of a science-fiction story to a more technical description does not dissipate the fears which, on the contrary, seem to be fed by the reference to political news. The study of popularization thus seems to be, "just as

---

21. "*autour d'une action racontée par un témoin [...]. Il s'agit de situer dans le temps et l'espace, un commencement. Cette action se doit d'être aventureuse, en rupture avec la banalité quotidienne. Enfin, des acteurs doivent être mis en place pour que se déroule l'action, et notamment le ou les héros*".

22. "*que la science paraît réaliser des miracles et que ses succès sont un facteur amplificateur de l'émerveillement en même temps qu'un facteur de réduction à un stade de mentalité "magique"*".

23. P. Bourdieu, *Sur la télévision: l'Emprise du Journalisme*, Raisons d'agir, Paris, 1996.

24. "*qui comme le fast food, nous empêche de penser, de réfléchir et de choisir [...] avec le fast thinking que nous, journalistes, imposons, la capacité d'élection culturelle et de développement d'un esprit critique social diminue de plus en plus*".

scientific research, indissociable from that of its social, psychological, economical and political context"[25] [FOU 02].

The "in-depth reorganization of knowledge" required when writing a popular science text, presents the difficulty "of simplifying and clarifying truth without sacrificing it" [JEA 95]. According to Daniel Jacobi, popular science literary works produced by researchers are inscribed in the diversity of social roles they assume. The article diverges from scientific article in a journal which he calls "primary":

> "its theme is less specific, in conclusion, we spread out to social preoccupations, the bibliography is less abundant, the results table or some demonstrations that would make the text unreadable are suppressed, illustrations pay a particular headlining role (…)"[26] [JAC 82].

In this author's opinion, popularization is a component of the scientific field:

> "On the one hand there is not a source scientific discourse, a discourse that is incomprehensible by the average public and, on the other hand, a second discourse, reformulation and paraphrase of the first destined for a wider audience, but a continuum, in which the writers, their texts and their diverse intentions are intimately mixed up"[27] [JAC 84].

He verified this hypothesis from observing effects of restricted distribution on targeted numbers of articles published in the *La Recherche* journal. The study focused on the written production of researchers having published *La Recherche* and in primary scientific journals on a similar topic. The work was completed by a survey from subscribers and interviews with authors. Being published in *La Recherche* is considered by the population asked as a consecration [JAC 82]. It therefore suggests replacing the popular science text in "the group of scientific discourse (on which it depends and from which it derives when it is not a variant of it)" [JAC 84]. The "reconditioning" implied by the reformulation for adapting to readers and work on the *figurabilité* of concepts, does not autonomize the popularization discourse of primary scientific discourse popularization [JAC 99]. Contextualized interdiscursive discourse therefore enables us to situate discourse in

25. "*tout comme pour la recherche scientifique, indissociable de celle de son contexte social, psychologique, économique et politique*".

26. "*son thème est moins spécifique, en conclusion on élargit à des préoccupations sociales, la bibliographie est moins abondante, on supprime les tableaux de résultats ou certaines démonstrations qui rendraient le texte illisible, les illustrations y jouent un rôle particulier d'accroche (...).*"

27. "*Il n'y a pas d'un côté un discours scientifique source, discours incompréhensible par le public moyen et de l'autre un discours second, reformulation et paraphrase du premier destiné au plus grand nombre, mais un continuum, dans lequel les scripteurs, leurs textes et leurs diverses intentions se mêlent intimement.*"

a more general theory of scientific communication. Furthermore, Yves Jeanneret emphasizes that the journal *Scientific American,* which "dominates the popular literature market", is a publication that is duly patented by the scientific institution" [JEA 94].

2.4. Specialized communication and forms of hybridization

Between communication among researchers and scientific popularization, a third path of research is born. It is based on new problematics that question the direct links existing between the worlds of professional practice and the world of research. Conducted ICS, the first works showed that communication between researchers can cause communication between practitioners to border on a unique medium and allow comings and goings between the two communities, leading to forms of mediation hybridization [COU 00].

2.4.1. *A multitude of writers*

Practitioners are confronted with the need to keep their achievements up to date. These achievements come from their professional training or result from their practice, they encounter the evolution of knowledge, machines and tools. The progress of information and communication technologies that penetrate all domains is also a major factor of the necessity for knowledge or know-how to be updated. In this context, practitioners participate actively in the maintenance and progress of their colleagues' training, most often in a grouping of associative form which represents them. The most experienced are therefore in charge of transmitting their experience, their critical view of the activity, and their point of view on new discoveries useful for solving concrete problems encountered in daily life or favoring adaptation to new situations.

Researchers contribute to this updating through the results of their work, first of all. Innovations produced by scientific research have repercussions for techniques implemented. Next, the ideas they inspire bring the help necessary for taking stock of and appropriating knowledge. Finally, they participate in constructing the feeling of belonging to a social group that is recognized as sharing a set of common knowledge and as a depository for this knowledge, i.e. responsible for its perpetuation and updating.

It is these two categories of participants, individual or collective, that are found in information media destined for the professional world. The author indeed plays an important role in the verbal act, in the sense that he/she assumes the truth of the utterance [MAI 91]. Belonging to a particular world in which the author and addressee recognize each other is invested with a certain legitimacy of speaking. The latter is also considered to be weak. In terms of disciplines, it also has many origins as the consequences of progress can be multiple. For example, the use of technology can have judicial implications and specifics for application to economic sectors. It is therefore necessary to know these consequences and the point of view of experts, whether scientists or practitioners.

Therefore, information destined for exercising a profession is located on the side of knowledge and the side of know-how at the same time. In time, the former have the authority to be transformed into the latter. Their authors are destined to meet. Does this meeting always imply that researchers should proceed to an intra-linguistic translation of their research?

This question led to an interest in the communication link held between a professional group of librarians and a group of information science researchers. The massive use of technological innovations by documentation users plunges practitioners into a situation of uncertainty, in terms of their professional future. Added to this is the encouragement to publish, which makes up the consideration of written production in attributing European certification. This certification is delivered by the French Association of Professionals of Information and Documentation (ADBS), which allows a label that is complementary to training to be obtained. In the same way, the need to distribute research, where information science universities are found, in the absence of a certified journal in the domain, invites us to observe the way in which these two fields interact to solve their respective problems. The existence, since 1964, of *Documentaliste-Science de l'Information* journal [*Specialized Librarian – Information Science*], created by the ADBS allows us to work the problematic on a relatively long-term basis.

The association of profession and research in a similar medium helps to position the reader. The presence of two different activities constructs a representation of the journal that allows it to be situated in the set of information science journals. In the same way, this representation participates in social and professional positioning of the person who reads it. At the same time, an article produced by a teacher-researcher will not be read in the same way by a professional and another researcher as:

> "we only truly understand what an agent engaged in a field (an economist, a writer, an artist, etc) is saying or doing if we are in a capacity to refer to the position he occupies in this field, if we know 'where he is coming from', as people used to say in a slightly vague way in 68"[28] [BOU 97].

28. "*nous ne comprenons vraiment ce que dit ou fait un agent engagé dans un champ (un économiste, un écrivain, un artiste, etc.) que si nous sommes en mesure de nous référer à la position qu'il occupe dans ce champ, si nous savons « d'où il parle » comme on disait de manière un peu vague en 68*".

Analysis of the communication link is focused on the origins of authors by focusing notably on the authorial paratext allowing us to identify the writer's position.

In the preamble, it is necessary to reveal the particularities of information documentation jobs. Whereas it seems easy enough to locate professors by the body of university professors or lecturers to which they belong, some teachers/researchers began their professional activity as documentation practitioners.

The opposite situation can also arise. Regarding professionals, the border between the activity of teaching and research, and professional activity can also be difficult to trace. Some, working in universities as senior lecturers or substitute teachers, called *personnel associé temporaire* (PAST), for example, are involved in science projects. Other study or research engineers in the documentation branch of activity also participate in teaching while managing large documentation services for researchers. If the activities cannot be confused, do they affect each other?

2.4.2. *Are the diffusion spaces juxtaposed?*

The practical world has its own places of distribution. Beyond the useful or obligatory standards, rules, technical specifications that emanate from specialized organizations, such as the Technical Center for Wood and Furniture, the Information Center for the Cement Industry for Architects or more institutional ones like the Directorate-General for Planning [COU 08], publishing houses produce collections of books aimed at professionals.

Furthermore, promotional forums, dedicated to a sector of activity, can reunite various forms of its "production". From the object manufactured to new work methods, including tools developed, promotion also includes researcher, university or industry public conferences. Documents – brochures, flyers, books, CDs, etc – are side by side with the reports at these conferences. In the same way, trade shows involving practitioners, often of high level, invite researchers to be part of the progress of their work. Considering only authors, it is therefore difficult to perceive the separation between research distribution and practice distribution for these display areas.

Periodical publications are not as clear cut as scientific journals either. Unlike the scientific ones, we can define professional journals – as does Louise Gagnon-Arguin (University of Montreal) – as being preoccupied with practical problems of the profession. They ensure the profession's good name and constitute a forum for exchange of experiences and debates [GAG 92]. The thematics periodicals take on are mainly linked to the news at the time of their appearance and are always associated with instrumental preoccupations, related to training or defending the interests of the profession.

Periodicals are often the publication of an association whose objective is to contribute to improving the social positioning of the activity they represent by ensuring its continued training, at least in part. However, they do not have the support of publishing specialists or grants from institutions[29] – except in exceptional cases.

Excluding newsletters between members of a group linked to an activity, and magazines, we notice that researchers are also present in journals. We can therefore wonder whether they are written only for professionals and whether their presence is linked to the need to publicize ideas brought forward or new processes developed during scientific investigations, or if they are only addressing the community to which they belong. In other words, whereas the scientific journal produced by researchers is aimed at researchers, and journals with a high level of popularization, in which researchers participate, are aimed both at a public that is well-informed and at the scientific community, are professional journals, in which researchers collaborate, written only for practitioners?

The essential difference between these two types of journal comes from their field of origin. For example, whereas neither of them use editorial professionals, the authors whose work they publish are not the same.

Initially, this question lead to an interest in the origin of the journal produced by the ADBS. This Association was created in April 1963 and has as its mission "to develop links and exchanges within the profession, to ensure that interests are defended, and the promotion and perfecting of all those who practice documentary activity" [30].

Since 1964, it has been equipped with the means to ensure that its works are widely distributed. It is for this reason that the first issue of *Documentaliste* was born. From 1967, the sub-title *Revue d'Information et de Techniques Documentaires* [*Journal of Documentary Techniques and Information*] was added. The editorial clearly announced its intention to be "the French documentation journal" and to make "information concerning the profession, documentary techniques, and the

29. In the publishing domain, the *Bulletin des Bibliothèques de France* arranges people specifically related to how they affect production.

30. Inside front cover of the special issue of *L'automatisation documentaire en France: méthodes, expériences, réalisations* [*Documentary automation in France: methods, experiences, realization*], 1st semester 1966.

evolution of information and documentation policy in France"[31] available to subscribers. Furthermore, if *Documentaliste/librarian – Sciences de l'Information*, wishes "to situate itself at a certain scientific level"[32], as stated by its director in 1983, how is the link between profession and research established?

In 1970, it published an initial article from an American professor. In 1974, it adopted the information communicated at a symposium organized by the Association under the direction of Jean Meyriat, its vice-president at the time. A new step in the interest for research was made in 1976, with *Documentaliste* completing with its *Sciences de l'Information* title. From that moment on, it received articles containing the results of French works in information sciences, and in 1977, two professors from ICS joined its editorial board. Since then, research has always been ready. It is shown in various angles, ranging from articles to advertisements for scientific events to information on researchers' productions or on the opening of new university training.

This union between librarians, such as information practitioners, and their academic discipline of reference was created from the title of the journal. Furthermore, the two fields, thus united, have different interests and preoccupations. It is necessary for the Association to raise and make us aware of the level of expertise of practitioners in their practice environment [COU 02].

It is one of the roles handed down to the professional journal. According to the professional journal, in the scientific environment, the research field needs to distribute the results of its investigations and submit them to peer criticism. This distribution of knowledge also allows researchers, as we have seen, to progress in their career and to accumulate symbolic capital. This role of distributor should sometimes be attributed to the scientific journal, as we have also seen, but to a lesser degree than the popular science journal. But these two fields also have a common interest. The research field needs to make its advances known to the professional field, which is interested in integrating them, from the point of view of improving practices and recognizing the level of expertise of the field.

Documentaliste – Sciences de l'information therefore has a few assets. Systematically indexed in the *Sciences de l'Information* base since 1984, and accessible in the Pascal and Francis databases, it is also present in a systematic way

31. *"un ensemble d'informations concernant la profession, les techniques documentaires et l'évolution de la politique de l'information et de la documentation en France"*, Editorial, *Documentaliste*, no. 2, 1, 1967.

32. *"se situer à un certain niveau scientifique"*, La Potterie Studies, "Vingt ans déjà" [Already twenty years], *Documentaliste-Sciences de l'information*, vol. 20, no. 6, p. 178, 1983.

in the UK database, Lisa. Some of its articles, issued by professionals or researchers, are indexed by the Information Center of the Spanish National Research Council. This document processing makes it famous outside of France. In France, it is found in all places where documentation training takes place, whether at undergraduate, graduate or postgraduate level, and is distributed to about 4,000 subscribers. Finally, it is distributed in 86 countries. For these reasons, researchers who publish in this journal are assured that their work will be distributed internationally. The media-reader relationship therefore needed to be studied in detail.

Between 1995 and 1997, an initial piece of research focused on two five-year periods, 1983–1987 and 1990–1994. It used the 45 regular issues distributed during that time to verify the hypothesis that the recent evolution of the journal tended to give more space to research.

Parting with the definition of the journal, the presentation, mode of production, status of authors and information on research activities in information sciences – advertisements for scholarly society meetings, descriptions and analyses of postgraduate diplomas, research reports, scientific seminar and symposium proceedings, researchers' publications – were observed.

The results brought to light two noticeably different profiles:

– The first profile (1983–1987) is that of a journal that is very oriented towards the profession and in which researchers have a part to play. The majority of authors are professionals, only professional diplomas increase the value; the presentation, although austere, has the features of a magazine.

– The second (1990–1994) is that of a journal that is more open to research and the university. Researchers' participation is greater in this profile. The value of research results is increased because of the stronger presence of theses and grey literature in general. The evolution of the verbal act mechanism constructs an image of a professional journal that is oriented towards a scientific journal. The increase in number of researchers who are writers and of the description of research in particular is noticeable [COU 97a].

This increase in research, which was perceptible from the physical form of the journal, had to be verified by an analysis of published articles and their form of writing.

2.4.3. *Hybrid mediations*

To our knowledge, there are no standards specifying the nature and structure of professional articles. Writing styles of the group of practitioners are based on the tradition of a certain discursive practice that has become the common rule of the group. By referring to the work of ICS researchers, it is possible to define a certain number of criteria helping to determine the layout and contents of "professional articles".

The CERTEIC/GERICO (Center for Research in Techniques of Expression, Information and Communication, University of Lille III) gathered researchers interested in professional writing, more particularly that of social workers. In this framework, Olivier Chantraine[33] defined six types of literary work in 1992. Three of them which were linked to types of literary work encountered in professional journals were retained:

> – "literary works tending to supply members of the profession with representations of the activity, or to intervene in the practice, its context, its means, its locations, such as articles innovative, prescriptive, defensive professional journals, depending on the case, making reference to a more or less idealised reality, more or less structured by the scientific construction of facts or the positivist findings of pseudo-realists"[34];
>
> – "testimonies in literary form of the lives of people in the profession: life stories, memoirs tending to cause specific experiences to exist in the common discursive space"[35];
>
> – finally "literary work tending to cause that which was perceived as 'acquired' in practice or technical elaboration of means and practice markers to be recognized in the scientific field"[36] [CHA 92].

---

33. The types of literary works we are not retaining here are:
– literary works that are more or less standardized in their layout, such as in their pattern of use and circulation, and which necessarily accompany professional acts, etc, "organization", "summaries", "reports", etc;
– literary works that have professional practices as their daily routine, "note taking", "log book", "*fiche de liaison*";
– literary works required by exams, initiation rites for access to the profession: theses, dissertations, or even essays called by diverse names.

34. "*les écrits tendant à fournir aux membres de la profession des représentations de l'activité, ou à intervenir sur la pratique, son contexte, ses moyens, ses repères, tels les articles des revues professionnelles, selon le cas innovantes, prescriptives ou défensives, faisant référence à un réel plus ou moins idéalisé, plus ou moins structuré par la construction scientifique de faits ou le constat positiviste de pseudo-réalités.*"

35. "*écrits-témoignages du vécu des acteurs de la profession: récits de vie, mémoires tendant à faire exister les expériences spécifiques dans l'espace discursif commun.*"

36. "*écrits tendant à faire reconnaître dans le champ scientifique ou politique ce qui a été perçu comme "acquis" dans la pratique ou l'élaboration technique des moyens et repères de la pratique.*"

The internal organization of accounts of experiments, which are applications of techniques or methods in a particular context, and are the majority discursive genre in journals, is explained in five points: experiment context, method used, implementation or experimentation, criticisms, aims and evaluation. These accounts present a particular interest to the extent that, by the explanation of one case, they invite us to relate know-how, acquired in the framework of repeated training or practice, and the environment constraints in which the experiment is situated. It is most often a matter of applying a well-situated, unpublished method, causing new tools to intervene.

Case studies have an important role in basic and further professional training, as shown by John Erkkila and Margaret Erkkila [ERK 91]. This is because they allow us to work data and situations in real life grandeur, but they can also be a risk for the learner, to the extent that they can incite identical reproduction more than innovation [JOB 90]. The experiment is only transferable if it is converted into knowledge, i.e. only if it leads to a theorization, a *mise en mots*, producing "a practice discourse" which the writer must transform into a discourse *about* practice. The writer does this "by re-placing it in the context of space and time which gave birth to it, then choosing the point of view from which the object is going to be looked at, to finally mobilize the built up knowledge that allows us to make a plural reading of it"[37] [JOB 90]. As a function of subjects and the way to approach them, these articles can be followed by bibliographic references highlighting other experiments, other approaches, or contributing to using theory to support the demonstration.

Other forms of literary work can be added to the basic discursive genres, adopted from Olivier Chantraines's work. The world of practice is particularly receptive to technological evolutions. As such, information on the novelties they suggest is part of major preoccupations. The descriptive professional article of these novelties reports the characteristics of the product, its functionalities, its performances and the changes to expect from it, from the point of view of the job and qualifications, and the necessary adaptations anticipated. Literary works similar to what Olivier Chantraine calls "patterns of use" (*modes d'emploi*), sometimes presented in the form of descriptive sheets accompanied by commentaries and criticisms, are inscribed in the same context of novelty.[38] The presentation is made up of a list of parameters (title, domains covered, products distributed, etc) filled in with words

37. "*en la replaçant dans le contexte d'espace et de temps qui lui a donné naissance, puis de choisir le point de vue à partir duquel l'objet va être regardé, de mobiliser enfin les savoirs constitués qui permettent d'en faire une lecture plurielle*".

38. They are professional writing as defined by Colette Sartout: "a description of real facts aimed at readers saving time". C. Sartout, *De l'Ecrit Universitaire à l'Ecrit Professionnel* [*From University Literary Work to Professional Literary Work*], les Editions d'Organisation, Paris, 1990, p.17.

more than sentences, limiting information to a strict minimum. They describe new machines or tools on these same subjects, but presented in a more elaborate manner. The comparative tables play an important part in the opinion of people who are well advised in the subject. Descriptions, patterns of use and comparative tables have a pragmatic interest and can be accompanied by complementary information such as rates, suppliers' addresses, glossaries, etc.

The greatest place given to the scientific information observed in the initial research conducted on *Documentaliste – Sciences de l'Information* led to the hypothesis that the proximity of research articles and the presence of researchers on the editorial board had an influence on the layout of professional articles. Retaining as identifiers the elements making up the authorial paratext – title, footnotes and most particularly, bibliographic references[39] – the layout of the content – description, thoughts, comparison, research results – and themes taken on, 130 articles were analyzed. The results obtained show that enunciation of articles confirms the openness to research perceived in the enunciation of journals. Consequently, it is possible to specify the two profiles established before:

– That of the 1983–1987 period, very oriented towards the profession, is reinforced by articles based on the desire to transmit personal experience or knowledge similar to practice, that of tools, materials, realizations or "guided tours" of national documentary networks or big information source sites. It therefore concerns strictly professional articles. Scientific articles are present in this period and stand out from the group by having their own presentation.

– That of the 1990–1994 period, when a tendency towards the uniformity of presentation attempts to erase differences, where the methods of approach minimize distance. From then on the article qualified as "professional" for the preceding period combines sharing of know-how and invitation to thought. Anchored in practice, it concerns information sciences, is supported by them, and internalizes, by borrowing physical dimensions, scientific practice.

At this stage, everything happens as if the greatest consideration of the model of the scientific article by librarians was to invite researchers to have a greater presence in journals and the presence of researchers invited librarians to consider research. The use of the medium and articles, a reflection of the partial integration of standards and values of the scientific community, places *Documentaliste – Sciences de l'Information* in an intermediary situation. Here scientific preoccupations and professional preoccupations rub shoulders with each other, sometimes interacting [COU 97b]. This journal is therefore revealed to be a complex mediating object.

---

39. The abstract which, forming part of what is called the authorial paratext, was not retained as here it is often written by the editor of the journal. Therefore it is a product of the editorial paratext.

Another piece of research, focusing on 34 years of publications (1964–1997), or 556 articles, allowed us to make a division between literary works having researchers or professors as authors (93 articles) and those having practitioners as authors (463). The former are essentially from ICS, but also from sociology, psychology, law. The majority of the latter are librarians, but also lawyers or doctors. This research put forward several hypotheses. The second position of *Sciences de l'Information* in the title is linked to history, i.e. to the intention to promote people exercising a certain profession. It indeed concerns "documentalist" and not "documentation" – an intention which produced the creation of the parent association of the journal. This mono-dimensional approach leads us to deduce that *Documentaliste – Sciences de l'information* is an exclusively professional journal.

Its use by researchers to distribute unpublished knowledge, however, lead to the formulation of another hypothesis based on a bi-dimensional approach: whereas researchers publishing in *Documentaliste – Sciences de l'Information* state research results, each community – that of professionals and that of researchers – addresses its own community. In other words, the hypen marks the interest one has for the other but each one follows a separate path. The communicational link is no longer made between research and profession, but from research to research and profession to profession. In this case, the second position of *Sciences de l'Information* in the title indicates that a bigger place is given to the profession. *Documentaliste – Sciences de l'Information* is a journal that is professional and scientific at the same time, conveying research results and not having a link with professional preoccupations. Communication is "*endogène intradsciplinaire*". It is characterized by the self-definition of the speaker and addressee as producers of knowledge in a similar scientific domain or in a similar professional domain. The two positions are therefore symmetrical [VER 97]. Each community exchanges information in a closed communicational circuit, where researchers and professionals cohabit.

However, this bi-dimensional approach still seemed insufficient for grasping the *Documentaliste – Sciences de l'Information* phenomenon in its heterogeneous, but combined constituents, and in their interactions. A third hypothesis was therefore favored. The hyphen present in the title establishes a multidirectional communication contributing to giving the reader representations of research, but also a reality of this research. The exchanges are established both from research towards profession and from profession towards research at the same time. This is shown by the analysis of two thematics worked by professionals on the one hand, and researchers on the other [COU 00][40]. But they are also established from

---

40. It concerns the internet and bibliometry and scientometry research and their applications, respectively.

profession to profession, and from research to research. *Documentaliste – Sciences de l'Information* is therefore a "hybrid journal", the term "hybrid" taken in the sense that this adjective has had since the 19th century: that "which is composed of two elements of a different nature, abnormally reunited"[41] and which "participates in two or more wholes"[42,43].

Hybridization signifies both separation and union at the same time. Because it is hybrid, it conveys representations of research, but also a reality of research and a reality of the professional activity allowing the speaker and addressee to each find therein their account. To adopt Eliseo Verón's terminology, communication is intradisciplinary and endogenous (information sciences "discipline") and trans-scientific and endogenous, but the two forms of communication are distinguished from each other. They are also completed by two other forms of communication: an intradisciplinary endogenous communication (documentation "discipline") and a trans-professional endogenous one, here also in the distinction. An open system where profession and research are in interaction can therefore be opposed to Eliseo Verón's closed system of scientific communication.

Media, therefore, while remaining faithful to their initial plan, can also become the medium of a multitude of mediations, in a well-defined context. From 2000, like its Canadian counterpart *Documentation et Bibliothèques* [*Documentation and Libraries*], it adopted modes of evaluation of articles belonging to scientific journals.

2.5. Conclusion

These diverse works lead us to question scientific communication. Can it be reduced to communication between researchers? At the current stage of research, if we limit ourselves to construction of knowledge it appears that it can indeed seem sufficient and can confine itself to the closed world of research. But it reveals itself to be insufficient for taking into account forms of distribution of knowledge in their complexity.

Whereas it is also a matter of taking into account social context, and the tensions that inhabit it, it seems necessary to introduce the notion of mediation to affirm the intermediary role of writing and medium. It is therefore possible to include scientific communication in a broader field that also includes popularizations and hybridizations. This field dedicated to specialized mediations, a piece of

41. "*qui est composé de deux éléments de nature différente anormalement réunis*"
42. *Dictionnaire Historique* [*Historical Dictionary*], op. cit., vol. 1, p. 984.
43. "*participe de deux ou plusieurs ensembles.*"

terminology we prefer to scientific and technical mediation, unites informational approaches and communicational approaches in a complementarity that authorizes belonging to a common discipline.

The rise in generality will, however, need to conduct empirical observations using other media of distribution of science and its applications in other professional domains. These pieces of research are revealed to be that much more necessary than the forms of distribution are diversified and than the modes of evaluation tend to uniformly organize themselves.

2.6. Bibliography

[AIT 85] S. Aït El Hadj, C. Bélisle (eds.), *Vulgarisation: un Défi ou un Mythe? La Communication Entre Spécialistes et Non-spécialistes*, Chronique sociale, Lyon, 1985.

[BAR 85] M. Barrère, "Les principales difficultés dans la vulgarisation scientifique viennent du milieu scientifique lui-même", in: Aït El Hadj S., Bélisle C. (eds), *Vulgarisation: un Défi ou un Mythe? La Communication Entre Spécialistes et Non-spécialistes*, Chronique sociale, Lyon, 1985, p. 27-31.

[BEL 85] C. Belisle, "Les objectifs de la vulgarisation" , in: S. Aït El Hadj, C. Bélisle (eds), *Vulgarisation: un défi ou un Mythe ? La Communication Entre Spécialistes et Non-spécialistes*, Chronique sociale, Lyon ,1985, p. 33-45.

[BOU 75] Bourdieu P., "La spécificité du champ scientifique et les conditions sociales du progrès de la raison", *Sociologie et Sociétés*, vol. 7, no. 1, p. 91-117, 1975.

[BOU 97] Bourdieu P., *Les Usages Sociaux de la Science: pour une Sociologie Clinique du Champ Scientifique*, INRA éditions, Paris, 1997.

[BOU 93] Boure R., "Le territoire incertain des revues scientifiques", *Réseaux*, vol. 58, p. 93-105, 1993.

[CAL 93] Callon M., Courtial J.-P., Penan H., *La Scientométrie*, PUF, Paris, 1993.

[CAR 90] Caro P., *La Vulgarisation Scientifique est-elle Possible?*, PUN, Nancy, 1990.

[CHA 92] Chantraine O., "Les écritures professionnelles ou la difficile synthèse de normes communicationnelles hétérogènes", *Études de communication* (*Bulletin du CERTEIC*), vol. 13, p. 139-155, 1992.

[COU 08] Courbiéres C., "Les dispositifs info-communicationnels en architecture: le recours à la documentation", in: V. Couzinet (ed), *Dispositifs Info-communicationnels: Questions de Médiations Documentaires*, Hermès, Paris, 2008.

[COU 97a] Couzinet V., "De l'information professionnelle à l'information scientifique: quelle place pour la recherche dans la revue *Documentaliste-Sciences de l'information*", *Documentaliste – Sciences de l'information*, vol. 34, no. 3, p. 147-154, 1997.

[COU 97b] COUZINET V., "Pratiques professionnelles, pratiques de recherche: les articles de la revue *Documentaliste-Sciences de l'information*", *Documentaliste – Sciences de l'Information*, vol. 34, no. 6, p. 289-299, 1997.

[COU 99] COUZINET V., "La revue électronique de sciences humaines et sociales: éléments pour une définition", *RIST, Revue d'information scientifique et technique*, vol. 2, p. 119-132, 1999.

[COU 00] COUZINET V., *Médiations Hybrides: le Documentaliste et le Chercheur en Sciences de l'Information*, ADBS Publications, Paris, 2000.

[COU 02] COUZINET V., "Expertise et association professionnelle: de la reconnaissance des documentalistes", *Questions de Communication*, vol. 2, p. 57-69, 2002.

[COU 03] COUZINET V., "Praticiens de l'information et chercheurs: parcours, terrains et étayages", *Documentaliste–Sciences de l'Information*, vol. 40, no. 2, p. 118-125, 2003.

[DAV 99] DAVALLON J., *L'Exposition à l'œuvre: Stratégies de Communication et Médiation Symbolique*, Collection Communication et Civilisation, L'Harmattan, Paris, 1999.

[ELI 08] ELIAS C., *Fundamentos de Periodismo Científico y Divulgación Mediática*, Alianza Publishing, Madrid, 2008.

[ESC 73] ESCARPIT R., *L'Écrit et la Communication*, coll. Que sais-je?, no. 1546, PUF, Paris, 1978.

[ERK 91] ERKKILA J., ERKKILA M., "Learning by others' experience: an analysis of library journal cases 1983–1989", *Education for Information*, vol. 9, no. 4, p. 269-283, 1991.

[FOU 02] FOUCAUD F., "La vulgarisation et la peur: le cas du laser dans *Science & vie*", *Communication & Langages*, vol. 133, p. 25-37 2002.

[FOU 88] FOURNIER M., GINGRAS Y., MATHURIN C., " L'évaluation par les pairs et la définition légitime de la recherche", *Actes de la Recherche en Sciences Sociales*, vol. 74, p. 47-54, 1988.

[FRA 06] FRAYSSE P., Le patrimoine monumental en images: des médiations informationnelles à la conversion monumentaire des documents, thesis, University of Toulouse II, 2006.

[GAG 92] GAGNON-ARGUIN L., "Réflexions sur les revues professionnelles: le cas de l'archivistique", *Documentation et Bibliothèques*, vol. 38, no. 4, p. 191-196, 1992.

[JAC 84] JACOBI D., "Sémiotique du discours de vulgarisation scientifique", *Semen*, vol. 2, p. 57-72, 1984.

[JAC 88] JACOBI D., SCHIELE B. "La vulgarisation scientifique: thèmes de recherche", in: D. JACOBI, B. SCHIELE (eds), *Vulgariser la Science: le Procès de l'Ignorance*, Champ Vallon, Seyssel, 1988, p. 12-46.

[JAC 99] JACOBI D., *La Communication Scientifique: Discours, Figures, Modèles*, PUG, Grenoble, 1999.

[JAC 05] JACOBI D., "Images originales et images de reproduction dans l'exposition", in : D. Jacobi, S. Lochot (eds), *Images d'Exposition, Exposition d'Images*, OCIM, Dijon, 2005, p. 90-107.

[JEA 94] JEANNERET Y., *Ecrire la Science: Formes et Enjeux de la Vulgarisation*, PUF, Paris, 1994.

[JEA 04] JEANNERET Y., "Le partage des savoirs entre métamorphose des medias et poétique des discours", *Médiation et Représentation des Savoirs*, Symposium Proceedings "Partage des savoirs", L'Harmattan, Paris, 2004, p. 15-32.

[JOB 90] JOBERT G., REVUZ C., "Ecrite, l'expérience est un capital", *Bulletin du CERTEIC*, vol. 11, p. 65-69, 1990.

[KUN 92] KUNTH D., "La place du chercheur dans la vulgarisation scientifique", Rapport à la Délégation à l'information Scientifique et Technique, Département Culture Scientifique et Technique, 1992.

[LAM 97] LAMIZET B., SILEM A., *Dictionnaire Encyclopédique des Sciences de l'Information et de la Communication*, Ellipses, Paris, 1997.

[LAT 79] LATOUR B., WOOLGAR S., *La vie de Laboratoire: la Production des Faits Scientifiques*, La Découverte, Paris, 1996.

[LAT 91] LATOUR B., "Le royaume de l'écrit scientifique", in : WITKOWSKI N. (ed), *L'état de Sciences et des Techniques*, La Découverte, Paris, 1991.

[LEF 03] LEFEBVRE M., "L'ambivalence des mathématiciens face à l'image: tension entre normes et usages", *Communication et Langages*, vol. 136, p. 75-82, 2003.

[MAI 91] MAINGUENEAU D., *L'Analyse du Discours: Introduction aux Lectures de l'Archive*, Hachette Supérieur, Paris, 1991.

[MAI 98] MAINGUENEAU D., *Analyser les Textes de Communication*, Dunod, Paris, 1998.

[MEY 81] MEYRIAT J., "Document, documentation, documentologie", *Schéma et Schématisation*, vol. 14, p. 51-63, 1981.

[SCH 85] SCHIELE B., "Les enjeux cachés de la vulgarisation scientifique ou la transformation du savoir en produit marchand", in: S. AÏT EL HADJ, C. BÉLISLE (eds), *Vulgarisation: un Défi ou un Mythe ? La Communication Entre Spécialistes et Non-spécialistes*, Lyon, 1985, p. 83-97.

[SEM 98] SEMIR V. de, "La dérive du journalisme scientifique: de l'acculturation à la déculturation", *Alliage*, vol. 37-38, p. 214-219, 1999.

[VER 97] VERON E., "Entre l'épistémologie et la communication ", *Hermès*, vol. 21, p. 25-32, 1997.

Chapter 3

Time, Memory and Document

3.1. Introduction

Document does not breed document, it becomes it. A document is not *a priori* a document, it is instituted as document by the addressee, reader, researcher or person retrieving information. It is therefore "from the past", like memory (*mémoire*); it can be from a near past or a distant one, like remembrance (*souvenirs*). It is a trace of an event or a past activity, entered in a more or less accessible place, as are remembrances in our memory. Access to information, to knowledge (*savoirs* and *connaissances*) cannot truly, or more "*véritativement*", be achieved without taking into consideration the "historical" character of sources questioned, the temporality of the documentation exploited.

In addition, knowledge does not present itself like a datum, which can simply be collected from consulting a group of specially selected sources. Any operation of document research or information retrieval is an operation of interpretation and construction, which is translated by production of a discourse.

This chapter is the result of a work of exploration of epistemological nature, still largely incomplete. This work trained me in the philosophy of history and led me to rub shoulders with authors like Paul Ricoeur, Michel Foucault, Carlo Ginsburg and Michel de Certeau. Sure, "information science" is not history or a discipline that borrows methods, presuppositions or perspectives from historical science. It has everything to gain, however, from knowing the historian's approach, its objects, resources, reasoning, the nature of its production. This is the case even if it is only

---

Chapter written by Jean-Paul METZGER.

because they have certain instruments in common (document, archive) and often have the tendency to search for concepts and methods in the same disciplines (language sciences, semiology, sociology, anthropology, philosophy).

First, I take on the issue of memory and the historian's approach so that I can then determine the place and role of the document in historical research. In the first two parts, Paul Ricœur [RIC 00] was of great assistance. The last part of this chapter is devoted mainly to the nature of the documentation device and the way it can be analyzed, interpreted and exploited. I finish with some reflection on the document research approach. This last part is laid out in the order of the discourse of Michel Foucault [FOU 69].

3.2. Memory and history

Human beings are capable of distinguishing between before and after. We perceive time by perceiving movement (Aristotle) or change (Hegel). But time is only perceived as different from movement or change if we can distinguish two moments in time: a prior moment and a past moment. For Aristotle, memory exists when time passes, memory exists with time. Memory is therefore indissociable from time and, in addition, "memory is past", while conjecture and waiting introduce the future, and sensation, or perception, marks the present.

In this first paragraph, different approaches to the notion of memory are evoked first, followed by some authors' reflections on time, and finally a presentation of the historian's approach that Michel de Certeau [CER 75] calls a historiographical operation, in its entirety.

3.2.1. *Memory and reminiscence*

3.2.1.1. *Remembrance*

According to Henri Bergson [BER 63], we must distinguish two forms of memory: habit memory and recollective memory. Like Augustin and the rhetoricians, Henri Bergson is placed in a situation of reciting a lesson learned by heart. Habitual memory is the memory we use when we recite this lesson, without evoking each of the successive readings from the learning period. The lesson learnt:

> "is a part of my present just like my habitual way of speaking or writing; it is experienced, and acted more than represented. Recitation is part of *savoir-faire*, such as knowing how to walk or knowing how to write. What different types of know-how have in common is that they are available without requiring the effort of learning again, of re-learning". [BER 63]

On the other hand, the remembrance of such a particular lesson, of such a moment of learning, does not present "any characteristics of habit". Henri Bergson says: "It is like an event in my life; its essence is to have a date and consequently to not be able to repeat itself". Therefore "remembrance of such a determined reading is a representation, and only a representation", whereas the lesson learned is "acted" more than "represented".

On the other hand, Henri Bergson distinguishes evocation and recall. Whereas evocation is the actual occurrence of something remembered, the maintaining presence of the absent perceived, felt, learned, recall is memory in practice, the overlapping of that which was perceived, felt or learned before. This recall can be "laborious" or "instantaneous"; the feeling of effort is present in one and absent in the other. On one hand, there is automatism, on the other, reflection, intelligent reconstruction; recall is therefore active retrieval. And recognition is the result of recall as well. Incidentally, a good part of the work of memory, of retrieval of the past, is devoted to the struggle against forgetting. Forgetting is an enigma because we do not know whether it is only prevention from evoking and finding "lost time" or if it is a result of the inescapable wear and tear, by time, of "traces" that unexpected events have left in us.

Henri Bergson also compares remembrance and image, memory and imagination. Imagination and memory have the presence of the absent as a common characteristic, and detachment from reality and the vision of an unreal life, on the one hand, the vision of a real past life, on the other, as a distinguishing characteristic. Whereas imagination can play with imaginary entities, remembrance lays down things of the past.

> "There exists an essential difference between the remembrance thesis and the image thesis. If I remember an event in my past life, I am not imagining it, I am calling it to mind, i.e. I am not laying it down as *donné-absent*, but as *donné-présent au passé*" [SAR 86].

In short, to remember is to welcome, to receive an image from the past; it is also to search for it, to do something.

3.2.1.2. *Memory exercise*

Remembrance is the fact that memory is exercised. One of the major aspects of memory exercise is memorization. Memorization is distinguished from recollection, the return of a recognized event to memory as having taken place before the moment memory declares having felt, learnt, perceived it by a work of learning focused on knowledge, *savoir-faire*, *pouvoir-faire*, in such a way that these are fixed and remain available for carrying out. Memorization researches economy of effort, the subject being exempt from learning to carry out and appropriate tasks again. Memorization leads to habit memory. The process of memorization, however, is determined by the character constructed from ways of learning.

Let us call to mind some of these learning processes. Learning experimental psychology consists of inciting a human being to acquire new behaviors not part of the repertoire of inherited *pouvoir-faires* or *savoir-faires*. Mastering the acquisition belongs to the experimenter conducting the manipulation; he/she sets the task, organizes punishments and rewards and thus conditions learning. The "by heart" already evoked is another way of learning. It is not the privilege of the school of old. Many a professional (doctors, jurors, scientists, etc) throughout their life resorts to a memorization photocopier of knowledge and *savoir-faire* relying on repertoires, lists, protocols. It is also practiced a lot in theater, in music and in dance, where execution is distinct from writing.

Let us end this brief overview of memorization techniques with "the art of memory". Initially it is a matter of mnemonic procedures recommended and practiced by Latin rhetoricians who combine images and places. The art of memory consists of associating images to organized places by a rigorous system, like a house, a public place, an architectural edifice. Images represent two things; and two neighboring images representing neighboring things are assigned to neighboring places. Images thus memorized are reputed to be easy to evoke at the opportune moment, with the order of places preserving the order of things. The things that appear are objects, characters, events, facts. Such procedures were abandoned as soon as literary work was able to substitute it.

A second aspect of memory exercise is the constraint it undergoes. Three types of constraint can weigh on this exercise:

– difficulty at the pathological level;

– manipulation at the practical level; and

– obligation at the political and ethical level.

Difficulty can be translated by a difficulty in recalling, by forgetting, or by melancholy, or by the difficulty in admitting the absence of a loved person (before mourning, for example). Memory and forgetting can also be forced by power holders; this memory manipulation can be manifest through a strong incitation for recollection of episodes of history held for founding events of an identity; it is often accompanied by diverse commemorations and a work of memorization. Similarly, the duty of memory exalts traumatizing remembrances and gives them an exemplary value: the work of memory becomes a plan. Traumatizing facts refer to the past; exemplary value refers to the future. The memory cult obliterates the question of the end, the ethical stake. The injunction to remember risks being understood as an invitation to neglect the historian's work, even if this work:

> "like all work on the past, never consists only of establishing facts but also choosing some of them as being the most salient and more meaningful than others, to then relate them to each other; furthermore this work of selection and combination is necessarily oriented by research, not of truth, but of good" [TOD 95].

3.2.1.3. *Individual memory, collective memory*

In the current debate, the question of the true subject of the activity of memory occupies the front of the stage. This question epistemologists are asked is: is its *vis-à-vis*, the place of memory, the memory of the main players taken one by one or that of groups considered as a whole? In other words, is memory primordially individual or collective? This alternative stems from a double movement that took shape after the test problematics and those of the quest for remembrance (Plato and Aristotle). On one hand is the appearance of the subjectivity problematic, on the other, the irruption of the concept of collective consciousness in the field of social sciences, introduced by sociology.

It is the emergence of a problematic subjectivity that put forward the concept of consciousness and provoked a movement of withdrawal of the concept into itself: intimate consciousness. To illustrate this approach of the "inside view", Paul Ricœur solicits three authors:

– Augustin (*Confessions* [AUG 62]),

– John Locke (*L'Invention de la Conscience* [*The Invention of Consciousness*] [LOC 98]) and

– Edmund Husserl (*La Conscience Intime du Temps* [*Intimate Consciousness of Time*] [HUS 64]).

For sociology, adopting an "objective" epistemological model analogous to that of life and earth sciences, collective consciousness is a reality whose ontological status is not called into question.

According to Maurice Halbwachs (*La Mémoire Collective* [*Collective Consciousness*] [HAL 50]), who forged the concept of "social framework of memory", in order to remember we need others; and our individual memory is necessarily derived from a collective memory. Attempting to reconcile the two apparently irreducible approaches, Paul Ricœur suggests introducing a third plan, that of close relations, and recognizing three subjects of memory attribution: ego, collectives and close relations [RIC 00].

3.2.2. *Historical time*

3.2.2.1. *Calendar time*

In [RIC 85], Paul Ricœur supports the idea that calendar time unifies cosmic time of movement of stars, and real, biological and social time. The calendar is born from this humanization of cosmic time and this "cosmologization" of real time. Calendar time is located between these two times. With it, historical time is put in place. Historical time, which organizes time along an axis that will enable man to be situated and situate events using a zero-moment, is a founding event (the birth of Christ, for example). With this axis, and a location at least on this axis, man can be oriented in time and move along the axis in either direction. Calendar time proceeds from a human need for orientation and social homogenization. Calendar time can be assimilated with Emile Benéviste's chronic time.

3.2.2.2. *Chronic time*

Emile Benvéniste defines chronic time in the following way:

– all events make reference to a founding event that defines the time axis;

– it is possible to move along time intervals in the two opposing directions of anteriority and posteriority in relation to date zero;

– constitution of a repertoire of units serves to name recurrent intervals:

- day,
- month,
- year, etc.

The dating operation, an operation of entry, belonging to historians but also economists, sociologists or political pundits, is not separate from a capacity for inherent dating that is inherent to live experience, and particularly to the sensation of distancing from the past and appreciation for time thickness. For all philosophers from the time of Aristotle to Henri Bergson, including Augustin, Immanuel Kant and Edmund Husserl, time extension seems a primitive fact, apprehension of duration is immanent in "intimate experience" of time. For memory time, the "*autrefois*" (of old) of time remembered is entered in the "*avant que*" (before) of the dated past, and the "*plus tard*" (later) of becoming is specified with the "*alors que*" (while) of the coincidence of an expected event with the schedule of dates to come.

The contribution of chronic time, like calendar time, consists of a temporal manner of entry, i.e. a system of dates extrinsic to events. The present moment with its absolute maintenance becomes some date among all those determined by some calendar or the other.

3.2.2.3. *Chronosophy*

Calendar time entered itself in *The Order of Time* where Krysztof Pomian [POM 84] distinguishes "four ways of visualizing time, of translating it into signs": chronometry, chronology, chronography and chronosophy. Chronosophy time refers to short or long cycles of circular time: day, week, month, year. Chronology time designates linear time of long periods: century, millennium, whose course is diversely emphasized by founding events. These two first times are measured by clocks and calendars. Chronology ignores separation between nature and history; it enables us to talk about cosmic history, history of the earth, history of life, human history. Chronography does without calendars. Episodes recorded are defined by their relation of succession compared to others.

By chronosophy, Krysztof Pomian means large periodizations, like those in Islam or Christianity, and their correspondence with chronology; during the Renaissance a periodization in terms of art eras, in the 13th, in terms of centuries, appeared. And in a big way, a "speculation of the order of time" is a vision of historic time in competition with others: cyclic or linear time, stationary, declining or progress time.

3.2.3. *Comprehension and representation*

After having evoked some of the principal philosophical issues related to memory and time in the two sections above, I take on, in the last part of this section, the two final phases of the historiographic operation, as defined by Michel de Certeau in *Ecriture de l'Histoire* [*The Writing of History*] [CER 75] and adapted by Paul Ricœur in *La Mémoire, l'Histoire, l'Oubli* [*Memory, History, Forgetting*] [RIC 00]. These three phases, or more so these three methodological components as they are directly interlinked, are:

– the documentary phase that sets the establishment of documentary proof as program;

– the explicative/documentary phase that sets the establishment of a response to the question "why?" (why did things happen this way?) as an objective;

– the representative phase, the shaping of discourse brought to the reader's knowledge, the production of a representation of the past "as it was produced".

Because we are particularly interested in the documentary phase, I will present its principle elements (testimony, archive, documentary proof) in section 3.3. Generally speaking, the explanation consists of answering the question "why". This retrieval of causes and reasons is common to all scientific disciplines, which run back to modeling procedures put to proving the verification. The models that explain use in historian practice, as a common characteristic, refer to human reality as a social fact, and stress change and the differences or gaps affecting the changes; and differences that have a manifested time dimension. It is for this reason that historical explication refers to the long term, the short term, the punctual event, etc.

3.2.3.1. *The archeology of knowledge and the writing of history*

On the subject of analysis and comprehension, two authors and two works can be solicited: Michel Foucault and his *Archéologie du Savoir* [*Archeology of Knowledge*] [FOU 69] and Michel de Certeau and his *Ecriture de l'Histoire* [*The Writing of History*].

The archeology of knowledge was initially supposed to be an alternative discipline to the history of ideas, which was unable to find its own voice. Archaeology does not seek to reconstruct the past, repeating what was, but "it is nothing more and nothing other than a rewriting, i.e. the maintained form of exteriority, a ruled transformation of what was already written". The descriptive capacity of archeology is exercised at four levels: novelty, contradiction, comparison and transformation. At the novelty level it seeks to distinguish the original, which is the breaking point with the *déjà-dit*, and the regular, which is the accumulation of *déjà-dit*. At the second level contradictions are objects for describing themselves, such as they appear in the interval, dissension, "rough edges of discourse". At the third level, that of comparison, archaeology becomes inter-discursive where different discourses, scientific for example, are articulated with each other in specific forms. Finally, at the last level, that of change and transformations,

> "archeology takes that which is normally taken as an obstacle as the object of its description and its analysis: its plan is not to overcome differences but to analyze them, to say what, rightfully, they consist of, and to differentiate them" [FOU 69].

It is the very idea of change that Michel Foucault asks us to give up, to the benefit of that of transformation. In this way it differentiates itself from the metaphor of flow. Therefore, Michel Foucault substitutes the ideology of the discontinuous for that of the continuous. With the two central ideas of the archive, as register for discursive training and for archaeology, and as description of interdiscursive transformations, Michel Foucault determines a neutral terrain from which all "subjectivizing" instances are absent, that of the statement without the speaker.

As for Michel de Certeau, he differs from MichelFoucault by leaving the absolute neutrality of a discourse on discourse and beginning to articulate this discourse on other practical signifiers. According to Paul Ricœur, what deeply separates Michel de Certeau from Michel Foucault is the anchoring of research from the first in a philosophical anthropology where reference to psychology and psychoanalysis is fundamental.

3.2.3.2. *History of representations*

The term representation designates both the evocation of an absent thing through the bias of a substituted thing which is the representative of it, and, at the same time, the exhibition of a presence, the visibility of the present thing tending to overshadow the operation of substitution. The notion of representation has progressively replaced the old notion of mentality in the evolution of history.

Upon encountering this, the idea of representation better expresses plurivocity, differentiation, multiple temporalization of social phenomena. This dialectic of representation is developed in an article by Carlo Ginzburg [GIN 91]. This definition is equivalent to the one suggested by the Greeks for the mnemonic image. Along with the economic, social and political, representation plays a role of favored referent in the field of social change, considered as the total object of historical discourse. For some historians, it is therefore a matter of not only analyzing the images that social agents construct of their environment and of the world they participate in, but also "updating the reflexivity resources of social agents in their attempts to understand themselves and their world".

3.2.3.3. *Writing knowledge*

The final phase of the historiographic operation is, as written above, that of the passage from explication/comprehension to literature, the book offered for reading by an interested public. This phase is not only a moment of writing but the moment when the historian declares his/her intention, his/her ambition for representing the past "in truth". This operation of representation must be distinguished from the representation-object of historian discourse and perhaps, in a second movement, move closer to this representation-object to the extent that the work of the historian is susceptible to mimicking the interpretive act of those who participate in the past, attempting to understand their world and understand themselves. The act of recollection, like the act of writing history, has this ambition, this re-vindication of representing the past, "in faith" this time. The memory's ambition of faithfulness therefore precedes history's ambition of truth. It is in terms of representation that the phenomenology of memory describes the mnemonic phenomenon, to the extent that remembrance presents itself as an image of what was seen, heard, learned and acquired. It is in terms of representation that the third phase of the historiographic operation is described. And, according to Paul Ricœur, this operation of representation of historical discourse is carried out through the bias of narration, argumentation and imagination at the same time. Narrative coherence gives readability to this discourse, the production of the past evoked gives sight, and the position-taking of the reader-addressee can respond to the worry of convincing.

3.3. Document and history

In this section, the historian conception of a document is approached; a conception ignored, to my knowledge, by "information science", and very influenced by information and communication technology. Following Paul Ricœur, before moving on to documents as such, I would like to discuss the notions of testimony and archive.

3.3.1. *Testimony*

> "With testimony, an epistemological process which parts from declared memory is opened, includes the archive and documents, and finishes on documentary proof." [RIC 00]

Renaud Dulong summarizes the main characters of the act of testifying in the following definition: "a certified autobiographical account of a past event, whether this account is carried out in informal or formal circumstances" [DUL 98].

3.3.1.1. *Assertion of reality and self-designation of testimony*

Testimony is first characterized by the assertion of the factual reality of the reported event, and by its presumed trustworthiness or authentification of declaration by its author's experience. The factuality attested is supposed to mark a frank boundary between reality and illusion. The phenomenology of memory shows that this border is always problematic, and that this trustworthiness must be submitted to doubt.

On the other hand, this assertion of reality is inseparable from self-designation of the testifying subject. That which is attested is indivisibly the pairing of the past thing and the presence of the witness on the places of the event. And it is the witness who declares him- or herself to be witness: "I was there". This self-referential feature inextricably links narration of past things to a personal history; and, therefore, the effective imprint of an event does not necessarily coincide with the importance accorded to it by the auditor of the testimony.

3.3.1.2. *Accreditation and confrontation*

This self-designation is inscribed in a situation of dialogue. The witness attests the reality of the scene that he/she is said to have attended before someone, and he/she is asking to be believed. Certification of testimony is only confirmed by the one who receives and accepts it. Testimony is therefore certified and, in addition, accredited. This accreditation poses the alternative between trust and suspicion. Doubt can focus on conditions of bad perception, of bad retention, of bad restitution and notably of what Sigmund Freud calls "secondary elaboration".

The eventual suspicion induces a space of controversy where several testimonies and several witnesses can be confronted. The witness is therefore the one who accepts being convened and participating in a debate that can be contradictory.

3.2.1.3. *A natural institution*

An extra dimension of testimony destined to reinforcing its credibility and faith is that of the possibility of its reiteration. A trustworthy testimony is maintained in duration and in the face of whoever solicits it. This stability of testimony makes it a security factor in all reports participating in the social link. This trustworthiness of testimony contributes to the general security, institutes it, sets it up in an institution. What makes an institution of it is the durability of the trustworthiness of the testimony that is ready to be reiterated and contributes to the solidity of the social link, which relies on confidence in the words of others. Renaud Dulong considers testimony as a "natural institution".

3.3.2. *The archive*

The archive is the central device of the historian's approach. The organized place where not only written testimonies are gathered, but also the written traces of human past activities.

3.3.2.1. *Archiving*

Before the consulted, constituted archive, there is archiving. This archiving brings a break in a continuous journey. Whereas testimony gives a narrative continuation to declarative memory, the story must be able to be detached from its narrator; the "said" must be able to be detached from the "saying" of any utterance. To this property which it shares with the story, testimony can be collected in writing, deposited, by virtue of the reiterable character conferred on it by its status of institution. This deposition thus conditions the possibility of specific institutions devoted to the collection, conservation and classification of a documentary mass in view of its consultation by qualified people. The archive is a physical place that shelters this sort of trace – the documentary trace – that must be well-distinguished from cerebral or affective traces. The archive is not only a physical, or spatial, place, but also a social place. It is a place that, according to Michel de Certeau [CER 75], establishes sources, redistributes space, authorizes or forbids this or that type of discourse in which purely cognitive operations are inscribed.

This act of isolating, gathering, collecting, is the object of a distinct discipline – archival science. Three phases can be distinguished on the subject of archive. First, we can distinguish the preservation by a physical or moral person of the traces of his/her own activity. Then comes the more or less systematic organization of materials thus constituted. These operations are carried out in view of the third moment, that of the consultation of materials in a determined statutory framework.

If we consider that the materials essentially consist of texts, and that we are devoted to those of them that are testimonies left by contemporaries having access to these materials, the change in status of oral testimony to that of archive document constitutes the first mutation in living memory submitted to examination. Such a document is open to whoever knows how to read; it does not have a designated addressee and it is not only silent, but also an orphan. It is detached from the authors who produced it. It is therefore left to the care of those who have the competence to question and defend it.

3.3.2.2. *Witnesses of the past*

In his examination of the historian's relationships to testimony, Marc Bloch distinguished two angles [BLO 74]: observation and criticism.

Observed objects are traces whose written testimonies represent a first sub-category. Written testimony is inscribed in a relation between past and present and in a movement of comprehension of the first through the second. Writing is the mediation of this fundamentally retrospective research. Furthermore, traces exist that are not written testimonies, that are also submitted to observation. It is a matter of vestiges of the past of all natures. Paul Ricœur calls them "unwritten testimonies".

This written/unwritten opposition is doubled with a distinction between voluntary testimonies and involuntary testimonies. The first are destined to posterity, the second are in spite of themselves. And according to Marc Bloch:

> "in the course of its development, historical research has gradually been lead to place more and more confidence in the second category of evidence, in the evidence of witnesses in spite of themselves".

Within this work of observation, Marc Bloch distinguishes two opposite methods: a lucidly reconstructive method, because of its active relation with witnesses, and a "positivist" method that avoids questioning and which he qualifies as "mental inertia".

The second angle of the relation of history to written or unwritten testimonies is that of "criticism". It is a matter of the testing of written traces and other vestiges of the past. This criticism is based on doubt, which is made for moving closer to Cartesian methodic doubt. The criticism approach consists of examining sources in order to distinguish the true from the false, about which we know witnesses may be mistaken, and "make speak" these witnesses in order to understand them [BLO 74].

3.3.2.3. *The evidential paradigm*

Marc Bloch's criticism can be likened to the index and Carlo Ginzburg's evidential paradigm [GIN 89]. Marc Bloch's analysis assimilates vestige, dear to the archeologist, in an unwritten testimony. Furthermore, vestige plays a central role in the corroboration and interpretation of oral and written testimonies. As for Carlo Ginzburg, he establishes an inventory of uses of the notion of the index; uses whose convergence authorizes their grouping under a single paradigm. He evokes Giovanni Morelli, the art lover, who had recourse to the examination of apparently negligible details (the outline of the earlobe) to distinguish copies of original paintings. This evidential method made the reputation of Sherlock Holmes and many other fictional police detectives. Psychoanalysis "accustomed to divine secret and concealed things from unconsidered or unnoticed details" [FRE 33] finds one of its sources there.

Medical semiology, with its concept of symptom, is also susceptible to come under the evidential paradigm. The writing itself is known as evidential. Several characteristics enable us to reunite these diverse disciplines under a similar paradigm: the singularity of the deciphered thing, the indirect and conjectural character of deciphering. History comes from this paradigm:

> "all this explains why history never became a Galilean science. […] As with the physician's, historical knowledge is indirect, presumptive, conjectural" [GIN 89].

And from the fact of the singularity of the index, historical knowledge has a probabilistic character. The domain covered by the evidential paradigm is very vast, and:

> "though reality may seem to be opaque, there are privileged zones – signs, clues – which allow us to penetrate it. This idea, which is the crux of the conjectural or semiotic paradigm, has made progress in the most varied cognitive circles and has deeply influenced the humane sciences" [GIN 89].

According to Paul Ricœur, the index and the testimony can therefore be considered as complementary. To the extent that the index is not of the verbal order, its "discourse" is not of the same nature as that of testimony, but the index completes, controls, reinforces or weakens the oral or written testimony. Carlo Ginsburg therefore introduces a testimony/index duality within the notion of clue and gives the concept of document its full dimension. The notion of clue can be considered as incorporating that of index and that of written testimony. And, therefore, the concept of document, gathering testimonies and indices, rejoin this notion of clue whose amplitudes are equivalent.

3.3.3. *Documentary proof*

3.3.3.1. *Questioning and document*

If the role of proof can be attached to consulted documents, it is because we are researching information with questions. The notions of questioning and questionnaire are therefore the first to set up in elaborating documentary proof. Armed with such questions, we engage in information retrieval.

Marc Bloch warns against what he holds as an epistemological naivety, i.e. the idea according to which there could be a first phase where the historian gathered documents, read them, and evaluated their authenticity and veracity, then a second phase where he/she implemented them. Antoine Prost [PRO 96], moving closer to Kantian conceptions, declares high and loud: no observation without hypothesis, no fact without questions. Documents are only a source of information if they are asked to verify, i.e. make true, some hypothesis. Facts, questions and documents are therefore interdependent. It is the question that constructs the historical object by proceeding to an original division in the unlimited universe of possible facts and documents [PRO 96]. The carving, or hypothesis, focuses on the phenomenon questioned and is inscribed in a research of explication and comprehension. In addition, this question carries in itself a certain conception of documentary sources and possible research procedures. Trace, document and question therefore form the base of knowledge.

This confrontation between question and document leads us back to the notion of document. Nothing as such is document, even if all residue of the past is potentially trace. The document is not simply given, it is sought and found. Then, it is circumscribed, constituted and instituted through the questioning. Everything can therefore become document, everything that can be questioned by a person in a situation of information retrieval.

3.3.3.2. *Fact*

From now on, what can be held as proved or confessed at the end of this confrontation between questions and documents? Facts; facts being able to be expressed by singular propositions. At this stage of the reflection on the elaboration of knowledge, and as emphasized by Paul Ricœur [RIC 00], we must not confuse the confessed fact and the unexpected event. The fact is not the event, itself the object of memory, but the contents of a statement aimed at representing it. Conceived in this way, fact is constructed through a procedure that extracts it from a set of documents; and we can say, in return, that these documents establish it. The propositional character of the fact governs the mode of truth or falsity affected by it. The terms true and false can be understood in the Popperian sense of refutable or verifiable.

3.3.3.3. *The event*

The world is everything that happens, writes Ludwig Wittgenstein in his *Tractatus Logico-philosophicus*; and what happens is the event. The event is the ultimate referent of knowledge. The event is what is spoken about, the thing on which knowledge is focused; whereas the fact, element of a discourse, is the thing said. The assertion of a fact marks the distance between the said, the thing said, and its intended referential that "turns discourse back to the world", according to Emile Benvéniste. A semiology inherited by Saussurean linguistics has long neglected the referent to the profit of the only signifying pair (narrative, rhetorical, imaginative) and the signified (the statement of the fact). The three-fold conception signifier, signified, referent now seems very generally admitted. Discourse, according to Emile Benvéniste, consists of someone saying something to someone about something according to the rules. In this outline, the event (the referent) is symmetrical to the researcher (the speaker).

3.4. Time and document

In this section, relying on Michel Foucault's *L'Archéologie du Savoir* [FOU 69], I take on the question of the documentation device on which "information science" is based. More briefly I cover document retrieval by referring in part to Georges Canguilhem's *Etudes d'Histoire et de Philosophie des Sciences* [*Studies in History and Philosophy of Science*] [CAN 83].

3.4.1. *Discursive documentation and formation*

3.4.1.1. *The documentation device*

Whether we call it documentation, material, corpus, base, or documentary collection, the symbolic material we are gathering, registering, processing, governing, questioning, developing, exploiting, is approached as a general rule in an empirical and practical way. Therefore, we do not really know what object it concerns, what its characteristics are, to what operations it can be submitted. And, above all, we only have one limited piece of knowledge of this set that is greater than the one from which it is extracted: what is its nature? What principles govern its formation, development, functioning, organization?

Several questions are regularly asked, faced with such an object. The first is that of the level of analysis of the documentation device, of its "granularity" – what is the minimum unit of description? And what are the connections between these units making up the set so that this material is described in its specificity, its formation and its use? Another question is that of the identification of diverse regularities that order such a group. Is it a disparate collection of heterogeneous elements, a jumbled list, or can rules or constraints conferred on it by a certain autonomy be revealed? Another question is that of its temporality. Is it a matter of an instantaneous or eternal object? A timeless and immobile object? Or a group in which successions, series or durations can be detected? In which a past, a present and a future can be distinguished?

On the methodological plane, when we are confronted with treatment, exploitation, questioning of such a material, we bump into many problems, some of which can be outlined here:

– the constitution of coherent and homogenous corpora (closed or open corpora, finite or indefinite) and therefore the establishment of a principle of choice, whether we are seeking to treat the documentation exhaustively, whether we are adopting a sampling according to statistical sampling methods, or whether we are attempting to determine the necessary or useful elements in advance;

– the identification of relevant marks, like numerical indications, references, explicit or not, to events, institutions, practices, words used with their rules of use and semantic fields they designate, or again the formal structure of propositions and types of chains that unite them;

– the delimitation of groups and sub-groups, which organizes our object (regions, periods, unitary processes, etc), and determines the relations that characterize them, whether it is a matter of numerical relations or logical ones, functional, causal or analogical relations, from signifier to signified.

3.4.1.2. *The statement*

Before having to deal, in all certitude, with a science or novels or political discourse or the work of an author or even a book, the material we have to process in its primary neutrality is a population of events in the space of discourse in general. Therefore, the description of discursive events is a preamble to the research of units formed therein. Let us agree to call such an event a statement.

A statement is an event that can never be completely exhausted, either by language or sense. An extraordinary event:

– first, because it is linked to a gesture of writing or the articulation of a speech, but it also opens itself a residual existence in the field of a memory or in the materiality of a manuscript, a book, or any form of recording;

– second because it is unique, like any event, but because it is offered to repetition, transformation, reactivation;

– because it is linked not only to situations that provoke it and consequences incited by it, but at the same time, and according to quite a different method, to statements that precede it and statements that follow it.

Therefore, the field of statements must be understood in its empirical modesty as the place of events, regularities, relations, determined modifications and systematic transformations. It must not be considered as the result or the trace of something else, but as an autonomous practical domain, though dependant, that can be described at its own level, although it must be articulated with something else. In addition, we must admit that a statement is the mode of existence belonging to a set made up of graphic, phonic or other signs. This mode enables it to be something other than a succession of marks on a substance, something other than some object manufactured by a human being. This mode enables it to be related to a referential, to prescribe a position on all possible subjects, to be situated among other statements, to finally be equipped with a repeatable materiality.

The referential is a domain where objects can appear and where relations can be assigned. This can be a domain of material objects possessing observable priorities or relations of perceptible grandeur. It can also be a domain of fictitious objects, equipped with arbitrary properties. Without authorities in charge of experimental or perceptive verification, this can still be a domain of spatial localization with coordinates, distances, non-hierarchical or inclusive relations, or a domain of symbolic belongings and secret relationships. The referential is not made up of things, facts, realities or beings, but of laws of possibility, rules of existence for objects who happen to be named, designated, described or represented therein, for relations that happen to be affirmed or denied therein.

The referential is the place, the condition, the filed of emergence, the authority in charge of the differentiation of individuals, objects, states, things and relations that are put into play by the statement itself. It is this set that characterizes the enunciative place of formulation and distinguishes it from its grammatical plane and its logical plane. As for the subject of the statement, it is neither the "speaking consciousness", a sort of collective and unified authority that produces speech, nor the author of the formulation, but a position that can be occupied under certain conditions by different individuals. Like the grammatical subject, the enunciative subject is not an authority outside the statement, but actually one of its components. This position, this determined and empty place, is not defined once and for all and is not maintained as such throughout a text, a book or a work. It varies in order to be able to be preserved, identical to itself, across several discursive sequences, to be modified with each one.

On the other hand, the statement emerges within a field, made up of other statements. This field is a domain of coexistence of the statement and other statements. It is therefore not a matter of the real context of formulation, of the situation in which it was articulated, but a matter of an enunciative context forming a complex web. This field is made up, first, by a series of other formulations among which it is inscribed, such as, for example, a game of counter-attacks forming a conversation, the architecture of a demonstration restricted by its premises and its conclusion, or the continuation of affirmations of a story.

It is also constituted by formulations to which the statement refers, explicitly or not, in order to repeat them or to modify or adapt them, or to be opposed to them: there is no statement that, in some way or other, does not update others. It is made up again by formulations whose future possibility is handled with care by the statement and that can follow it like its consequence, natural continuation, or counter-attack. It is made up, finally, by formulations with which the statement shares it status (judicial, political, religious, scientific, etc.), and among which it takes place without considering order, formulations with which it will be erased or, on the contrary, developed, conserved or made sacred. Therefore, a group of signs is only a statement if it is emerged in an enunciative field where it appears as a singular element.

Finally, the accuracy of a statement is not only the substance or the medium of the articulation, but a status, rules of transcription, possibilities of use or re-use. The regime of accuracy that statements obey is in order of institution more than spatio-temporal localization; the regime defines more the possibilities of re-inscription and transcription compared to limited and perishable individualities. Instead of being a spoken or shown thing once and for all, the statement comes out in its accuracy and, from then on, appears with a status, enters networks, is placed in fields of use, is offered to transfers and possible modifications and is integrated to operations and strategies where its identity persists or is erased.

3.4.1.3. *Discursive formation and archive*

Formation is the central object of analysis of the archaeology of knowledge. It is a group of sentences that can be defined neither by the object, the concepts, or the theme that changes and transforms over time. Michel Foucault defines it as a system of dispersion, a discursive space governed by the rules of possibility of existence for statements and diverse relations they are susceptible to entertain. A space where strategies, changes and transformations can be detected. The Michel Foucault archive is therefore the register of discursive formations on which archeology can be exercised. Let us note that archeology is of an absolute neutrality from which all intervention outside of the discourse is banned.

3.4.2. ***The time of discourse***

Discourse is historical through and through. Its temporality is its essential dimension. After a brief return to time, or more to the future, I now present the principle temporal characteristics of statements.

3.4.2.1. *Change and transformation*

A true future is something other and more than the sum of changes. Its unit claims the types of of change do not remain eternally identical to themselves. It also claims that its appearance is not an absolute beginning, neither its disappearance an annihilation. Change must change.

The future is the change of change, and the deep connection between all the changes. Therefore, energy transformations represent the passage to diverse levels of change; the death of an animal is the transfer from the biological level to the simply chemical level of the future.

Georg Hegel meticulously analyzed this change of change: it is a reversal – the jump from one change to another – qualitatively distinct. This jump is produced when a certain degree of quantitative modification of the first change is achieved. The increase in quantity leads to the mutation of quality. And, in return, all quantitative modification is operated by repeated adjunction of units, singularities, and qualitatives.

Georg Hegel gave many examples of this qualitative change and quantitative change. Therefore, the progressive dropping of the temperature of water provokes, at zero degrees, the mutation of liquid into solid; and at 100°C, the mutation of vapour into liquid. Technically, it is by operating on the quantity of change that the expected transformation of quality is obtained.

But quantitative change of qualities assures the unity and continuity of the future at the same time that it takes breaks into account. An absolute continuity, or an absolute discontinuity, of change would deprive us of all possibility of knowing it and would prevent all action on it. The future is therefore presented as the continuity of a discontinuity in time and space, like the unity of a diversity. It is the link of breaks. Fist hidden, but fundamental, it is "the link of the link and of the non-link".

3.4.2.2. *Succession and additivity*

In its transformations, in its successive series, in its derivations, the field of statements does not obey the temporality of human consciousness like its necessary model. The time of discourse is not the translation, in a visible chronology, of the obscure time of thought.

It is not a matter of treating what is given as successive, as simultaneous, nor of freeze time and substitute correlations that designate an immobile shape for its flow of events. It is not a matter of supposing that the succession is an absolute either: a premier and integral linking to which discourse would be submitted, nor a matter of considering that, in discourse, there is only one form and only one level of succession. On the contrary, it is a matter of making diverse forms of succession that are superimposed in discourse, and the way in which successions thus revealed are articulated and appear at the same time.

Instead of following the line of an original calendar, compared to which the chronology of successive or simultaneous events is established, the chronology of short- or long-lasting processes, that of instantaneous phenomena or that of permanences, it must be shown how there can be succession, and at what different levels distinct successions are found. And, instead of considering that discourse makes only one series of homogenous events, i.e. individual formulations, several planes of events have to be able to be distinguished in the thickness of discourse:

– the plane of statements themselves in their emergence;

– the plane of the appearance of objects;

– of types of enunciation;

– of concepts;

– of strategic choices;

– the plane of the derivation of new rules of formation from rules already at work; and

– the plane of substitution from one discursive formation to the next.

Furthermore, the types of groupings between successive statements are not the same everywhere, and they never proceed by simple piling or juxtaposition of successive elements. Mathematical statements are not added among them like religious texts or acts of jurisprudence. Each has a specific way of being composed, cancelling each other out, being incompatible, complementing each other, forming more or less indissociable groups and groups equipped with singular properties. In addition, these forms of additivity are not given once and for all, for a determined category of statements: medical observations of today form a corpus that does not obey the same laws of composition as the collection of cases from the 18th century; modern mathematics does not accumulate its statements on the same model as Euclidian geometry.

3.4.2.3. *Recurrence and remnance*

All statements have a field of past elements in relation to which they are situated, but which they have the power to reorganize and redistribute according to new relations. It makes up its past, defines it in what precedes its own relations, redesigns what makes it possible or necessary, excludes what cannot be compatible with it. And it poses this enunciative past as acquired truth, like an event that is produced, like a form that can be modified, like a material to be transformed or even like an object that can be spoken about. Compared to all these possibilities of recurrence, memory and forgetting, the rediscovery of meaning or its repression, are not fundamental laws; they are only singular figures.

Statements must also be considered in the remnance that belongs to them, and which is not that of the always updatable return to past events of their formulation. To say that a statement is remnant is not to say that it remains in the field of memory or that its meaning can be found. It means that it is conserved thanks to material supports and techniques (of which the book is only one example), according to certain types of institution (the library among others), and with certain statutory methods (which are not the same, depending on whether it concerns a religious text, a rule of law, or a scientific truth). It also means they are invested in the techniques that put them into practice, in practices that derive from them, in social relations that are made up or modified across them. It means, finally, that things no longer have completely the same mode of existence, the same system of relations with what surrounds them, the same schemes of use, or the same possibilities of transformation after they were said.

As far as this maintenance across time is the accidental or happy prolonging of an existence made to pass with the moment, remnance rightfully belongs to the statement. Forgetting and destruction are only the zero degrees of this remnance, to a certain extent.

3.4.3. *Documentary time*

Document retrieval, the reconstruction of some knowledge from a piece of documentation, cannot ignore the temporality of the latter, the temporality of the discursive formation it came from. Research time is nevertheless not assimilated to that of discourse. Documentary research has its own temporality. It progresses to its own rhythm and possesses its own time.

3.4.3.1. *A critical analysis of concepts*

Documentary research, i.e. the discovery and comprehension of a piece of knowledge through the bias of exploration and the interpretation of a piece of documentation, can undoubtedly distinguish and assume several levels of objects in the specific theoretical domain it constitutes. These levels include documents for indexing, methods and questions to be interpreted, instruments and techniques to be described, and concepts to be analyzed and criticized. This last task alone confers on the documentation their true *raison d'être* and their scientific quality. Being ironic about the importance accorded to concepts is easier than understanding why, without them, there is no true constituted knowledge. It is at the level of methods, questions, concepts that a piece of knowledge is formed. Documentary science concerns an axiological activity, a search for the truth.

3.4.3.2. *The documentary object*

The documentary object is not a scientific object. This object is not given, it is an object "for which incompleteness is essential"[1]. The theoretical place in which documentary science is going to find an object does not have to be sought outside documentary science itself. It is this science, and this science only, that constitutes the specific domain where theoretical questions find their place, through the practice of elaboration of a piece of knowledge, in its future.

---

1. To adopt Georges Canghilhem's formulation in the introduction of his *Etudes d'Histoire et de Philosophie des Sciences* [CAN 83].

3.4.3.3. *A non-logical beat*

Therefore, this discipline, whose object is incomplete by essence, possesses its own rhythm and time. Documentary time – the time of documentary research – is not civil time, that of the chronology of results of knowledge or of tools. It does not follow the regular and universal time of general history. Documentary time is that of the advent of scientific truth; or of socially established truth. Access to a piece of knowledge consists of understanding the way in which this knowledge was elaborated, and not only assuming its results and reconstructing the journey, the procrastination, the impasses and the breakthroughs that lead to what is assumed today.

Documentary time is not a logical time, i.e. that of a pure reasoning that establishes truth relations and whose propositions are inferred from other propositions. Logical time that leads to ignoring of the indefinite process of knowledge elaboration, to carry out artificial and anachronic comparisons and introduce this notion of "precursor" as fought by Alexandre Koyré [KOY77]:

> "not being aware of the fact [the precursor] is a creature of the history of sciences and not an agent of the progress of science, it is to accept as real its condition of possibility, the imaginary simultaneity of the before and the after in a sort of logical space".

Documentary research is not a science and its object is not scientific. To carry out documentary research, in the most operative sense of the term, is one of the functions of epistemology. A critical analysis of texts and works brought closer by the telescoping of heuristic duration did not explicitly establish that there is identity of the question and of the intention of research, identity of meaning of principle concepts, identity of the conceptual system from where the latter take their meaning. It is artificial and erroneous to place two scientific plans in a logical succession from beginning to end, or from anticipation to realization.

On the other hand, a piece of knowledge in emergence promotes a misunderstood discourse at the moment it appears and cancels out other discourses. Furthermore, the meaning of the breaks and relationships can only come to the researcher through his/her contact with contemporary knowledge. There is no possible definition of a piece of knowledge, whether it was well-established, before the succession, still ongoing, of discoveries, inventions and decisions that constitute it. "Mathematics are a future", wrote Jean Cavaillès. In these conditions the researcher of information can only take the provisional definition of the knowledge concerned from the specialist researcher of today.

3.5. Conclusion

Through the journey that led us from a reflection on memory to some propositions on documentary research, passing through a study of the historian's approach, it seems that the elaboration of theoretical bases for "information science" cannot make the economy of a detailed epistemological work. If one of the main objects of this "science" is the sharing and the transmission of knowledge, then it has to be directly associated with epistemology. Perhaps not the epistemology of the history of sciences, nor the genetic epistemology of Jean Piaget, but an epistemology of the mediation and transmission of knowledge.

3.6. Bibliography

[AUG 62] SAINT AUGUSTIN., *Confessions*, "Augustinian Library", Desclée de Brouwer, Paris, 1962.

[BER 63] H. BERGSON , *Matière et Mémoire. Essai sur la Relation du Corps à l'Esprit*, PUF, Paris, 1963.

[BLO 74] M. BLOCH, *Apologie pour l'Histoire ou Métier d'Historien,* Armand Colin, Paris, 1974.

[CAN 83] G. CANGUILHEM, *Etudes d'Histoire et de Philosophie des Sciences*, Vrin, Paris, 1983.

[CER 75] M. DE CERTEAU, *L'Ecriture de l'Histoire* "History Library", Gallimard, Paris, 1975.

[DUL 98] R. DULONG, *Le Témoin Oculaire. Les Conditions Sociales de l'Attestation Personnelle* [*The Eye Witness: Social Conditions of Personal Testimony*], EHESS, Paris, 1998.

[FOU 69] M. FOUCAULT *et al.*, *L'Archéologie du Savoir* , Gallimard, Paris, 1969.

[FRE 33] S. FREUD, "Le Moïse de Michel-Ange", in *Essais de Psychanalyse Appliquée*, Gallimard, Paris, 1933

[GIN 89] C. GINZBURG, "Traces, racines d'un paradigme indiciaire", in: *Mythes, Emblèmes, Traces, Morphologie et Histoire*, "New Scientific Library", Flammarion, Paris, 1989.

[HAL 50] M. HALBWACHS, *La Mémoire Collective*, PUF, Paris, 1950.

[HUS 64] E. HUSSERL, *Leçon pour une Phénoménologie de la Conscience Intime du Temps* , "Epiméthée", PUF, Paris, 1964.

[KOY 77] A. KOYRÉ, "Du monde de l'à-peu-près à l'univers de la précision", *Etudes d'Histoire de la Pensée Philosophique*, Gallimard, Paris, 1977.

[LOC 98] J. LOCKE, *Identité et Différence. L'Invention de la Conscience*, Le Seuil, Paris, 1998.

[POM 84] K. POMIAN, *L'Ordre du Temps* , "History Libraries", Gallimard, Paris, 1984.

[PRO 96] A. PROST, *Douze Leçons sur l'Histoire* , "Points Histoire", Le Seuil, Paris, 1996.

[RIC 85] P. RICŒUR, *Temps et Récit. III: Le Temps Raconté*, Le Seuil, Paris, 1985.

[RIC 00] P. RICŒUR,, *La Mémoire, l'Histoire, l'Oubli*, "The Philisophical Order", Le Seuil, Paris, 2000.

[SAR 86] J.-P. SARTRE., *L'Imaginaire*, "Folio Essay", Gallimard, Paris, 1986.

[TOD 95] T. TODOROV, *Les Abus de la Mémoire* , Arléa, Paris, 1995.

Chapter 4

Document and Network

4.1. Introduction

It is probably neither possible nor desirable to make the emergence of new scientific problematics a subject of study as such. The proposition is, on the other hand, opportune for bringing out an originality in information and communication sciences (ICS), its game of relations with other scientific discourses, and its original role in a social context that brings relations between language, technique and human interactions to the forefront. Currently, the conceptual purity of disciplines or their combination, their theoretical quality or their operational potential are alternatively enhanced, depending on whether the framework is that of academic evaluation or social relevance. In such a framework it is useful to remember the liability of ICS. It is interested in social objects, the media, discourses and communication systems, which are, themselves, social practices and commentaries on social practices at the same time. Reflexive practice, meta-language – ICS is defined less by its density than by its extent. Today, it covers a very vast terrain which, far from dissociating it, disperses it across the entire span of social life, from natural interactions to digital mediations. The facts of communication determine face-to-face relationships, industrial organization and uses of technique as much as digital, computer, social and documentary environments.

With mixed semiotics, polyphonic and fragmented documents, digital hybrids that do not distinguish human objects from non-human ones, the current communication situations overwhelm the course of activity, and the temporal and spatial regimes. They call into question scientific methods, disciplinary separations,

---

Chapter written by Sophie PÈNE.

and many undiscussed subjects in human sciences. Modifications are at work in the relationship with space, time and others. Two phenomena, i.e. two observables – the document and the network – carry the mark of these changes.

The document, its integrity, the means by which it is described, are called into question by its treatment on the web. The network becomes the carrier of sense, the means for textual migration, and even a continuous description of the world, from commentaries to judgments and tags. This vernacular indexation activity announces a gigantic documentarization of all objects, individuals included.

In the following pages it will be shown that comparing document and network creates a sort of explosion; in a landscape where the social network is installed as a downright entertaining metaphor of social life, conjoining document and network is done silently. Today the Internet, in which digital identity, here the description that makes someone or something recognizable, will take on a function of a meeting point. ICS is the best suited of the human sciences for taking into consideration this convergence between texts and social link. This is because its examination solicits two of the extreme branches – documentary science on the one hand, the study of interactions on the other – currently almost still strangers to each other. It must operate an epistemological critique of its interdisciplinary position for this. It also has to reunite the competences that can help it design, once again, sociodocumentary objects and no longer sociotechnical ones. This work, already undertaken by some of the researchers, could become a focus for the discipline. It will compare them to their fields of origin to treat three themes: cognition, innovation and human work, whose internal convergence (linked to document and network) and external ones (linked to social conditions) will undoubtedly be confirmed.

4.2. Critique of ICS as an interdiscipline

It would only be possible to describe new problematics in relation to something presented by a preceding inventory. We do not have this inventory. Even if we did, it would not help to approach the particularities of an interdiscipline. Unfavorable in the eyes of current scientific evaluation practices that enhance homogeneous and circumscribed fields, this characteristic of re-vindicated interdiscipline leads to a paradox. ICS inscribe their specificity in the mediations and enrichment they suggest to other sciences. Let us clarify this affirmation with an example:

– Patrick Chareaudeau [CHA 07] will approach the media through the bias of discourse analysis and sociopolitics;

– François Jost [JOS 04], from image semiotics;

– others through the history of techniques and systems of production or through that of press groups;

– others still, like Valérie Jeanne-Perrier [JEA 02], through the study of professional entities or like Dominique Cotte [COT 04] through their modification under the effect of technical and symbolic changes;

– studying mediations between social groups or analyzing news fabrication in press agencies, as done by Michael Palmer [PAL 01], can be added to this.

This diversity of angles does not alter the coherence of the only object, the media, at which these analyses are aimed. It concerns the high part of this object, the most manifest part, the part most in contact with society. It is the one that takes on economic and technical reception, influence, interaction, and complexity of discourse industries. If we reach a deeper layer of the media, archives and indexation of funds constitutes a new object, and another specialty, that of documentation science.

Information, documentation and production systems will be an even deeper, organizational and computer layer. This will compare the media and digital libraries to sports communication, combining video and audio productions to text, to iconography, to communication media in a dynamic and unlimited digital convergence. This capacity for drilling in communication systems, combining techniques to a communication pragmatic, is a property of ICS. Today, it gives them a unique potential.

4.2.1. *Unity of object, diversity of means*

This confusion of social and technical objects and the disciplinary division that accompanies it are actually a characteristic of ICS. It would not make sense to describe sociology using the same angle. But sociology organized its sectors of work, media and political sociology, a long time ago in order to achieve fine thematics, such as sociology of co-operation, of networks, of genre. Can "information and communication science of work" be imagined? Already mixed up in their denomination, composed of four nouns, one preposition, one coordinating conjunction and no determiners, ICS was able to remain reasonable.

As divided as they may be, ICS maintained convergence of their specialties by being interested in a global object, information and communication systems, and the way in which they affect the social state. It is why we risk speaking of a unified discipline despite the apparent dispersion. The stakeholders in the discipline held their ground and maintained a unity of object, combined with a wide dispersion of methods. Today the convergence of social information systems and digital information systems, the symmetry of different layers of these systems and the echoes they address change the order. A danger of splitting up, and a chance to reinforce the scientificity of the discipline around this capacity to take all the levels of information systems exist at the same time. The affirmation of this competence would enable us to deepen the scientific program around three key words – "semiology", "technique" and "policy".

The analysis of information and communication systems had to couple the production of signs with digital production from then on, and integrate the consequences that ensue from it with social organization, organization of powers, changes of place, negotiations, violence and cooperations with this view. ICS takes on objects that became central in the cultural industry, education and political and economic activity. They describe them and seize them as a dynamic of data circulation and actions provoked by this circulation.

4.2.1.1. *The invisibility of ICS*

Whereas an ICS researcher contributed to the analysis of network communication during the 2007 presidential campaign via the Internet, the results will be read as a contribution to political science. The originality of the methodological and heuristic approach specific to ICS will be erased. They will remain in the blind spot of the construction of the survey. They will not achieve the same visibility as that of the interpretation of political science it will have contributed to establishing.

And yet the study of political blogs as a system of communication implying a network analysis, a discourse analysis, a sociotechnical analysis, is revealed to be the only means of constituting information in the field, for human sciences that do not have the methodology adapted to digital territories. Information, in this case, cannot be given by classical means of sociology (interview, questionnaire, observation, documentary analysis). Because the data are displaced: that which participants explain in their style has less value and relevance than that which is determined by communication, ploysemiotic and polyphonic frameworks. What the technical device produces, like communication facts, becomes a component of the "ground". This ground can only be taken up by an analysis mediated by its communicational layer.

The problematic of political science debated during this presidential campaign focused on the development of the participatory democracy in the face of a model of proven and discredited representative democracy. The blogosphere, i.e. the constellation of blogs and sites, carried the discursive and technical marks of this debate.

4.2.1.2. *Political ground disrupted by digital technology*

The sociological data available for observing this ground were important. But political sociology was powerless for observing the essentially digital events of the object, of which only ICS seize the discursive and dynamic material. The medium is no longer the visible page. Or more so, the territory of the page is only understood by its cartography. It is the hypertext constituted by the network of links. It is "the ground".

New methodological approaches are designed, deeply impregnated by ICS. Among the thematics of the campaign, the contesting of representative democracy through a participatory democracy promotion was a central point of the web campaign. This democracy publicized this ancient questioning, clearly synthesized by Sintomer [SIN 07].

To follow this debate it was necessary to analyze communication productions and processes at the same time. ICS researchers enabled the deconfinement of these data because they showed the cooperative architecture of blogs and information dispersion mechanisms. They were able to organize the arguments and justifications carried by contributors to blogs (control of the action of politics through portable television, explicitation by politicians of their origin of actions and their system of values) and to illustrate this instrumentalization of the web as an electoral arena.

By becoming a medium of political action, and not only of political communication, the blogosphere contributed to designing a new form of political action; a semiotization of politics, like an activity and not only as an analysis. It could be said that politics, that aspect of the political campaign, functioned as metapolitics. By publishing critical analyses of its own functioning on a daily basis, by taking a pragmatic value from the interpretation of the campaign, the blogosphere had a double dimension of symptom and observatory. The phenomenon of participative communication, blogs and the group of web discourse, design the communication angle for which the group of human sciences is preparing.

ICS intervene like a mediation for political science: as methodological mediation, they help to describe and analyze the ground. As theoretical mediation, they help to design the communication device, which is pragmatic (producing a do, a make do, a make believe and a duty) and meta-linguistic (feeding itself from its own observations to increase its pragmatic efficiency) at the same time.

4.2.2. *The media as meta-media*

These particular relationships between political science and information and communication science could be transposed to other disciplinary couples. Media analyses only leave ICS a discrete place, whereas the preoccupation of the analysis is becoming an intrinsic part of the activity of the media. The media attempt to inhabit an intermediary zone between production and critique. "Deciphering" [AIM 06], like a meta-informational activity, is a sign of it. Commentary programs like "*Arrêt sur Images*"[1] also testify to it.

The unveiling of what was not known implies the critique of the system of production of publicized facts. On this account, the *Canard Enchaîné*[2] assumes a double role of critique of the political class and the journalistic class. Information is a piece of meta-information, which invests the field of updating of the sense production device. Numerous titles that today have a digital form are placed on a plane of political and communicational analysis: political because it is communicational.

This general survey suggests that ICS are victims of two ambiguities: collaborating with other human sciences, ICS become necessary for them to analyze communication interfaces, faced with a semiotization of grounds that make all enquiry spaces mediated worlds. Communication systems infusing the group of public devices, ICS find themselves, according to another movement, popularized by para- and meta-informational media.

Evidently with any other finalities, these media absorb the interest of publics for the critical dimension. They deprive ICS of their chance to be manifest in the social field as a science – the science perhaps? – capable of intervening on fundamental problematics in the knowledge-based society: the value of information, the industry of its production, the mechanisms of its dispersion, participation and circulation, the relation between computer code and text, the variation of the code and the text.

Accompanying the semiotics of the world and documentarization of social spaces [ERT 07], ICS cannot be satisfied with this incorporation by vernacular critiques of the media, or being in similar disciplines. How can this paradoxical situation be explained? An affirmation of scientific problematics and a strategy of publicization could reinforce the identification of ICS in the social and scientific community.

---

1. "*Arrêt sur images*" began as a weekly French television program about deciphering the media. Television broadcasting stopped in 2007 and the concept gave birth to a website, which began broadcasting online in 2008. There is now a television channel with the same name and also a literary program.

2. The *Canard Enchaîné* is a weekly satirical newspaper in France. It features investigative journalism and leaks from sources in the French political and business world, as well as numerous jokes and cartoons.

4.3. ICS and ICT: an exceptional encounter

Another factor intervenes in the current configuration of ICS – that of their closeness with information and communication technology (ICT). Objects and links between objects that compose the social, scientific and technical environment of ICS, have continued to be enriched and displaced these last few years. ICT played a role in this transformation of the landscape. ICT widened the field of ICS, by making it visible by media production mechanisms. Blogs, already mentioned above, give a materiality to human networks. They artificially build networks up, to the point that, by a curious reversal, the expression "social network" from then on seemed to belong to computer applications, such as Facebook or LinkedIn, which develop social networks on an industrial scale.

4.3.1. *The technique stolen by ICST*

ICT amplified the ICS field. But it also contributed to making them opaque. ICST, communication science and technologies, are fighting with ICS for ground. A large number of computing theses currently supported are referenced in ICS. Document computing, the modeling of social groups, the conception of intelligent agent systems, and computing associated with the genesis of texts and forms, affirm their proximity with ICS. Even if they are strictly information and are not incorporated in any natural practice of communication, they are counted as theses linked with ICS.

The word "technical" makes all the difference. Inscribed in the heart of ICS, the *technê* refers to the machine through which the message is transmitted. Digital technology introduced machinery of a particular nature. This machine, the code, reveals, may be better than the pen, the profoundly semiotic nature of all *technê*, whether it is materialized by a digital network or before digital communication by waves, frequencies, smoke signals or light. According to Anne-Marie Christin's theory [CHR 01], the reader invents the writing. Following the image of the "starry sky" she puts forward, the interpretation prevails over the text, and the medium prevails over the layout. The technical system of sign production is actually second to interpretation, like a semiotic system, of a layout on a medium.

Regarding the origin of writing, the idea received is that it would have been dependent on an economic need. Under the effect of beginnings of administrative organization, an accounting system would have been necessary in Mesopotamia 5,000 years ago. It is in response to this administrative need that a system for counting animals and harvests, houses and men would have been invented. Writing would have been born of vertical lines drawn in clay and stone through which one proceeded to inventories. Cuneiform characters would keep the outline and, further enable thinking about ritual formulae, epic poetry, evolving into transcription of the spoken chain.

4.3.1.1. *The reader invents writing, the semiologist prevails over the technician*

Anne-Marie Christin does not allow us to go against this origin of writing by putting forward a well-known argument. Without neglecting economic and notorious uses of writing, patrimonial and symbolic at the same time, the success of which is evident, she suggests a completely different reasoning which she judges much closer to the reality of civilization. It is because the world, the sky and the sand were perceived as media strewn with signs that writing was able to be invented. The spaces between the stars, visible on the celestial vault and the folds of sand left by the wind captured the attention of man. They were able to pre-judge that this disposition had a meaning; priests and soothsayers suggested interpreting them. It is in this way that signs make sense, relying on the hypothesis of regularity and variability of the signifying chain. The entrails interpreted by the auspice become signs because they find their reader.

All communication *technê* is based on an ability to interpret. Communicating machines [PER 88] began as interpreting machines. Evidently, in response to this need for sense, today digital machines are created prior to encoding machines. The volume of data processed and their connection capacity make the *techné* balance on the side of encoding. The variation between ICS and ICST places the "T" on the side of encoding. Implicitly, ICS claim their "T", without being placed on the side of technical system creation. The neighboring, which they need, plays in their disfavor. ICST take benefits from the current enhancing of the technique, even if what the technique covers and delimits is little known.

In the same way, computing technique contaminates the fragile field of ICS. ICS are not really invited so much to invest in the territory of technique. They did not find, if not in the field of documentation science, dialog spaces and spaces of co-development to the extent of what they could bring.

The current forms of the web include interpreter activity, whether interpreters are seeking to capture in order to make a technical and semantic enriching of it. In the case of open-source developments, it is the technical user who suggests his/her know-how to accelerate the development of professionals. These gifts of know-how, outside of all explicit paid context, deconfined an entire professional sector. These gifts enabled us to cross development techniques, and techniques of improvement on the level of informaticians by leading them to cooperation and self-training practices. These alliances have had important effects on development technique and software economy, without having an origin in technical competence at all, but much more in the social organization of production, even in the situation of insufficiencies of technique, its slowness, its rigidities, its poverties.

4.3.2. *Towards the reorganization of technique through its social organization*

We clearly see that technique, even if we are placed on the computing upstream of programs, is not limited to the code. It has even exceeded its competence to model organizations. Organizational computing began its career by reproducing procedure. It was revealed as an analyzer of organizations. Computerization constraints contributed to administrative rationalization, even more so than the computerization it produced.

Today, computing integrates the event, i.e. the plasticity of practices and the interest there is in being able to memorize accidents and apparent organizational dysfunctioning, in order that programs are enriched from it. Still better, computing is interested in the strategy and anticipation of needs that the human organization does not know how to fill. It only succeeds in doing it by leaving the gangue of the code, by implying the description of complex states desired in the program, and by therefore becoming an executive of strategic utopia.

Socially contextualized from the professional culture of practitioners, it is also contextualized with regards to its modes of applicative conception. Today, it is the observation of real life courses of action that draw deeply contextualized developments.

4.3.2.1. *A text industry, based on "contribution"*

Wikipedia, an example so often used, is the simplest proof there is of the efficiency of industrial contribution of interpreters. Volunteers interested in an entry in this encyclopedia "contribute", i.e. bring their tribute, their resource to a group of information already in place. Their gift, their discourse, is added, aggregated, substituted and causes the discourse already in place to vary. The very fine work of putting knowledge into words, the writing of insertion links of one discourse in another, are sophisticated discursive techniques. Words find their translation in computer code, through HTML tags and digital signals. It is a matter of composite techniques, in which the human subject intervenes, as a collection of subjects, and works industrially to a continually-ongoing collective construction

Determining the respective territories of ICS and ICST is therefore delicate. The increasingly social use of the web should arouse the necessary dialogs for the harmonious development of communicational studies that have one single question in common: "How and why is the world becoming digital?" [BER 08].

Surely the same ambiguities and the same overlapping exist in other disciplinary fields? Management sciences welcome work concerning administrative data processing and information systems among organizational, managerial, financial or accounting studies, and can consider ICT as cutting down their disciplinary identity.

ICS can devote the forces necessary for ensuring its development and specifying its relation to ICT to the epistemology of their discipline. The request for proposals text "forms and mutations of communication. Processes, competences, uses", expresses the restlessness of the French National Research Agency, and the need for restoring balance in the face of the domination of ICT over ICS. The interest for historical approaches to communication, for considering the social link, is indicated:

> "At the time when communication is very often associated with technology and most particularly the internet and computing, this request for proposals wishes to highlight the interest of works that focus on more traditional media and on non-mediated communication situations".[3]

Whereas it seems useless to imagine drawing the digital component of the work of ICS researchers, this injunction translates the discomfort of the institution in the face of a technophilia which, in some regards, subordinates ICS to ICST. We can also just as well think that the strong social dimension currently introduced in the web prepares a new reversal. Discursive productions reveal the social nature of computer communications. They can dialectically introduce an evolution of ICST which can from now on reason because of natural languages and orientations of social groups, as erratic as they seem, to those who model.

4.3.3. *Social science of digital networks*

ICS have a tendency to badly live out the multiple consanguinities they have undergone or desired if they are judged by the double discourse they display. On one hand, they make a force and a trademark out of it, inscribed from the origin, by thinking of themselves as an "interdisciplinary". On the other hand, they are worried about it. Devoting themselves in phases to repeating the fundamentals of their interdiscipline, they protest against the indifference of sociology. This sociology seizes the "grammar of practices" or "forms of collective action" and digs into the forgotten part that had been described by Anni Borzeix [BOR 01]. This forgotten part is communication language, interactions and practices, by getting very close to ICS territories without deigning to recognize ICS and without ever citing the works in question.

On the ICT front, disorientation, as we saw above, is equivalent. The field of "uses", a strange expression that installs practice as a consequence subordinate to the tool, is dominated by technical productions. These productions are treated as fixed states from which use – and its observation – are to be constructed. The apparent consideration for "users" continues to be restricted to a study of needs and

3 From http://www.agence-nationale-recherche.fr/AAP-184-Communication.html.

to tests. Neither the socialization of technique, nor consideration of users from conception are real changes.

The user reveals him- or herself, first, by adopting his/her exteriority, taking control of collective publication systems. The current complementarity between indexation by librarians (according to standards such as Dublin Core or Dewey) and indexation by spontaneous user tags (so-called folksonomy) does show the reversal through which the user invades conception and organization. Communication systems found their mirror image on ICS. But ICS are often on the wrong side of the mirror, and see without being seen: heuristic and reflexive practice, or diagnostic and conception tool, ICS struggle – and sometimes hesitate – to promote their autonomy and uniqueness. Their composite character between techniques and society, between languages and communications, make them particularly apt for seizing the current dynamics of discourse circulation.

ICS, in all their dimensions, are a science of networks of relations between individuals, no matter what their materials, their forms or the means chosen to ensure their continuity. In a world that rejoices at being described as a network, from economics to geopolitics, passing through financial systems, terrorism, education, organization of production, etc, ICS should give up being declared an "inter-discipline" and affirm their efficiency of meta-discipline. It causes the greater communicational turn of human sciences, that makes the "grounds" less and less seized by direct observation, and more and more attracted by the mediation of systems of signs:

– clothes;

– language;

– behavior of subjects;

but also the map and territory and the ways of living and moving, are more and more semi-politically approached and less and less phenomenologically so. Whereas the behavior in a waiting line at a ticket machine [BREV 05] can become the material used to interpret the feeling of risk in our society, it is good that the researcher considers the waiting line as a semiologist and not as an ethnologist. The twisting of bodies, the foreclosure that operates on the neighboring body which is too close, the concealment of your bank code, are less interesting as the symbolic translation of a fear of the other. Two key objects of the ICS field, the document and the network, are exposed to the same questions. Should they be approached as phenomena? Are they main themes of the social and productive reorganizations that we are in the process of experiencing? Are they semi-political indicators?

It is around these two poles that the reflection starts. The presentation of negotiations and reconfigurations of disciplinary fields actually leads to a scientific proposition. Reconfiguring the document under the effect of digital technology, pulverizing of documentary closure [BAL 04], the hold of social networks over documents are the first element of this couple. The social network is the second element: itself a documentary space, indexed and molded by the marks of digital identity and digital reputation. The human network is mixed with the digital paste, therefore suggesting a social illusion. The mark of human readings is seen on the document, the mark of documentarization is printed on human action. This combinatorial analysis affects documentary spaces and social spaces in an unexpected manner. This suggests to ICS a site, whose opening they have to orchestrate, as meta-discipline more than as inter-discipline.

4.4. The stakeholder network, visited by digital technology

In 1995, Nicolas Dodier therefore introduced his work *Les Hommes et les Machines*: "Social sciences can no longer ignore the fact that links between humans, or between humans and the world, henceforth largely pass through technical objects whose presence is affirmed at the same time as the vitality of techniques capable of putting forward innovations that are incessantly arising, in a world whose waiting horizons are furthermore shaken. For a long time and on several fronts, social sciences caused a critical voice against this technicization of the world to be heard: a voice against the violence of signs denounced by semiological analyses of consumption, against distancing of modernity pinned by philosophical critique, and against the inhumanity of industrial work finally, notably in its Taylorian form, which sociology of work amply showed" [DOD 95 , p. 1].

The vitality of the technical object, (its *virtus*, the energy which makes it change its state), is evoked by Nicholas Dodier in a way that places the object at the intersection of two tendencies and invites us to make indexes of ongoing change from it: the technical object unites man with nature, by giving him/her the means to perceive it other than through the eye only (the microscope, the magnifying glass), to touch it other than by the hands (a haptic arm, a crane), to transform it (a factory, a machine, a pestle, a bulldozer). At the same time machine separates man from nature: it symbolizes transformations and alterations of an imaginarily harmonious relationship. It also represents, as Nicholas Dodier reminds us, the distancing of man from machines and represents forces that organize production.

The history of relationships of man and machine is as long as that of human sciences. It is in many respects the founding myth. Stiegler [STI 04] supports that the expression "philosophy of technique" should not be, affirming that philosophy should originate from its very relationship to technique, while philosophy is, on the contrary, constituted on an evacuation of this *technê*. The object is the layer that the sociology of translation places at the heart of negotiations and translations [AKR 06].

But is the digital object not a mediation? Is the relationship between man and technique not disrupted by man and object hybridization, digital code and language hybridization? In this context of instrumented communication, let us remember the importance of two domains – that of man/machine communication and that of mediation, to show the changes – of the notion of object, in the context of social networks.

4.4.1. *Aphids on humans*

Man/machine communication causes four states to meet: machine design, software design, interface design, and usage accompaniment. The landscape is so well installed in the field of ICS that it boils down to one single view of the man/machine dialog: man in a head-to-head with the screen, reading a digitized text. This image slowed down comprehension of the emergence of the Internet by human sciences. Is the man/machine object not in the process of vanishing in order to be reconfigured? In the process of going from a macro-world to a micro-world? The object is inserted in the body at such a small scale that it is no longer defined by its being outside the human body.

Invisible prosthesis, the nanochip introduces code in cellular functioning and neuronal in the mathematical code. "Aphids[4]" make industrial or biological objects deeply computer-related. Today they are installed under the skin. In the future they could be grafted on the neuronal scale. Objects enter human networks through computer ubiquity. Humans enter the network of objects through computer tags and identity documentarization. The thought of technique, the thought of document, the representation of the splits between nature and industry, semantic object and functional, biological and technical object are complexified under the effect of the NBIC[5] convergence (nanobiotechnology). This NBIC convergence has an impact on the anthropology of technique, and specifically on ICS. The antagonism between animate and inanimate is followed by a mixture of matters, which the ICS division described above is apt to face.

This mixture henceforth devaluated the "computer", historical representative of the relationship between man and computer science. For human sciences, this object

4. This is what Berry calls computer chips that invade the biological and objects.

5. NBIC, is an emerging and converging technology that refers to Nanotechnology, Bbiotechnology, Information technology and Cognitive science.

layer arbitrated for 10 years during which relations between the reader and digitized data, between human intelligence and machines was debated. It was able to be inserted, without too much difficulty, into the tradition of mechanization of writing on the one hand [LAU 82], and the sociology of technique on the other. But the keyboard and the screen, which will have structured our first techno-semantic visions and oriented all cognitive problems towards reading from the screen and towards forms of navigation associated with it, are in the process of a limitation period. In any case they lose all heuristic power and mask new, invisible, nanoscopic, mobile, cumulative objects that solicit ICS. This binarization (man on one side, code on the other), mediated by the screen, contributed to slowing down the comprehension of what social networks oblige us to consider: hybridization of objects and humans materializes the theoretical reality described by the sociology of translation [AKR 06] and theoreticians of mediation in the ICS field [DUF 01], in an observable social reality. All the effort made by communicational anthropology for 20 years is revealed as the adequate socle for approaching the semiotic terrains evoked above.

4.4.2. *A mutation masked by the psychologization of networks*

Social networks are spaces of transition. As educational spaces, they liberate us from the computer, in the sense that they break the imaginary technician and help to create of a mixture of communication systems, in all their relational, identity, and imaginary stakes.

In an intranet of the groupware type, i.e. the business hall of the web, of which the years 1996-2005 witnessed the birth and maturing, the home page is a portal in which the user is oriented, from the time he/she connects, and according to rights, towards applications and documents. He/she is lead all at once towards a personal space. This form of "hall" where, by successive selections, the requester constructs his/her path is becoming obsolete. Depending on the model of need for information, which research must satisfy, it functions from the big towards the small, form the general to the unique. The "social network", new written form and software in the process of installation expresses a new polarity that somewhat sets back the need for information. It substitutes the need with a serendipity scenario: "enter and go, you will find something that will respond to the need you do not know".

The lexical variation which currently causes us to slide from "intranet" to "social network" is not really explained by differences in functionalities. Wikis and blogs can be available on the intranet as they are on a social network. On the other hand, the variation expresses a change in polarity. The explicit query is no longer the only way to retrieve a piece of information. The intranet is an environment. It remains a place metaphor. We speak of the "architecture" of a site. Signage orients us from one public space towards diverse suitable places. It is a centered informational ecology. Whereas the point of entry that governs exposure remains the same, identification (name and password), the social network is, itself, focused on the individual as a whole and not as a point in a whole.

Does the individual come off best? That is to be seen. Let us agree on its digital definition. The new point of entry is the subscriber's profile. For several years, ICS perceived this new polarity and accompanied it with many works that bring out the relation of the personal diary and the blog, which set the foundation of electronic communication in the social link and the quest for affection [LAR 04, LIC 07, SEI 08]. Marrying the path opened by comprehensive sociology [KAU 04], they submit electronic diarim to the scholarly and popular idea often explored by sociology, of a contemporary development of individualism [SIN 06].

Strong critiques can be made about this tendency of ICS. It is certain that between the "individualism" described by sociology and that which can be observed on the web, the resemblance is strong. This means that when a feature exposed above is found, the tendency of ICS is to analyze communication facts by implicitly submitting them to sociological facts. On the phenomena plane, the convergence does not cause doubt. But this convergence tends to limit the interpretation of social networks to a psychological angle, a tendency that is confirmed with the theme of digital identity. This identity is approached from its theatre angle, a Goffmanian Marivaudage[6] or an anthropomorphic representation of games of masking and unveiling [CAR 08]. The thesis we are exploring is completely different. Intimacy, in this framework, is a glimmer. It causes specific and possibly new analyses to go missing. The description of ourselves with which we lead social networks is an informational stimulation, whose goals are grossly expressed by documentarization of human objects' collective education.

4.4.3. *Documentarization of human objects*

The subscriber arrives on "his/her" page. But this individualized representation is an illusion. The sensitive and personal world of this subscriber has no value. The supposed conviviality, the eventual psychologization, are a condition of the environment. It is of the same level as heating an amphitheatre in winter, which is supposed to favor learning conditions. The operating system does not seek its benefits in this direction. Socialization is a metaphor. It is the means for obtaining

6. Marivaudage is the style of writing of French novelist and dramatist Pierre de Marivaux who, for example, uses a familiar phrase where dignified language would be expected or uses words that would not normally go together and making them fit.

the subject's consent and especially his/her good mood for providing the data, which the whole exercise the network demands.

The individual, his/her photo, his/her personal description are a point of entry in a network. But why, then, the need for such a fine description of the person? The division of the object creates an information resource that multiplies the semantic possibilities of interfacing between objects. It therefore increases the quality of contacts between objects. It intensifies the density of points linked. It weakens the information given, because different participants, from different points on the system, co-describe and co-validate the same objects according to different views.

On Plaxo[7], a social network that aims to replace Facebook and introduce computerized social networks in the daily lives of businesses, the second stage in the registration procedure consists of a proposition which suggests trusting the Plaxo system with exploring other networks such as LinkedIn or Yahoo. It places itself as "heir" of content of all other networks and does not suggest any particular new description: these are already available in pre-informed networks. The third stage is a dive in Gmail web messaging: the robot presents, in seconds, hundreds of contacts listed in an e-mail in two groups – Gmail addresses already linked to a Plaxo account, and Gmail addresses not yet linked to a Plaxo account. The subscriber is invited to send a proposition to the latter. Two humanized information resources are therefore explored with great rapidity. "Humanized?" As we say very naturally, it is the "contacts", i.e. objects that have a particular property, represented by the link of two e-mail addresses, the property of having exchanged at least one piece of information. This property incorporates them in the information object in the process of being described.

On the surface it seems to be a matter of saving the subscriber the fastidious work of inviting his/her contacts to discover this new network. But is it only a matter of simplifying an approach that the new satisfied subscriber would do quite naturally? This proposition is made to him/her at the start of the process, even if he/she him/herself only had very little personal information to give: his/her name, his/her business, his/her e-mail, his/her date and month of birth. The year of birth is not requested. Symbolically a certain number of facts are signified to him/her in this way: he/she him/herself is interested less than the network he/she is attracting.

---

7. Plaxo is a network that has existed for several years and is based on sending visiting cards to be filled out, which then circulate from one contact to the other. A new version reconfigured as social network places this functionality of identity description at the heart of a network system of systems. It offers the subscriber the possibility of reuniting his/her presence on different searchable macro social networks in this aggregator of linked identities. Plaxo's site: http://www.plaxo.com/ (accessed October 5, 2009).

His/her worth, his/her presence, are linked to his/her social interfacing. The digital description of him/herself already available is henceforth sufficient.

Networks have arrived at a sort of maturity that brings the criteria of their competition to light. The winning network is the one that, for a given period, can be constituted into a meta-network capable of inheriting information properties of prior networks. How do they inherit some of them? By automating the harvest of other networks. This automation is a facilitation. It systemizes exploration. It accelerates it. It suspends the evaluation of the opportunity: "Should I invite this one?". Documentary density being acquired, we are no longer proceeding to a new inquiry, which would be a disorientation and a dissipation. The system harvests and brings this harvest in the form of a very easily examinable list for the subscriber. Refusing being cognitively more costly than accepting, the presentation being done in the most natural form possible, we can believe that the presentation will be appreciated by the subscriber and that he/she will accept the proposition.

Except if he/she is surprised and hit by the brutality of the message. Even if he/she were accustomed to these entertaining networks, an open secret is cruelly revealed to him/her by the apparent modesty of the solicitation he/she undergoes. If he/she is attentive to the processes in which Plaxo integrates him/her, he/she can understand that his/her person is worth nothing and his/her network is worth everything. Here, digital identity represents a crossroads of links. Capturing it causes capital to be inherited from links tangled up around the "person". The precision of subscribers' personal descriptions enables us to constitute information objects, which are refined in numerous faucets and are therefore going to increase connectivity between small worlds [MIL 67]. Small worlds that are becoming more and more dense, as if we were leaning to a nanodimension description of subscribers' centers of interest.

4.5. Dating, metaphor of indexation

The first popularized model of this interfacing between human objects is that of electronic meeting services. Between 2000 and 2005, electronic meeting services definitively came from the telematics era of France's pre-Internet online service, Minitel. Opening out in multisemiotic interfaces on the one hand and dynamic databases on the other, they constitute a particularly precious transition space, in order to understand a development on two levels: a hypostasis of seduction, and its objectivation in document. Seduction has been transformed by electronic dating, with two people's information making them stand out to each other in the online crowd. Similarly it's emergence heralded the acceptance of the indexed portrait, and a digital identity serving as a referent for reuniting multisemiotic links on one's name.

The mutation witnessed was cultural transgression: searching for a match has moved from private contemplation to public exploration of "profiles", giving up the attached authenticity for the idea of "falling in love", to proceed by progressive adjustments, not by familiarizing yourself with only one elected object, but by testing degrees of adequacy with a series of objects. The remarkable mutation was the essential transgression. People have accepted the Internet by voluntarily defining its humanity in binary code that can be integrated in bases. On the side of the evolution of intimacy are, the paradox of powerful tools capable of industrializing the incomparable, respective attraction between two people, and "increasing the chances". On the side of evolution of the object, is the simplification enabling access to a social documentarization, without the embarrassments of whichever rules are enacted by the French Data Protection Authority, CNIL[8].

4.5.1. *Seduction – the face of transition between dating and connection*

The two evolutions went together. Metaphor of dating, the exploration of profiles on online dating and chat sites, Meetic or Net Club, was a scenario of selection that simulated "initial contact": "who do you look like?", "how tall are you?", "how much do you weigh?", "what color are your eyes?", "what do you like to eat?". It was therefore about making intuition and taste stand out – I am going to like this one, that one even more – in structured elements in databases. That surely represented unsuitable questioning, but the lack of realism and relevance did not inhibit subscribers.

The most boorish man does not ask a woman her weight when she is introduced to him. Immediate perception goes beyond quantitative indicators. Beyond this awkwardness, these personal descriptions – auto and alter – modeled the different points of view and moments of dating. "What I believe myself to be", "how I would like to appear", "who I imagine wishing to date". Even a principle of reality intervenes. "The one I am looking for is never the one I am imagining". Because two functionalities of Meetic introduce first, an accident – channel hopping randomly extracts images of people from the base, independently of stated queries – and secondly, a rationality – the shaker calculates the conformity between dream and reality by extracting from the base of "profiles", of which conformity with the query is measured according to the percentage of items carrying convergent responses. If you want to know the one who thinks they want to know a completely different person, well, the convergence and discordance between expectation (the profile

8. The CNIL (*Commission Nationale de l'Informatique et des Libertés*) is an independent institution in charge of watching over respect for human identity, private life, and liberties in a digital world.

solicited) and response (the counter-profile expected by the solicited profile) will be measured as a percentage and will sound like an oracle.

Moment of transition, to what? These different arithmetic filters capable of converting dreams into percentages can be interpreted in diverse ways. We can be interested, following Giddens [GID 92], in feeding a history of sensitivity and emotions. It is surprising that the need for affection, confined in the tacit, is therefore deconfined, publicized, quantified, materialized and made visible. It is surprising that private counsel enters a public arena. Hypotheses on the rituals of address, pick-up lines, and evolution of forms of communication will be taken from them. The implementation of computerized dating databases could therefore seem like a simple organizational rationalization of matrimonial agencies. But some facts incite another reading.

4.5.2. *Dating spaces are not sociological objects*

As in all contemporary computer innovations, dating sites drop human intermediation and give the initiative to the subscriber. Related through their computer structure of auction sale sites such as E-bay, these dating sites lend to a classic analogy between seduction and commerce. The temptation to evoke a communicational situation of online sale is great, with the vendor selling him/herself, in any case his/her web image, like a third-party object, and trying to evaluate the exchange value of this image against another image. Two clients negotiate live from objects described in the best way possible, thanks to mediations induced by distance, caution and technique.

The image of a person, as he or she is presented by the site, is an initial description to which dialogs will bring contextual richness, to the point of making them evolve and adjust to other images. In this case the "falling in love" no longer concerns the unveiling of an object held hidden, but the voluntary co-construction of a sufficiently acceptable fiction, which will make the link. Two documentary objects semantically describe their connotations. There is an interesting reversal. Where animosity is expected, there is a decision, where uncertainty is expected, we would have a measure of the predictable. Evidently, faced with such a scenario, it is important that the image is not taken for the thing represented. Therefore, let us avoid highlighting the defaults of a society that compensates its members' solitude with alliances whose strong sexual character predicts the worse. What can such approaches bring, if not the completely foreign psychologization of a machine? It is nevertheless good, just as studies of "love encounters on the internet", proceed. Nevertheless the strength of ICS is to be able to approach such objects by avoiding analyzing a communicational system according to categories imported from a completely different system. Speaking of the Internet system as a continuous or discontinuous prolonging of the social world seems a total methodological aberration that projects the naturalness of the social and psychological world on the digital objects.

When Berry [BER 08] asks: "How does the world become digital?", he is restricting himself to describing the mathematical structure of an Internet that is practiced by humans but that has most of all, for major efficiency, to be dispersed in objects. Is it not an aporia to treat social networks as digitized projections of real life social networks or like updating of potential networks? And to incessantly compare the real world and the virtual world, like symmetrical terms, by comparing the respective inconveniences and advantages of face-to-face situations and digital mediations, the different forms of management of temporality and spatiality?

4.5.2.1. *The "sociomorphy" obstacle*

Looking at this calculation of the relationship as an industrial manifestation of the documentarization of domains of life is a lot more heuristic. By suggesting that we consider dating sites as a moment of transition, we evoke precisely this articulation between an extreme psychologization of digital worlds and the documentarization of social worlds. Or at the very least the start of this documentarization. When Durkheim takes suicide as the object, he operates a stroke of methodological force. The least of this is not to choose an act representing the absolute of free will, giving oneself death, to constitute it in an event that can be interpreted from determinants that introduce comparability where subjectivity, the *raptus*, the harmful accident seemed to bring explanations that nothing could make converge. It was a barrier that was falling, an impression of immanence that was resolved in tables. One hundred years later the severing of an equivalent barrier seems to be represented.

The psychologization of digital technology is two-fold: it focuses on the nature of relational propositions made to users. It also focuses on interpretive tools. Why do social science researchers have the tendency to treat social networks as social facts and not as digital facts? Why is the enormous work of spontaneous description of human groups not seen for what it is – a hybrid object similar to calculability and sociability, in an overriding that could call to mind the Durkheimian stroke of force? Why is the social digital world treated as a compensatory society, responding to the link deficit through a virtual affectivity and to the fear of contact by a set of masks? Nothing new under the sun to this account. ICS are completely prepared to treat this emergent object, it will perhaps represent, for this field, a stroke of strength capable of causing us to understand how the Internet is in the process of organizing itself.

It is significant that dating sites were the visible preludes preparing the inscription of social networks of the years 2006-2007. They imaginarily marked the conquest, through computation, of its "dark continent", the affect. Within our communication society, the power of computation is continuously being improved. We know Moore's law, according to which, every two years computation power will double in relation to the physical surface occupied by a processor. Completely understood in management, finance, industrial design, health contexts, the stake of data processing seems to escape analysts – and users – as soon as it is a matter of a social network. It is as if the name itself made the system into a sanctuary by making the technique an auxiliary means and not the substance of the phenomenon.

4.5.3. *Towards the removal of profiles*

Depending on the date different networks appeared, the social metaphor is more or less strong. Among the most ancient social networks[9], two models were in competition, MySpace and LinkedIn, one projecting in public space the world of intimate pastimes, the other attempting to graft the referent of the professional social world, based on a nucleus of curriculum vitae, in the web world. In both cases, growth of the network depends on the link. But LinkedIn requires individuals to know each other in the social world[10], while MySpace believes in the attraction created by the pages visited.

On LinkedIn, people "find each other" and notice that they have quite a few acquaintances in common: it is the image of little worlds. The idea is that, all united, we share the marks of businesses in which we have worked, universities at which we have studied. We list our backgrounds on the front page and, from group to group, we increase the potential to develop a relationship, which has the potential to become a solid friendship with further benefits (finding each other, helping each other, comparing each other and linking with each other).

MySpace has more of a visible impact; success stories are not lacking: it is from her MySpace page that some young singer who recorded her first album at her home became known worldwide. A point worth noting here that is constant in all of the networks, you make yourself known under your own name. Pseudonyms therefore are rarely used in the digital world. This does not prevent the adoption of false identities and identity theft, as there is no verification system. It is in the capacity of "oneself" that the person participating in the network can intervene. Making your

9. Here we are using, without critique, the vernacular designation "social network" with the meaning designated in about 2006: a group linked to personal pages based on the description of people and their desire to develop "friends".

10. LinkedIn restricts the selection of friends in two ways: 1) by a question whose answer is obligatory, "how do you know this person?"; 2) by the obligatory validation of this response on the target page. It is explicitly asked that people contact only people they actually know and not people they would like to have in their network.

digital network fruitful in social spaces by combining the virtual and real means you need to be recognizable.

Networks whose notoriety is more recent also cause the rivalry of two models that mark a progressive emancipation compared to the metaphor of identity as a psychic representative to go towards an object node identity.

The first model, of which Ziki is an example, uses identity (photo and elementary profile) as a portal. Ziki brings together various pieces of information across online websites and links them to the user's identity. Ziki therefore does not offer functionalities of content creation. It requests that the subscriber reunite on his/her page the flow of diverse documents that he/she creates on scattered sites. The goal is the construction of repetition: Ziki is represented as a referencer. By the number of profiles housed, by keywords and tags used, Ziki increases the rate of use of correct names. With digital identity, the ability to identify someone from their online profile is one of its fundamental features. It is a brand that can be enhanced, according to the large volume of associated content and the quality of its indexation.

The second model, represented by Facebook, operates a displacement that is also important, but of another nature. The online identity, or portrait, is used here to create a large number of links. The information provided on Facebook is reduced to a photo, to the indication of sex, relationship status (single, attached, married), and an e-mail address.

4.5.4. *The social network as ready made*

The object of the description is no longer used to feed a base whose connections are constructed term by term according to the documentary analysis of subscribers. It is the linked objects, titles of films, books and published photos, that will be the mediations between subscribers and will generate the development of connections. The content is created on Facebook itself. It is limited to brief invitations to participate in some activity, whose artificial character is the bait: to adhere to groups "my president is a riffraff", "for exchanging Sarkozy with Ingrid Betancourt", "for the family of each soldier who died in Pharsale by CM-2".

These invitations circulate at the speed of the network. The more absurd they are, the more successful they are. The derision acts as an accelerator of links. Because the title of the group suggested is represents a critical state of mind, but also pushes the idea of adhering to the absurd, the network seems to be based on irony, adhesion through antiphrase and to counter-use. It suggests the parody of the power of the network: Facebook is a network *à la Duchamp*, a ready-made, everyday computer structure of packets of data, circulating at all speeds. Data "pings" between users and reveals the structure of a production, of which exhibition and dynamism reveal the *raison d'être* of the network.

By emulation, the lists published on linked pages by other subscribers, from which it is suggested a person completes his/her own, are limitlessly enriched, corrected to be accurate, and grow into an enormous and artificial document. This document installs, without making a sound, a new model of acquaintance, performance and relation between subjects and objects. The interfacing relies on a sharing economy, whose apparently mediocre added value, is acceleration and expansion. The important interfacing is created from the comings and goings of content: internal e-mail, "Super Wall" receiving mischievous messages that are also sent to all "friends", or are at least visible from their sites. A thread of action notifying the most modest changes made on the page and making an object of collective attention out of the absurd liability of a network. The content, on "my" page, is that put up by my contacts.

Facebook is characterized by numerous light applications, installed as quickly as they are removed, which each subscriber can install on his/her page. Graphic, entertaining and creative, they have in common the lightening speed, originality, and above all the capacity to represent the network: graphic map of contacts, random table of photos of individuals cited on all linked pages, collections of digital objects to offer. These are digital eggs whose animal content is only revealed to the happy receiver once the shell is broken. Games soliciting vast tribes and giving rise to scores. Almost everything that is inscribed on a page is circulated on the pages of all other pages linked by the "contract".

How can this amalgamation of fluid documents, mixing objects, images, and animations, be other than it seems? Why should it be considered as the ambassador of the Internet of things? With a mobile phone, such as is conceived by Japanese mobile communications operator NTT DoCoMo today. Consider a man walking through a town. He scans the coded description of an object on a form in the street with a laser and orders it. He sends its reference to his friends and he classes it among his preferences or favorites. He gets in a taxi and pays with his digital bank cards, details of which are included in the same telephone. He stops in front of a shop that publishes the updated prices of articles he previously bought on his screen. He orients himself with his integrated GPS, and in passing picks up the addresses of individuals, businesses and cultural places that are pointed out to him in the streets he crosses. He couples his journey with taking photos that document his experiences and puts them on websites. These photos contain information that his geolocalization automatically records. At the same time, he records a program through his TNT mobile. Thanks to his radio-frequency identification (RFID) chip he accesses controlled websites that recognize him, without difficulty. He programs different home automation elements and remains connected to his "networks".

Incidentally, simultaneously, he sends e-mails and makes voice calls. A tagged object in a world of tagged objects, identified by a code "unique to the world" is like a digital fingerprint, like a DNA code or a biometric print of the iris. The individual faces digital objects initiating events, posing as subjects of interaction, and provoking interactions.

How can this permanent percolation [LEL 06] be cognitively borne? How can we socially endure with a calm state of mind and a capacity of reaction and production, life within frameworks that fit together and are unstable, on a permanent bevel that slides along from action to action, according to a spate of course? How can a differentiation between organic and inorganic be morally maintained when we feel progressively constituted of mobile computers, administrating packets of digital invitations, in a simple reaction, via digital crossroads recognized as a grade of excellence, like a "semiotic hub", through the digital infrastructure of the "City"?

4.6. Conclusion

The grounds of ICS, meta-discipline accompanying the semiotization of social sciences, are particularly concerned with the observation of this flashing interface. The coupling of the document and the network open four fields of reflection that it is important to consider together:

– *Economics and ICS*: the implication of new organizations of competence, productivity and performance in this dynamic of the link. Current economic models demand a capacity for innovation, an introduction of externalities [MOU 07] of which the document/network is an instrument;

– *Sociology of work and ICS*: the updating of the analysis of work: stress at work, intensification of tasks, the cognitive swivel of production and the over-implication of individuals create worrying conditions whose analysis demands the taking of "digital life" into account;

– *Cognition and ICS*: a metaphor of the neuronal abundance and axons targeting other axons is substituted for the "intranet" metaphor of the site as a work space. The digital social network aimlessly sends objects and texts, simply seeking the microscopic and random interfacing. It is a retrieval of resources in cognition or invention is analogous to the model of creative percolation already cited;

– *ICT and ICS, ethical and political*: in these new combinations of semiotics of objects and technicization of dialogs, ethical questions appear. How is our culture similar to these intense and radical modifications that touch all our space, time and relationship frameworks, that reach the undisputed separation of man and machine?

How are public spaces, modes of debate, and participation in decision configured by these fine networks of living information?

Being recomposed of inter-discipline in meta-discipline, ICS as a language, form of information and communication sciences can profit from the proximity with human sciences on one hand and information science on the other. In this way it can contribute to the reconfiguration of "grounds" and scientific objects, overwhelmed as much by documentarization of the social as by singularization of objects.

4.7. Bibliography

[AIM 06] O. AIM, "La transparence rendue visible", S. PÈNE (ed.), *Communication et Langages*, Armand Colin, Paris, 2004, p. 31-46.

[AKR 06] M. AKRICH, M. CALLON, and B. LATOUR, *Sociologie de la Traduction,* Mines Paris, Paris, 2006.

[BER 08] G. BERRY, Cours au Collège de France, Chaire d'innovation technologique Liliane Bettencourt, Leçon inaugurale, Paris, January 2008.

[BOR 01] A. BORZEIX, "Le travail et sa sociologie à l'épreuve du langage", *Langage et Travail, Cognition, Action, Communication*, CNRS Editions, Paris, 2001.

[BRE 04] M. BREVIGLIERI, "La coopération spontanée. Entraides techniques autour d'un automate technique", in: B. CONEIN AND L. THÉVENOT (eds), *Raisons Pratiques*, no. 8, p. 123-148, 1997.

[CAN 07] E. CANDEL and V. JEANNE-PERRIER, "Les blogs de peu et la politique ordinaire", no. 140, p. 31-42, 2007.

[CHA 94] P. CHAREAUDEAU, *Le Discours d'Information Médiatique*, Hachette, Paris, 1994.

[CHR 01] A-M. CHRISTIN *L'Image Ecrite ou la Déraison Graphique*, Flammarion, Paris, 2001.

[COT 04] D. COTTE, "Le concept de document numérique", *Communications & Langage*, no. 140, p. 31-42, 2004.

[DES 08] O. DESSEILLIGNY, "Du journal intime au blog: quelles métamorphoses du texte?", *Communication & Langages*, no. 155, p. 45-62, 2008.

[DOD 95] N. DODIER, *Les Hommes et les Machines*, Métailié, Paris, 1995.

[DUF 01] B. DUFRENE and M. GELLEREAU, "La médiation culturelle, métaphore ou concept? Propositions de repères", *Actes du XIIème Congrès National des Sciences de l'Information et de la Communication*, p. 233-240, 2001.

[ERT 07] O. ERTZSCHEID, "*L'Homme est un Document Comme les Autres*", available at: http://www.slideshare.net/olivier/lhomme-est-un-document-come-les-autres, accessed October 6, 2009.

[FOU 07] G. FOUETILLOU, *L'Observatoire de la Présidentielle, Blog*, available at: http://blog.observatoire-presidentielle.fr/ (active from September 2007 to May 2008), accessed October 6, 2009.

[GID 06] A. GIDDENS, *The Transformation of Intimacy: Sexuality, Love and Eroticism in Modern Society*, Stanford University Press, Stanford, 2006.

[JEA 02] V., JEANNE-PERRIER V., "Le rôle du journaliste au prisme de l'internet: le passage de l'écrivant-auteur à l'autorisant-animateur", in: B. DAMIAN, R. RINGOOT, D. THIERRY and R. RUELLAN (eds), *Inform@tion. Le Paysage Médiatique Régional à l'ère Électronique*, L'Harmattan, Paris, 2002.

[JOS 04] F. JOST, *Introduction à l'Analyse de la Télévision*, Ellipses, Paris, 2004.

[KAU 04] J-C. KAUFFMANN, *L'Invention de Soi,* Armand Colin, Paris, 2004.

[LAR 04 P. LARDELLIER, *Le Cœur Net,* Belin, Paris, 2004.

[LEL 06] S. LELEU-MERVIEL, "La structure du Aha. De la fulgurance comme une percolation", *8th International Conference H2PTM'05 - Hypertexts and Hypermedia. Create, play, exchange: network experiences*, p. 59-76, Paris (France), November 29 to December 1, 2005.

[LIC 07] C. LICOPPE, "De la communication interpersonnelle aux communautés épistémiques: le développement des TIC et l'enracinement du paradigme de la distribution", *Paroles publiques, communiquer dans la cité*, Hermès vol. 47, p. 59-68, 2007.

[MOU 07] MOULIER-BOUTANG Y., *Le Capitalisme Cognitif, la Nouvelle Grande Transformation*, Edition Multitudes, Amsterdam, 2007.

[JOS 04] JOSEPH I., *Erving Goffman et la Microsociologie*, PUF, Paris, 1998.

[PAL 00] PALMER M., "Les journalistes-agenciers et les normes langagières de l'ubiquité", in: S. PENE, A. BORZEIX and B. FRAENKEL (eds), *Le Langage dans les Organisations, une Nouvelle Donne,* L'Harmattan, Paris, 2001 p. 159-180.

[PEN 05] S. PÈNE, " La vie des "hommes infâmes" dans la société de disponibilité", *Etudes de Communication – "Organisation, Dispositif, Dujet"*, vol. 28, p. 107-124, Lille, 2005.

[PEN 05] S. PÈNE, Société de disponibilité. La vie quotidienne des communautés artificielles, habilitation à diriger des recherches, Paris 4 Sorbonne, Celsa, 2005. Available at: http://tel.archives-ouvertes.fr/tel-00132522/en/, accessed October 6, 2009.

[PEN 07] S. PÈNE, "Bloguer la politique", *Communications & Langage,* vol. 140, p. 31-42, 2007.

[PER 89] J. PERRIAULT, *La Logique de l'Usage. Essai sur les Machines à Communiquer*, Flammarion, Paris, 1989.

[QUE 04] L. QUERE., "La situation toujours négligée?", *Réseaux*, vol. 85, p. 163-192, 1997.

[SIN 06] F. DE SINGLY, *Les Adonaissants*, Armand Colin, Paris, 2006.

[SIN 06] Y. SINTOMER, *Le Pouvoir au Peuple. Jurys Citoyens, Tirage au sort et Démocratie Participative*, La Découverte, Paris, 2007.

[STI 04] B. STIEGLER, *Entretiens avec Elie During, Philosopher par Accident*, Galilée, Paris, 2004.

Chapter 5

Information Culture

5.1. Introduction

Can information culture be considered as a problematic emerging in information science? In order to respond to this question and thus justify the presence of this chapter in this book, it is probably best to decompose the different elements.

What is "information culture"? How can it be defined? Before providing our own answer, we will give some terminological and semantic markers on an expression that is still badly defined, by recalling its origins.

Is it about a truly new, emerging thematic? It is neither a new concept, nor a recent expression since it has inspired a number of researchers, works and publications for several years. "There is no information society without information culture", said Claude Baltz, in 1997 during a study day of the Association des Professionnels de l'Information et de la Documentation (ADBS). Information culture, of which a certain number of "conceptual nodes" had been defined by Baltz in a text that can be qualified as founding [BAL 98], is therefore not exactly a new idea in information science. It is much less so if it is considered as one of the possible translations of information literacy, a thematic that is already 30 years old. We will try to show however, that the expression itself as well as its content and its meaning remain thematics "in emergence", if emergence of a phenomenon is understood as an uncertain, un-mastered process being able to come under an average-length story and, above all, as it happens, like an incomplete process. Bibliometric analyses on scientific publications as well as a brief presentation of

---

Chapter written by Alexandre SERRES.

work in progress will help us to measure this emerging character of a continuously renewed thematic.

But for all that, does it constitute a theoretical "problematic", a new scientific object? In what conditions does a thematic, an expression like this one, become a true research "problematic"? We will see that the answer to this question depends on the preliminary design made of information culture.

Should problematic be spoken of in the singular or the plural? Is information culture not more filled with different problematics corresponding to several undecided questions: questions of epistemological pre-suppositions, finalities, content, territories, stakeholders, etc? We will attempt to identify pending questions that today cross the field of information culture.

Finally, to what extent does (or do) this (or these) problematic(s) come first under information science? And does it come under information science exclusively, or is information culture situated at a large interdisciplinary crossroads? Whereas, from close up, it concerns information and communication sciences, we will plead finally that this interest is more reciprocal.

5.2. What is information culture?

It is advisable to first supply some markers on the abundant terminology (information literacy, *maîtrise de l'information*, information culture, etc.), on the origins and the diverse meanings of an expression still in search of a definition.

5.2.1. *The terminological debate on information literacy in France*

Without limiting ourselves to it, we cannot avoid mentioning the expression "information literacy" when attempting to define information culture. Since its appearance in 1974, and most of all its definition in 1989 by the American Library Association, the expression "information literacy" has known growing success on the international plane. It has become, at the same time, a generic term enveloping different sub-notions (information competencies, information skills, user training, documentary methodology, etc). It has become a semantic and theoretical node, around which numerous related terms and notions gravitate, as shown by Paul Bernhard since 2001[1]. Several literacies thus appeared successively (media,

1. P. Bernhard, *Maîtrise de l'Information et Notions Associées* [*Information Literacy and Related Notions*], 2001. Available at: http://mapageweb.umontreal.ca/bernh/TICI/termino.html, accessed on September 26, 2009.

computer, digital, critical, visual, etc.), enriching a notional landscape and making it more complex to the point of making it abundant, even confused.

The French translation of this canonical expression, 'information literacy', has never been simple and continues to regularly cause debates in the field of professionals concerned[2]. We must recall that the first difficulty comes from the absence of a true French equivalent of the term 'literacy', translated, in the strict sense, by *alphabétisation*. Several specialists recalled that the term '*alphabétisation*' did not take into account the cultural, specific and richer universe of literacy for the Anglo-Saxons. The recent linguistic innovation of France's General Commission of Terminology and Neology[3], which created the term *littérisme*[4] in August 2005, as an antonym for illiteracy, has not really enabled this problem of translation to be resolved. The expression *littérisme informationnelle* (which could be the most correct "literal" translation of 'information literacy') was not adopted by the community of stakeholders.

Like Sylvie Chevillotte [CHE 07] recalls, the terminological debate on the French translation is doubled as a theoretical debate on underlying designs. Because "*maîtrise de l'information*", "*formation des usagers*", "*méthodologie documentaire*", "*intelligence informationnelle*"[5], "*culture informationnelle*" or "*culture de l'information*", sometimes used to translate 'information literacy' into French, are not equivalent expressions and correspond to different approaches and realities.

The first problem encountered is: is "*culture informationnelle*" (information culture) not only a translation into French, among others, of 'information literacy'? And, to respond to the challenge of translation, if the question was asked differently, in other words, if we first parted from the different conceptions at play behind the expressions, to eventually find a solution to the terminological question? For our part, we have sliced the question of translation by the following choice. On one

---

2. Like on distribution lists, blogs, etc. See, for example, the 2006 debate on the librarians' distribution list *Biblio.fr*.

3. France's General Commission for Terminology and Neology is described as the "cornerstone of the enriching device of the French language". Its office was opened by the French Prime Minister in 1997 and renewed in 2000. It has 19 members and meets once a month. Each year it establishes a summary report on actions carried out by administrations for enriching the French language. Its website (in French) is: http://www.culture.gouv.fr/culture/dglf/dispositif-enrichissement.htm, accessed on September 26, 2009.

4. "Capacity to read a simple text and understand it, to use and communicate a piece of written information in everyday life (...). Foreign equivalent: 'literacy'." Available at: http://www.legifrance.gouv.fr/WAspad/UnTexteDeJorf?numjo=CTNX0508668X, accessed on September 26, 2009.

5. Notably put forward by Diane Poirier [POI 00].

hand, we will use the expression "*maîtrise de l'information*" here as the standard translation of "information literacy". On the other hand, in order to get it out of terminological quarrels, we will make "*culture informationnelle*" (information culture) the denomination of a thematic in emergence, of a particular conception, even a problematic that overhangs and exceeds the sole information literacy.

5.2.2. *Three origins and three complementary approaches*

Information literacy gave rise, about 20 years ago, to a rich anthology of definitions. It has abundant scientific terms, especially in literature written in the English language, recently analyzed in France by Laure Endrizzi [END 06], Sylvie Chevillotte [CHE 05, CHE 07] and Olivier Le Deuff [LED 07].

Without carrying out here a recension of all these definitions, we find it interesting to recall the three origins brought out by Olivier le Deuff [LED 07] that correspond to the three specific, but complementary, approaches to information literacy: business, library and citizen designs. This three-way split was already present in 1989 because the American Library Association, in its final report on information literacy, which will, as a result, become one of the founding texts of the domain, developed "the importance of information literacy to individuals, business and citizenship" [ALA 89].

It is in the business world, we sometimes forget, that expression and notion are born at the same time: actually, the term "information literate" had been used for the first time in 1974 by Paul Zurkowski, president of the Information Industry Association (IIA). He therefore suggested this first definition:

> "People trained in the application of information resources to their work can be called information literates. They have learned techniques and skills for utilizing the wide range of information tools as well as primary sources in molding information-solutions to their problems"[6] [BEH 94].

Since then "information literacy" was extensively adopted, notably in the world of economic and business intelligence, to characterize the competencies necessary for professional use of information. This economic design refers to the numerous information stakes in businesses, confronted with the moving universe of track digitization, information explosion and the globalization of exchanges.

The vision of libraries, dominant in specialized literature, also appeared in the 70s and was the object, in 1989, of a first official definition in the United States, in

6. http://www.slais.ubc.ca/courses/libr500/01-02-wt2/www/D_Lee/history.htm, accessed on September 26, 2009.

the final report of the Presidential Committee on Information Literacy of the American Library Association:

> "To be information literate, a person must be able to recognize when information is needed and have the ability to locate, evaluate, and use effectively the needed information." [ALA 89]

This definition, which has become canonical, had been adopted and developed some years later in another report of the Ocotillo Information Literacy Group, in 1995:

> "Information literacy is the ability to identify what information is needed and the ability to locate, evaluate, and use information in solving problems and composing discourse. It encompasses a set of competencies that will provide for survival and success in an information technology environment. [It is identified] as one of five essential skills that the workplace will demand of employees of the future. Teaching information literacy involves communicating the power and scope of information as well as explaining how information is organized, how it is retrieved through a variety of access sources and tools, and how to evaluate, organize, and apply information to a variety of problems and situations." [INF 95]

This conception of "information literacy" as "a set of competencies" is found in most of the later definitions, notably that of the *Grand Dictionnaire Terminologique* of the *Office Québecois de la Langue Française* (Quebec Office of the French Language), which in 2002 thus defined the culture of information as a:

> "set of competencies enabling us to recognize the existence of a need for information, to identify adequate information, to find it, to evaluate it and to exploit it in relation to a given situation, in a perspective of resolution of the problem"[7].

A note specifies that

> "the culture of information has to enable people to become aware of their information needs and provide them with the relevant competencies of identification, evaluation and use of the results of their research. Information culture will enable us, thanks to these competencies, to survive and have

---

7. "*ensemble de compétences permettant de reconnaître l'existence d'un besoin d'information, d'identifier l'information adéquate, de la trouver, de l'évaluer et de l'exploiter en relation avec une situation donnée, dans une perspective de résolution de problème.*"

success in the information society, notably through mastering technologies giving access to this information."[8]

We will note the congruence of the two approaches as regards the presumed role of information literacy as a condition of employability and surviving in the "information society".

Finally the citizen design is also quite old because it can be dated from 1976, from the proposals of Major R. Owens, American librarian, who, as a result, will have a political career:

> "Information literacy is needed to guarantee the survival of democratic institutions. All men are created equal, but voters with information resources are in a position to make more intelligent decisions than citizens who are information illiterates. The application of information resources to the process of decision-making to fulfill civic responsibilities is a vital necessity." [OWE][9]

Necessary for business productivity, for the survival and blooming of individuals in the "information society" and for democratic life, information literacy continued to be equipped with numerous virtues throughout the years. Thus, the *Prague Declaration* of September 2003 affirmed:

> "Information Literacy encompasses knowledge of one's information concerns and needs, and the ability to identify, locate, evaluate, organize and effectively create, use and communicate information to address issues or problems at hand; it is a prerequisite for participating effectively in the Information Society, and *is part of the basic human right of life long learning*"[10] (our italics).

Two years after, the *Alexandria Proclamation on Information Literacy*, adopted in November 2005 by the International Federation of Library Associations

---

8. http://www.granddictionnaire.com/BTML/FRA/r_Motclef/index1024_1.asp, accessed September 26, 2009.

9. See also: http://www.ala.org/ala/acrl/acrlpubs/whitepapers/presidential.cfm, accessed September 26, 2009.

10. The Prague Declaration, "Towards an information literate society", was elaborated during a conference of experts, coming from 23 countries, on the notion of information competency, a conference organized by the National Commission on Library and Information Science and the National Forum on Information Literacy in Prague, from September 20-23, 2003, with the support of UNESCO; article available at: http://portal.unesco.org/ci/en/files/19636/11228863531PragueDeclaration.pdf/PragueDeclaration.pdf, accessed September 26, 2009.

and UNESCO, drives the information literacy nail in even more as the new right of man:

> "Information Literacy lies at the core of lifelong learning. It empowers people in all walks of life to seek, evaluate, use and create information effectively to achieve their personal, social, occupational and educational goals. It is a basic human right in a digital world and promotes social inclusion of all nations." [IFL 05] (our italics)

These two very strong declarations, *Prague* and *Alexandria*, to which the numerous texts and papers of UNESCO in this domain should be added[11], therefore make information literacy a new fundamental law, a necessary condition of employability, a political and social stake of struggle against the digital divide. Whereas they show an evident continuity compared to the first declarations of the 70s, they show a progressive widening and an openly political dimension of the notion.

We could (provisionally) conclude this evocation of successive definitions with the new concept, of "transliteracy":

> "Transliteracy is the ability to read, write and interact across a range of platforms, tools and media from signing and orality through handwriting, print, TV, radio and film, to digital social networks." [THO 07]

And by this declaration, also recent, of a group of experts of the European Commission, in December 2007:

> "Media literacy relates to all types of media, including television, cinema, video, websites, radio, video games and virtual communities. It can be summed up as the ability to access, understand, evaluate and create media content."[12]

All these definitions and declarations on information literacy make up as much "discourse", the "archeology" of which should be done using Foucault's method[13],

---

11. See also the US Information for All Program available at: http://portal.unesco.org/ci/en/ev.php-URL_ID=1627&URL_DO=DO_TOPIC&URL_SECTION=201.html, accessed September 26, 2009.

12. "Media literacy: do people really understand how to make the most of blogs, search engines or interactive TV?", European Commission, *Europa*, December 20, 2007. Available at: http://www.europa.eu/rapid/pressReleasesAction.do?reference=IP/07/1970&format=HTML&aged=0&language=EN&guiLanguage=en, accessed September 26, 2009.

13. M. Foucault, *L'Archéologie du savoir* [*The Archeology of Knowledge*], Gallimard, Paris, 1969.

by observing the genesis, content, circulation and transformation of the most outstanding statements. It is already possible to locate an evident ideological dimension in these discourses; a dimension marked at the same time by the primacy accorded to communication and information, a certain "positivist" vision of the so-called information society and the affirmation of "adaptation" as a categorical requirement of this information society. But it is not our intention here to criticize the ideological presuppositions of discourses and the representations of information literacy, which are outlined in another text [SER 08].

Nevertheless, "under the discourses, the stakes": discourses show, in deep-lying or in a very explicit way, the diversity and depth of the stakes (educational, social, professional, political, etc) to which information literacy is supposed to respond. The analysis of the stakes remains a fundamental task, still to be lead, because nothing less than these two central, directly overlapping, questions depend on it: the question of finalities, to which information culture should respond and, parting, that of its content. To define the stakes would therefore be a preliminary to the definition of finalities, too often overshadowed, or simply considered as "*allants-de-soi*". The axiological dimension of information culture appears here as one of the live questions of this thematic, still insufficiently detailed. Whereas this analysis of the stakes does not have its place here, we will come back to the double question of finalities and content later.

5.3. Is information culture truly an emergent thematic?

We have seen it: the first works and writings on information literacy go back more than 20 years. Replaced in this short history, "information culture" is inscribed in continuity and at the same time represents an emergent notion, possibly a new stage to come, in the process of being defined. We must distinguish here the two faces of our object of study:

– On one hand, the linguistic expression, the phrase "information culture", whose novelty characteristic, or lack thereof, in scientific publications we can measure, in a relatively objective way, by the means of information retrieval and bibliometric studies on different tools. This will be the object of the work we will present below.

– On the other hand, beyond terminology, the thematic itself: using a brief presentation of some ongoing works in France, we will try to show of what and how information culture constitutes today a research domain in the process of constitution.

5.3.1. *Interest in bibliometric observations*

Without pretending to replace a true bibliometric study, systematically leading on to databanks, the theses and all the scientific publications [NAZ 07], we proceeded to consider different pieces of research on the presence, or lack thereof, of terms linked to information culture. We looked at a certain number of tools, as well as the number and evolution of publications and citations. We present here the summary of results of this research[14], made up of four different bibliometric analyses.

An initial comparative and very simple research was organized from the following queries: *culture de l'information* (culture of information), *culture informationnelle* (information culture), *maîtrise de l'information* (information literacy), *formation des utilisateurs* or *formation des usagers* (user training), focused on seven different sources and tools[15], in order to measure the variation of results on these close expressions. The analysis of the results revealed the following observations:

– The overwhelming predominance of the expression 'information literacy' (20,494 results) in relation to the various French translations (1,229 for "*culture de l'information*"), which emphasizes *a contrario* the weakness of scientific publications in French on this thematic. Quick examination of the results, notably on Google Scholar, enables us to easily verify the hegemony of publications in the English language.

– The importance of the expression "*culture de l'information*", clearly preferred to "*culture informationnelle*" (1,229 results compared to 147), and which wins even over "*maîtrise de l'information*" (1,113 results), which is considered generally to be the most standard French translation of 'information literacy'.

– The great weakness of the open archives (HAL, Tel, ArchiveSic, Memsic) on these themes: 50 results with all archives mixed[16].

– The domination of Google Scholar over the other sources (apart from, undoubtedly Article@Inist for articles on the culture of information).

A second series of queries, focusing on the same expressions (except for 'information literacy', very little utilized in Sudoc), had also been carried in the

14. This work, with the complete results and their analysis, is available at: http://www.uhb.fr/urfist/files/Etude_bibliometrie_culture_informationnelle.A%20Serres.doc (website accessed in 2006).

15. Google Scholar, Sudoc, Article@inist, Tel (online thesis), ArchiveSic, HAL (hyper articles online), Memsic.

16. This figure of 50 does not in the least mean 50 distinct publications, because a similar text is often indexed with several of these key words in the open archives.

Sudoc catalog[17], uniquely on theses. It notably revealed two interesting observations:

– concerning the indexation of theses and dissertations in the Sudoc, the key word retained for *maîtrise de l'information*, in the classical sense of information literacy, is first "*formation des utilisateurs*"[18] (24 theses compared to 14 indexed with *maîtrise de l'information*);

– a very clear increase from the year 2000, for all the queries, notably "*formation des utilisateurs*", that went from two theses before 2000 to 22 since then. The progression observed since 2003, for theses on the "*formation des utilisateurs*" or "*culture de l'information*", furthermore constitutes one of the indicators of the emergence of these thematics.

This finding of the "turning point" of the year 2000 is confirmed by the third piece of research, focusing this time on journal articles in the Article@inist base[19], the catalog of the Institute for Scientific and Technical Information (INIST). The same queries also showed a very clear majority of results after 2000, especially for articles on the culture of information, with a "peak" in 2004. In the same way, analyzing the INSIT catalog confirms the importance of the results with "information literacy" (654), but also with "*culture de l'information*" (540). It thusreveals a different choice than that of Sudoc in the indexation: that of the using "*culture de l'information*" more than "*maîtrise de l'information*" or "*formation des utilisateurs*".

This third piece of research also emphasized the almost non-existent use by the INIST, of the expression "*culture informationnelle*" (12 results) as indexation key word. Finally, it confirmed the weakness of results in French (17 results in French out of 540 for "*culture de l'information*", 14 out of 654 for "information literacy"). Itmust be noted, however, that the expressions "*maîtrise de l'information*" (49 out of 57) and especially "*culture informationnelle*" (9 out of 12) concerns more of the articles in French.

---

17. Sudoc is the collective catalog of university libraries and research in France, and also identifies almost all the theses supported in France; it is accessible at: http://www.sudoc.abes.fr.
18. Therefore, out of the total of 19 theses found with key phrase "*maîtrise de l'information*", 14 theses focused on information literacy in the business or the search and only three on user training in libraries; on the other hand, 24 theses or dissertations were found with "*formation des utilisateurs*".
19. Article@inist, which gathers catalogs from the documentary fund of the INIST, is accessible at: http://services.inist.fr/public/fre/conslt.htm, accessed September 26, 2009.

Finally a fourth, more important, piece of research was conducted with a liberated and free bibliometry tool, *Harzing Publish or Perish*[20], which, from the Google Scholar results, calculates and analyzes the citations between publications. Here it was a matter of carrying out a longitudinal study on the evolution of the number of citations, indexed in Google Scholar[21] and focusing on the same expressions: information culture, culture of information, *maîtrise de l'information* and information literacy.

Four indicators kept our attention:

– the number of publications found according to the four expressions;

– their number of citations;

– their evolution in time; and

– the origin of publications according to language.

We present the main conclusions of this study in Table 5.1, of which we can only show the most synthetic results here, across the table below.

The following statements can be made, not only based on this table but on more complete results, available on the Rennes URFIST[22] (Regional Unit for Training in Scientific and Technical Information) website:

– First and foremost, the crushing domination of 'information literacy' over other expressions, in numbers of publications (8,754 results compared to 835 for "*maîtrise de l'information*") as well as in numbers of citations (34,577 citations). Harzing PoP thus supplies the report of 13.35 citations per publication for results on 'information literacy', whereas it is established at 5.14 for "*culture de*

20. *Harzing PoP* (*Publish or Perish*) is a computer download tool; it is free and accessible at: http://www.harzing.com/resources.htm#/pop.htm (accessed September 26, 2009). For each query carried out in Google Scholar, Harzing PoP gives not only the number of results found, but also the number of citations received through publications, thus permitting us to measure the impact of a particular publication, author or group found. The tool also gives the complete list of results, with its number of citations, its rank, and several other bibliometric indicators, for each.

21. Google Scholar is the specialized module of Google on scientific information and constitutes today one of the most important universal access points for global scientific literature, of all disciplines and all media. Unlike Sudoc, Article@inist, or the open archives, indexation is made here automatically on the full text, the résumé or the metadata of documents.

22. URFIST is an interacademic training and research organization destined to develop scientific information use and literacy in higher education teaching as well as digital resources. The URFIST website (in French) is: http://www.sites.univ-rennes2.fr/urfist/, accessed September 26, 2009.

l'information", and falls to 0.58 and 0.56 for "*maîtrise de l'information*" and "*culture informationnelle*" respectively.

– The paradoxal difference between "*culture*" and "*maîtrise de l'information*": whereas publications of "*culture de l'information*" (408) are two times less numerous than those of "*maîtrise de l'information*" (835), they nonetheless have a bibliometric impact that is very clearly superior, with a total of citations that is four times higher (2,098 compared to 486).

Phrase used	Total public-ations	Dated public-ations	% of "non-dated" publications [23]	% of public-ations > 2000	Total citation s	Citations / per public-ation
Culture informationnelle	115	36	69 %	83 %	64	0.56
Culture de l'information	408	193	53 %	69 %	2,098	5.14
Maîtrise de l'information	835	311	63 %	65 %	486	0.58
Information literacy[24]	---	8,754	---	---	34,577	13.35

Table 5.1. *Analysis of the number of citations, indexed in Google Scholar*

– The weakness of the expression "*culture informationnelle*" (115 publications and 64 citations only).

23. Google Scholar allows us to search by date of publication of indexed documents, but it only seems to take into account the "official" date of publication provided by the editors. Therefore, many documents, otherwise dated, cannot be found from their date of publication: reports, pre-prints, etc.

24. Google Scholar only posts and enables results to be processed in a limit of 1,000, even if it can announce a lot more in the total figure indicated. Therefore, the number of results on information literacy is from 996 on Harzing PoP, corresponding to 996 results posted on Google Scholar, whereas the total number is actually 22,200! From this fact, almost all the queries for information literacy were biased by this limitation to 1,000, which explains the difficulty, even impossibility, to relate "dated" results and "non-dated" ones; the figure of 8,754 was obtained by adding query results on each year since 2000.

– The very important percentage of "un-dated" publications (according to Google Scholar's criteria) for results on "*culture informationnelle*" (69%) and "*maîtrise de l'information*" (63%). This means that, beyond the sometimes incoherent and inexplicable aspects of the functioning of Google Scholar, the majority of these publications stem from open archives (pre-prints, communications, etc), from the professional press, different badly recognized documents, or out of the institutional framework of scientific journals.This finding is particularly striking for results on "*culture informationnelle*", which is another way of emphasizing the still-emerging character of this furthermore largely "Franco-French", thematic.

– The important progression of publications from 2000: for all the groups of results, the difference is very clear between the results before and after 2000. Eighty-three per cent of the results for "*culture informationnelle*" have been published since 2000, and 69% for "*culture de l'information*". This spectacular progression is without any doubt the main sign of the emergence of these thematics, in the landscape of specialized literature.

– The supremacy of publications in English or Anglo-Saxon appears even more clearly here, notably upon examination of results on "information literacy"; it is certainly not a surprise, but the proportions (difficult to measure statistically) are impressive. At least two-thirds of results on "information literacy" stem from American, British, Australian, etc, publications.

– A very important portion (sometimes almost a third) of the results stem from Asian, Chinese or Japanese publications.

– And finally, the almost insignificant part of French language publications, notably on "information literacy": thus out of 977 results listed for the year 2007, there were no French publications!

Our quick bibliometric research confirms at least four striking facts, of which the first three are further confirmed by Mohammad Nazim and Moin Ahmad's [NAZ 07] recent (even more important) study:

– the absolute hegemony of English language, notably American, literature in the field of information literacy;

– the very weak, even laughable, part represented by French publications[25];

– the turning of the new millennium, from which a general increase in publications is observed, confirming the rise in strength of these themes;

– finally, the still timid emergence in France, of the expression "*culture informationnelle*" in the group of publications on "*maîtrise de l'information*".

25. Out of a total of 607 articles analyzed by Nazim and Ahmad, only 10 articles come from France! [NAZ 07].

5.3.2. *An abundance of research work*

The bibliometric research carried out, as instructive as it may be, cannot take into account the emergence or lack thereof of a new field of research. The true measure would consist, without any doubt, of enumeration and observation of works in progress on these thematics. But it should overcome several obstacles to draw up a complete inventory. First and foremost, the spreading and splitting up of information culture research. This would cross several disciplinary fields, like media literacy, which touches education sciences and information and communication sciences (ICS) at the same time, or information and communication technology (ICT) training, which is the object of many works. Then it effects the diversity of approaches (pedagogic, didactic, sociological, etc) of the question of pupil and student training (in addition to the differences between superior and secondary assignments) in information. We should also take into account the blurring of boundaries between the three spheres of professional (university library personnel), pedagogic (teacher-documentalists) and scientific (professors in ICS and in education sciences). All three are directly concerned, but according to different modalities, through questions linked to information culture. Finally, to all these difficulties is added the abundance of works of research that focus on ICT, their uses, their stakes, their evolutions, etc. Furthermore, a number of these works, notably in ICS, approach in a more or less direct manner the question of information culture, whether it is a matter of that of users or someone who should be the object of training.

All these reasons make an exhaustive or synthetic presentation of research works, focusing on a thematic that is at the same time as large as it is badly defined, very difficult or even impossible. A solution therefore consists of coming back to information culture in its specifically "info-documentary" version, notably across the research currently being led in the framework of an ERTé[26]. Launched following the National Conference for Education to Information, held in Paris in 2003, this ERTé was officially created in the Charles de Gaulle University – Lille III in 2006[27] and took the name "Information Culture and Documentary Curriculum", clearly displaying its research objects. In the long term, its aim is indeed the construction of a curriculum in documentation, i.e. a statement of the principles and an analysis of case studies and situations contributing to a didactic progression, allowing the

---

26. Cherche en technologie éducative [Educational Technology Research Team].

27. Piloted by Annette Béguin and relying on two research laboratories, the GERIICO (Lille III) and the CIVIIC (University of Rouen), the ERTé regroups about 15 ICS professors, several doctoral students and associated professionals and six representatives of organizations or associations implicated in information training (FORMIST, URFIST networks, CNDP, Rouen and Lille IUFM, FADBEN, INRP). It is now in the middle of its contract and will present its works in an international symposium in autumn 2008.

learners to acquire information literacy throughout their school and university journey. The end object is of educational order, from the perspective of the information curriculum. Research works engaged in by the six regional ERTé teams, however, focus on institutional, political and social stakes of information culture. They cover the uses, practices and representation of information-documentation, the didactic approaches, notably the reflection on the notions and info-documentary learning, and the professionalization and training of teacher-librarians at the same time.

As diversified and as active as it may be, the "Information Culture and Documentary Curriculum" ERTé, which would not know how to represent all the richness and abundance of works in progress, lead on these thematics. Thus, whereas our little bibliometric study showed the very clear progression of the number of theses already supported, it was not able to measure the number, in strong growth, of theses, masters dissertations and professional dissertations currently concerned with questions of user training, information culture, etc. We should also mention the constant success of the annual FORMIST (French network for information use training) meetings for the past seven years. This has led to the growing number of study days, symposiums and seminars, and the multiplication of works, not only research works in the academic sense, but also "research-action" works, or simply professional reflection works, which flourish in the secondary teaching teacher-librarian domain. Works, actions, conferences, symposiums, etc, focus notably on a precise aspect of the vast domain of information literacy: the didactic question of "school knowledge", i.e. the content belonging to a true information education.

This question of a didactic of information has formed the object, for the past few years, of a multitude of texts, writings, and diverse initiatives[28]. It constitutes one of the main research objects of the ERTé, and beyond the different divergences or approaches it raises among stakeholders of the domain it probably represents a turning in the short history of French information literacy. For in our eyes the didactic of information constitutes the manifest sign of emergence in progress of a new thematic. It notably testifies to a movement in the long term towards autonomous teaching of the contents of information-documentation. This is a movement of which it is impossible today to predict the origin (new discipline, cross teachings, specific modules?), but that is partly linked to a recognition of information culture as one of the basic learnings of the 21st century.

---

28. On this subject see the Didactique Information Documentation at: http://documentaliste.ac-rouen.fr/spip/spip.php?rubrique66&lang=fr

5.4. Is it truly a (research) "problematic"?

That information literacy is a research theme is not an easily contestable fact. The bibliometric observations gave an idea, even partial, of the abundance of publications, both scientific and professional, that are devoted to information literacy and to its various French translations. Information user training (pupils and students) aroused, for two decades, not only a rich scientific literature [VIR 03], but also the birth of specialized organizations, journals, stakeholders, regular encounters, networks, etc[29]. The qualifier of a research domain can therefore also be conferred to this vast international group, despite its sometimes reduced visibility, as well as to social and scientific planes. As regards France, it is less advanced in the building of the field and structures and communities comparable to those of Anglo-Saxon countries, for example[30], do not exist yet.

For all that, by limiting ourselves to the specific thematic of information culture and to its approach in France, can it be considered a true research problematic, like a scientific object giving rise to a diversity of outlooks, of epistemologically and theoretically founded "points of view"? It is necessary here to distinguish first two different and complementary approaches.

On one hand, the educational pedagogic approach: information culture is viewed there as the group of knowledge, know-how, information competencies to acquire, to reach a true literacy – intellectual and practical at the same time – of information and documentation. In this perspective, *culture informationnelle* is one of the possible translations of the expression information literacy, and it entertains

29. To get an idea of the richness of the domain, simply consult the following:
– in Canada, the Canadian Research Libraries Information Literacy Portal:
http://apps.medialab.uwindsor.ca/crlil/wiki/FrontPage/
– in the United States, the ACRL website, Information literacy:
http://www.ala.org/ala/acrl/acrlissues/acrlinfolit/informationliteracy.cfm
– in Great Britain, the list of research papers on the Sheila Webber site:
http://dis.shef.ac.uk/literacy/research.htm
– in France, the FORMIST site, the FOURMI repertoire of the URFIST of Paris, etc.
– for Europe, the European Observatory on IL Policies and Research: http://www.ceris.cnr.it/Basili/EnIL/gateway/gatewayhome.htm
– and for UNESCO, the International Information Literacy Resources Directory: http://portal.unesco.org/ci/en/ev.php-URL_ID=22444&URL_DO=DO_TOPIC&URL_SECTION=201.html
(websites accessed September 26, 2009.)

30. We can cite the two examples of the National Forum on Information Literacy (http://www.infolit.org/) in the United States and the international scientific journal JeLit, Journal of eLiteracy (http://www.jelit.org/index.html) in the UK, which do not have equivalents in France. (Websites accessed September 26, 2009.)

historical and direct links with the methodological training of students in higher education, and the documentary training of secondary school pupils. Are these pedagogical and educational dimensions, evident and recognized by all the stakeholders, sufficient to qualify it as a possible theoretical problematic? In our eyes, no. In order to truly be able to give it the status of research problematic, we would have to remove information culture form its origins and its educational dimensions, without so much separating as cutting it from them. This is because a set of competencies, learning and documentary teachings cannot constitute a research problematic, in the strong sense of the term. Certainly, this set of practices and pedagogical contents represents an object of research, like any aspect of the world of education. Thus numerous research conducted in the field of information literacy have as object the study of documentary teachings, their efficiency, their modalities and their institutionalization. But this does not make information culture, as such, a research problematic that is partially complete.

On the other hand, a second, more "sociologizing" approach: information culture is seen there as the set of information practices and representations, at work in different categories of populations: we will therefore speak about the information culture of youth, students, teachers, executives, etc. Culture is to be taken here in the anthropological, sociological sense of the term, like a set of practices, uses or representations, more or less spontaneous. In this perspective, is information culture something other than a particular branch of the sociology of uses? How can it become an autonomous theoretical problematic?

In what conditions could information culture therefore become a research problematic, i.e. a construction of research object(s) from "points of view"? The answer will depend on the preliminary conception that we can have of it. In other words, whereas information culture remains understood as a set of competencies and knowledge for transmission (educational approach), or as a set of uses and practices for observation (sociological approach), therefore the answer will be, according to us, negative. Information culture will remain, at best, a subject of interrogation, of theoretical or political reflection. On the other hand, if we consider information culture like a set comprising, all at the same time, explicitated epistemological presuppositions, identified theoretical questions, definite and delimited didactics – all referring to precise scientific disciplines –information culture could be able to exceed its status in the field, domain or object of research, to access that of a true problematic. We are still far from it.

5.5. One or more problematics?

Information culture, conceived here as an educational plan (and not as the only observation of information uses and practices) and as a research problematic (and not as a simple "domain) at the same time, asks, according to us, six big types of questions. The inventory of these questions will allow us to better identify many sub-problematics, which make up perhaps as many "research fronts". They can thus schematically be summarized here:

– the epistemological presuppositions;

– the axiological dimension of finalities;

– the "territorial" problem of boundaries with close cultures;

– the didactic question of content and learning to transmit;

– the pedagogical dimension of teaching methods, and;

– the question of stakeholders of this information culture.

Let us take them up one by one, according to our own order of priority.

5.5.1. *The question of epistemological and scientific foundations*

We adopt the word of the historian Gerard Noiriel[31], "all 'points of view' rely on presuppositions". Theepistemological question is always first, whatever the object or the domain of research may be. This constant necessity to clarify the epistemological foundations of any problematic or theory is here even more alive, considering the permanent interference in the notion of information, or "concept chameleon" as it is known. In the all-purpose expressions, "information technologies, information society, information retrieval, culture of information", it is not about the same information and the confusion of meaning is general between the diverse categories of information. Notably between "machine-information" (info-data) and "social information" (including info-news and info-knowledge) [BOU 95]. Between the two types of information, that are directly inter-linked on the network, "there is naturally an essential difference", as Yves Jeanneret very justly explains it:

> "They are even exactly the contrary of each other, because information, in the social sense of the term, has as a condition, the interpretation, that mathematical information has as a benefit to eliminate." [JEA 00]

All that is well known in ICS, but this essential difference needs to be constantly recalled in the different "educations", the confusion between the two meanings and the illusions on information which are so spread out. These epistemological clarifications should be part of the educational necessities of information culture,

31. G. NOIRIEL, *Sur la "crise" de l'histoire* [*On the "Crisis" of History*], p. 194, Belin, Paris, 1996.

which would have a double job to do: on one hand, to recall the ambivalence and polysemy of the notion of information, from the epistemological point of view at the same time as the disciplinary point of view; on the other hand to situate the specificity, definition and place of information in the documentary sense, in the more vast "notional set" of information.

The "epistemological question" of information is certainly not new, and a literature, as abundant as it is prestigious, has already deeply ploughed the terrain[32]. The new fact, with the information culture plan, is to have to re-specify, re-work and above all to distribute all these notions until then reserved to ICS. Even more so if we are seeking to develop a widened vision of information culture, enveloping the three "educations" that are linked to them: computer literacy, characterized by info-data and ICT training, info-news, and media literacy, information-documentation culture, relying on info-knowledge and giving rise to information literacy.

Whereas people are starting to talk about "transliteracy" [THO 07], on the subject of the necessity to provide the elements of a global culture of computer tools, media and their messages and methodologies of information, could the notion of information culture not be able to designate this vast group, on the condition of explaining each time what information it is a question of? On the epistemological plane, information culture, in the widest sense of the term, should be able to show all the complexity, richness, depth and diversity of the concept of information. And at the time when Google wants "to organize all the information in the world", we must continuously give up the epistemic illusions or mistranslations: Google is organizing nothing other than computer data, which are incarnate in information data, which will only become information in the eyes of users. And this mass of information could not be confused with culture[33].

5.5.2. *The axiological dimension*

In what should pupils of the so-called digital native generation be trained, in information material? In practical use, intellectual literacy, critical distance of digital tools and networks? What should be placed at the head of the educational objectives and finalities of information culture? "Adaptation" to the "information society", and to its permanent innovations, as the majority of discourse on information literacy implies? First we must question, in such a political way, the purpose, first of information training, but also more largely of education. This question, which is

32. We are thinking notably of the works, "founding" in ICS, of Escarpit, Morin, Mattelart, Bougnoux, Jeanneret, etc.

33. On this point see Barbara CASSIN, *Google-me. The Second Mission of America,* Albin Michel, Paris, 2007.

only beginning to be developed by the stakeholders concerned and which is hardly emergent in society, should rely on a true collective, socio-political reflection, of which the works of Bernard Stiegler make up here the most precious tool of the moment. This is because the reflection on the finalities of information culture also comes back to asking, as Stiegler does [STI 06], the following question: what policy of "technologies of the mind"[34] do we want to develop? And what training belonging to these technologies? To ask the question of finalities of information culture comes back to asking the question of values, always delicate in a scientific field, because of being part-linked with "morals", or worse, opinion. But if we consider the problematic of information culture, as an educational *plan* – in other words as the necessity to transmit a certain amount of learning, knowledge, permitting not only "to adapt itself to" but above all to understand and criticize the "information society" – therefore we must assume this axiological dimension and defend a conception of information culture based on a certain number of values, clearly identified.

The axiological dimension is also asked at another level of the ladder – meso- as well as micro-level: that of the necessary legitimation, social, political, institutional, professional, pedagogical at the same time of an "education" or a "teaching of" information, from the different spheres (political deciders, media, people responsible in universities, teachers, information professionals, etc).

All the participants of documentary training know from experience the properly military dimension of their action and the permanent efforts to convince different partners of interest to give documentary training to pupils and students. One of the main reasons for the weakness, or the backwardness of France in the domain of information literacy sticks, without a doubt, to the inadequacy of networks of stakeholders, capable of creating, organizing, structuring and maintaining all the devices necessary in this field: training, teaching paths, specialized journals, institutions, research networks, etc. But this explanation, part tautological, places the axiological question of the motives of such an education belonging to information in a deep-lying place. How can the other partners, the deciders, be convinced if these two elements are missing: on one hand the shared, social awareness of the stakes of an information training still far from being acquired[35], on the other hand a solid socio-political argument, relying on the strengths, even the network-stakeholders, not less solid? The axiological question, in our opinion, remains one of the main priorities of the information culture problematic. And the collective

34. The "technologies of the mind" encompass the vast totality of media, cultural industries, telecommunications, learning and cognition technologies.

35. We could be able to make the comparison here with another "education to", durable environment and development education, which seem to have more of a social and political resemblance, considering the gravity and urgency of the climate stakes.

elaboration of "the social argument" passes through a triple procedure: the in-depth analysis of the stakes linked to information and communication technologies, the reflection on the values that we want to defend collectively, and the explanation of the finalities of information culture. We can only raise the question here without answering it.

5.5.3. *Content, borders, stakeholders, pedagogy*

The problematic of information culture finally covers four questions, better known and often dealt with in specialized literature. We will evoke them only to provide a recap.

With the didactic question, maybe the most lively today by the number of works carried out, the question of the content of information training is asked: on what learning, what notions should a teaching of information be constructed, how should it be organized according to a curricular progression? The "didactic shanty" [SER 07] is however open and several works have already been carried out on this question[36]. Let us note only that the didactic question, of the choice of teaching content and its didactization, reflects a specific conception of information culture, putting in the forefront of pedagogical objectives, the acquisition of the keys to understanding digital universes, more than their only practical use.

The "question of boundaries" designates the delimitation of the "territories" of information culture, in its info-documentary version, and above all its relations with two neighboring cultures: media literacy and ICT training. This question, crossed by epistemological, axiological and didactic dimensions, is asked today with a particular acuity in secondary school teaching, around the reflection on relations between B2i (information technology and the Internet) documentary teachings. It is also now being asked in higher education teaching around C2i. For example, how to share information retrieval training, between computer and documentary teaching? On a more theoretical plane, this "territorial question" obliges us to detail the definition of information culture, to better track its contours, to identify its different components. We must note that this reflection, emergent for holders of information

36. Let us cite, for example, the works of Pascal Duplessis (see the blog on http://esmeree.fr/lestroiscouronnes/idoc/blog/page/1) and Ivana Ballarini in the Nantes academy, the work lead within the French Federation of Associations of Teacher-Documentalist of National Education in 2006-2007 on the "Seven essential notions in information-documentation", research in progress within the ERTé, the works carried out within the French Information Culture and Didactics Research Group, presented at: http://culturedel.info/grcdi/.

literacy, is also engaged, by stakeholders in computer culture, notably around the EPI (Public and Computer Teaching) at the same time as those of media literacy[37].

The analysis of the stakes, the explicitation of objectives, the definition of content, the layout of the boundaries of information culture: all these strategies of reflection inevitably re-ask the question of the stakeholders. Under what do these different types of training come, on what research communities can the collective reflection rely? How can the necessary interactions between such distant universes be established? Because it is a truism to note the few footpaths between stakeholders of these three cultures of the media, computer and information literacy. In other words, the interactions occur between media literacy specialists, computer science teachers and information-documentation professionals.

Finally the pedagogical question, which, on the theoretical plane, comes under education sciences and, on the practical plane, from the collective experience of supply teachers and trainers, should not be under-estimated. This is because true information training clearly cannot make the impasse on its own pedagogical methods, considering the representations and obstacles stemming from social practices, and this in the very use of information and communication technologies. Here, notably, the entire ODL[38] problematic and conception of distance-learning media have to be used, coming to complete the face-to-face training. Object of study and training tool at the same time, ICT reveal all their potentials here.

5.6. And ICS?

Evidently, information culture, in the widened sense which we sought to give it, is located at an inter-disciplinary crossroads; it interests and convenes several disciplinary fields and several communities of stakeholders – computer science, sociology of media, information, but also of communication science, education science, economy and law of information, etc: the list of disciplinary belonging is long and potentially concerned with the development of a true information culture. This inter-disciplinarity, due to the transverse nature of information, is an asset and a weakness at the same time. It is an asset by the richness of specific contributions of each discipline, the complementarity of outlooks on information, and the plurality of knowledge mobilized. It is a weakness through the greater difficulty in combining interactions, partnerships and exchanges. The problem is not new and, without any

37. See notably: CLEMI (Center for Liason Between Teaching and Information Media), 2001, *Education à l'Information: un Apprentissage Fundamental* [*Education to Information: a Fundamental Learning*]. Available at:
http://www.clemi.org/organisme/ rapports/RA2001/tgb.rtf (accessed on September 26, 2009).
38. Open and Distance Learning.

doubt, a long time will elapse before we see a common problematic emerge around information culture.

As for ICS, they have a central place in this problematic: information and communication epistemology specialists, but also those of the media and information-documentation and researchers in ICS, already implicated on diverse accounts, should become the spearheads of a culture of information and communication. By their very nature, information and communication sciences have authority to be the scientific discipline of reference, for a systematic teaching of an information culture, at the different levels of schooling. This role of scientific and institutional culture is certainly far from being filled today, considering the marginal enough place which the information literacy user training thematic occupies in the general landscape of ICS (we are of course talking about the French situation).

A greater implication of ICS in this thematic would however have a doubly beneficial effect. On the side of information culture, it would be a matter of a reinforcement of weight for the current stakeholders of the thematic, too often isolated, and of a decisive scientific legitimation, to reinforce social legitimation of an information science teaching in society. For ICS themselves, on the other hand, the development of such a teaching would inevitably have a large number of positive spin-offs – institutional, professional, scientific, budgetary, etc – at the same time. The constitution of an autonomous information teaching and maybe a discipline in the long run, as the researchers Bill Johnston and Sheila Webber [JOH 06] wished, is a long-lasting movement, which cannot be thought of without a permanent interaction with the scientific field from which this discipline stems.

5.7. Bibliography

[ABR 05] CARL (Canadian Association of Research Libraries), CARL information literacy policay statement, 2005.
Available at: http://www.carl-abrc.ca/projects/information_literacy/IL_policy_statement-e.html, accessed September 26, 2009.

[ALA 89] ALA (American Library Association), *Presidential Committee on Information Literacy: Final Report*, ALA, 1989.

[BAL 98] C. BALTZ, "Une culture pour la société de l'information? Position théorique, définition, enjeux", *Documentaliste – Sciences de l'Information*, vol. 35, no. 2, p. 75-82, 1998.

[BEH 94] S. BEHRENS, "A conceptual analysis and historical overview of information literacy", *College & Research Libraries*, vol. 55, no. 4, p. 311, July 1994.

[BOU 95] D. BOUGNOUX, *La Communication Contre l'Information*, Hachette, Paris, 1995.

[CHE 05] S. CHEVILLOTTE, "Bibliothèques et information literacy: un état de l'art", *BBF*, vol. 2, p. 42-48, 2005. Available at: http://bbf.enssib.fr, accessed September 26, 2009.

[CHE 07] S. CHEVILLOTTE, "Maîtrise de l'information? Education à l'information? Culture informationnelle?", *Les Dossiers de l'Ingénierie Educative*, vol. 57, p. 16-19, 2007.

[END 06] L. ENDRIZZI, "Information education", *La Lettre d'Information*, vol. 17, April 2006.Available at the following address: http://www.inrp.fr/vst/LettreVST/avril2006.htm.

[IFL 05] International Federation of Library Associations and Institutions, *The Alexandria Proclamation on Information Literacy and Life Long Learning*, IFLA, November 2005. Available at: http://archive.ifla.org/III/wsis/BeaconInfSoc.html, accessed September 26, 2009

[INF 95] INFORMATION LITERACY COMMITTEE, "Information literacy", *Ocotillo Report '94*, Arizona, USA, Maricopa Center for Learning and Instruction (MCLI), 1995. Available at: http://hakatai.mcli.dist.maricopa.edu/ocotillo/report94/rep7.html, accessed September 26, 2009.

[JEA 00] Y. JEANNERET, *Y a-t-il Vraiment des Technologies de l'Information?*, Septentrion University Press, Paris, 2000.

[JOH 06] B. JOHNSTON, S. WEBBER, "As we may think: Information literacy as a discipline for the information age", *Research Strategies*, vol. 20, p. 108-121, 2006.

[LED 07] O. LE DEUFF, "La culture de l'information: quelles "littératies" pour quelles conceptions de l'information?", VIth ISKO Symposium-France 2007, June 7-8, 2007, Toulouse, Paul Sabatier University IUT, 2007 (to appear in the acts).

[NAZ 07] M. NAZIM, M. AHMAD, "Research trends in information literacy: A bibliometric study", *SRELS Journal of Information Management*, vol. 44, no. 1, pp. 53-62, 2007. Available at: http://eprints.rclis.org/archive/00012388/01/ Research_trends_in_IL.doc, accessed September 26, 2009.

[OWE 76] M. OWENS, "State Government and Libraries", *Library Journal*, vol. 101, p. 27, 1976.

[SER 08] A. SERRES, "Questions autour de la culture informationnelle", *La Revue Canadienne des Sciences de l'Information*, vol. 31, no. 1, p. 69-85, available at: http://www.inrp.fr/vst/LettreVST/avril2006.htm, March 2007.

[SER 06] A. SERRES, "Information literacy in the university: the didactic shanty", *History and Knowledge symposiums. Symposium no. 1. Knowledge and Stakeholder Training*, Workshop no. 5: Knowledge and information-documentation, CIVIIC Laboratory, University of Rouen, Rouen, May 18-20, 2007. Available at: http://archivesic .ccsd.cnrs.fr/sic_00177325/fr/, accessed September 26, 2009.

[STI 06] B. STIEGLER and ARS INDUSTRIALIS, *Réenchanter le Monde – La Valeur Esprit Contre le Populisme Industriel*, Flammarion, Paris, 2006.

[THO 07] S. THOMAS, C. JOSEPH, J. LACCETTI *et al.*, "Transliteracy: Crossing divides", *First Monday*, vol. 12, no. 12, 2007.
Available at address: http://www.uic.edu/htbin/cgiwrap/bin/ojs/index.php/fm/article/viewArticle/2060/1908, accessed September 26, 2009.

[VIR 03] S. VIRKUS, "Information literacy in Europe: a literature review", *Information Research*, vol. 8, no. 4, July 2003.
Available at: http://informationr.net/ir/8-4/paper159.html, accessed September 26, 2009.

Chapter 6

Relevance in Information Science Different Models, one Theory?

6.1. Introduction

In information science, the concept of relevance has long been a preoccupation of researchers. Although having been the object of numerous publications, it still remains an ambiguous notion and is periodically re-questioned: whereas it is at the centre of the information retrieval problematic, being able to better define it would certainly enable a better understanding of the way individuals behave when they are searching for information. Since the end of the 1990s, this concept has been suggested as a possible candidate for the elaboration of a theory enabling us to unify the works on the retrieval behavior of information users (in human and social sciences) and those seeking to conceive operational computerized systems to help them in their queries (in computer science and in artificial intelligence) in a common framework. Scientists indeed agree on this point: the goal of an information retrieval system (IRS) is to enable an individual to (re)discover the relevant information, which is supposed to be present in a collection of documents.

The notion of relevance is intimately linked to the notion of need for information. Individuals' needs for information are of different natures and are more or less explicit. Therefore, a need for information can be visceral, adopting Taylor's term, i.e. vaguely felt, or conscious, i.e. better defined by the one who is feeling it. This need is expressed through a demand, when the user asks a third party in the

---

Chapter written by Brigitte SIMONNOT.

usual language or by a query when the user uses a IRS. The query is a translation of the demand in a language that can be interpreted by the IRS: it is the formulation stage. During formulation, needs are generally misrepresented (it is the label effect revealed by Taylor). On the one hand the individual only expresses what he/she thinks is important for getting an answer, and on the other hand, he/she has the tendency to say the least possible about his/her information needs. Querying by key words also obligates the user to evacuate a part of the meaning of his/her query. Formulation is therefore affected by the vocabulary used, the diversity and ambiguity of the natural language: the problems of homonymy and synonymy, but also of specificity and generality well-known by librarians.

To answer the query, IRS present the user with a set of results. These results are generally first presented in the form of a list of short descriptions. These descriptions can be excerpts of library catalogue notices or, in the results pages of publication banks, short series of descriptive elements (often taking the format of bibliographic references). They can also take the form of snippets like in search engines where the title, URL address of the document, and sometimes its date of publication, are found as well as a brief summary or a few lines from the document including the terms of the query.

Information retrieval researches have long focused on the best ways to represent documents and on matching algorithms between a set of documents and a given query. We will not discuss the different algorithmic solutions here, nor will we cover the way to represent documents: all these have greatly evolved from structured library catalogs to full-text retrieval in huge collections of documents. For a historical summary of these approaches, the reader can refer to [CHI 07] (in French).

Human science researches have discussed and challenged the objective of IRS since the 1990s: whereas early systems had as a goal to answer an isolated query, it seemed important to make them evolve so that they attempt to respond to the user's information need. With the development of IRSs dedicated to a wider public – of which online search engines are the latest avatars – such an issue rises with more acuity. Early softwares were conceived to be used by people trained in documentation, who were supposed to be able to formulate appropriate queries. Current IRSs, dedicated to a wider audience, cannot rely upon the expertise of the user in matters of formulation and use of documentation languages.

Satisfying an information user is achieved by suggesting relevant documents to him/her. But what exactly is relevance? Going deeper into this concept leads to a long quest where vocabulary literacy is not the smallest obstacle. Whereas each person, in an intuitive way, understands well what relevance is about, the question becomes more complex when we aim to develop a model of it. The English language distinguishes two terms: relevance and pertinence. Researchers do not all exactly agree on the precise definition of these two terms. The English term "relevance", through its etymology, is related to the French verb "*relever*" in the sense of "to fall within the competence of"[1] but also "to accentuate"[2]. "Relevance" would be what, for a given question, would enable us to differentiate one information object from others. The English term "pertinence" comes from the Latin term *pertinere*, composed from the verb *tenere*, which means "to recollect something" but also "to understand, to keep in one's mind" and of the prefix *per* which means "across, through". It etymologically designates the action or the fact of understanding thanks to something. From the same verb *tenere* the term "attention" (to set one's mind to) is also derived.

Generally, "relevance" means the appropriateness of a document or an information object for an information need or a request for information in general. "Pertinence" is considered as the adequacy of a document or of a piece of information for the request of a given individual in a situation: in order for a relevant document to be pertinent for this individual, he/she must be able to understand it and to link it to the knowledge he/she has on the subject.

6.2. The nature of relevance

Better defining the nature of relevance, has been the object of much research in human and social sciences, especially to advocate for a better consideration of users in IRS design.

6.2.1. *Topicality*

Early IRS were settled for matching the terms of the query to those describing – or, in the case of full-text retrieval, appearing in – the documents of the collection according to the following hypothesis: if a term or a group of terms are found in the query and in a document (or its description) at the same time, this document is relevant to the query. As soon as collections became so much more enormous – and with the development of web information retrieval – it became important to suggest to the user an ordered group of the candidate documents by presenting the "best" documents first. It was no longer enough to retrieve the documents likely to be relevant but to find the way to distinguish them, and to rank them. Topicality had long been the only criterion taken into account in algorithms. We must say that this

1. "*être du ressort de*".

2. "*mettre en relief*".

was true in the days when documents were manually indexed by librarians who were seeking to determine its topic and subject (aboutness).

In the 1990s a number of scientists, in the field of human information behavior, showed that topicality was not the only criterion to consider in order to answer the user's information need. Harter [HAR 92] stressed that the common meaning of relevance did not tally to topicality: actually, a document that does not deal with the subject expressed in the user's query can also be relevant for it. Topicality is only one criterion among others, even if it remains very important in most retrieval situations [GRE 95]. In an attempt to identify other variables that intervene in relevance judgments, numerous empirical studies were conducted on users, in laboratory or in real context.

6.2.2. *The dynamic nature of relevance*

An information retrieval process was first modeled in a linear form by a series of steps: formulation of a query – matching the query with the collection of documents – and displaying results. It became rapidly apparent that such a process was not linear but iterative. In information retrieval, Rocchio has introduced, in 1966, the principle of relevance feedback which enabled us to implement an automatic reformulation of the initial query in IRSs based on relevance judgments of the user. Markey and Atherton (1978) had also noticed that information searchers take a leaf of terms contained in the first documents they find to broaden, pursue or refine their search.

The relevance feedback mechanism focus either on whole documents or, more often, on terms describing documents chosen or rejected by the user. These attempts were mainly a matter of helping the user in his/her query process by focusing on vocabulary used to query the IRS. But when someone searches for information, the documents he/she finds can modify not only the knowledge of the appropriate vocabulary to query the system but also his/her need, increasingly the need is vague and not well defined. If the IRS must answer to a need and not only to the query as it is formulated at a given time, it is important to take this evolution into account.

Marcia Bates [BAT 89] strongly challenged a vision of a retrieval process where the user's need would always remain the same. In real life, humans proceed by successive steps, and the information they collect at each step modifies or brings new questions. She introduced a model of information behavior called "berry-picking": people solve their problem by gathering successive pieces of information. Like in the forest, berries are not picked by whole branches. The picker takes some berries here and there to fill his/her basket and try to choose the best.

Harter [HAR 92] has also analyzed the dynamicity of relevance: inspired by Dan Sperber and Dierdre Wilson's [SPE 86] relevance theory, he develops the vision of an information search during which the individual moves on from an initial context, with a certain representation of his/her need for information to other contexts that he/she constructs little by little. Therefore, the important thing is to consider the complete retrieval session – and not simply the submission of an isolated query – to conceive IRSs that answer to a information need. During a retrieval session, relevant documents are those that help somebody to better define his/her problem, to ask questions in a different way, and those that carry the necessary information to solve the problem at hand at the same time.

6.2.3. *The situational nature of relevance*

Patrick Wilson seems to have been the first to emphasize the importance of considering the situation of the information searcher to help him/her in his/her search. Situational relevance refers to the way in which humans use information and to the real effects of information changing their vision of their problem. It covers the usefulness or the pragmatic value of a document for a task or a problem to be resolved [XU 06]. For a similar query (i.e. formulated within the same terms), it is not necessarily the same group of documents that will be relevant for persons who have different tasks to achieve or even for the same person in two different situations.

But how can the context of information search be defined and characterized? Whereas librarians can question the user about what he/she wants to do with the information found to better help him/her, implementing such functionalities in a IRS poses many issues. In cognitive psychology the context has mainly been defined from the task that the searcher has to do. From a bibliometric point of view, the context can include documents that surround or are linked to a relevant document, for example through citations. From a technological point of view the context takes into account the technical and material environment the individual has at hand to present him/her documents in adapted formats (for example, such as the small screen of a mobile phone can display).

From the geographical point of view, the notion of context can give rise to local searches: whereas an individual searches for a particular service, he/she can prefer that this service be close to his/her current location. In brief, the notion of context in information retrieval is multiple and its meanings differ.

6.3. Multidimensional models of relevance

To characterize the different aspects of relevance, researchers have first and foremost tried to break up the concept into sub-categories. It actually quickly appeared that relevance manifests itself at different levels during a search process and that at each level, different elements affect users' relevance judgments. Tefko Saracevic has taken particular attention in analyzing the manifestations of relevance to distinguish its different attributes. His model was revisited by Erica Cosign and Peter Ingwersen. Stephano Mizzaro suggested an neat model integrating different relations of relevance. Finally, Peiling Wang and Dagobert Soergel analyzed users' decision-making processes when they are choosing or rejecting a document suggested by a IRS. We will now go into more detail on these different modeling endeavors where relevance plays a central role.

6.3.1. *Saracevic's stratified model of interaction (1996)*

Tefko Saracevic worked a lot on the concept of relevance since 1975. Taking inspiration from the writings of Alfred Schütz in philosophy and from those of Dan Sperber and Deirdre Wilson in linguistic pragmatics, he stresses that the cognitive notion of relevance implies that interactive and dynamic relations are done by inference[3], the user having intentions and being situated in a certain context. According to Saracevic, relevance can be characterized by a number of attributes: relation, intention and motivation, context, inference – most often grasped through gradual judgments about efficiency or about the degree to which a given relation is maximized – and interaction. He suggests to model the interaction between the user and the IRS as a sequence of processes occurring in a system of strata [SAR 96; 97]; see Figure 6.1. His stratified model [SAR 97] distinguishes different kinds of manifestations of relevance:

– system or algorithmic relevance, i.e. the relation inferred by the system about the adequacy of a document for a query;

– topicality or subject relevance, a relation of aboutness between the subject of the query and that covered by the document;

– cognitive relevance or pertinence, i.e. the relation between the state of knowledge of the user and his/her cognitive information need and texts; it is inferred from informativeness, novelty, information quality, and the connection with the user's knowledge (the information should be adapted to the user level of comprehension);

3. Inference in psychology differs from reasoning in that the underlying elements are not necessarily explicit.

– situational relevance or utility is the relation between the task or problem at hand and the texts retrieved; it is inferred from their usefulness in decision-making, appropriateness of information to solve the problem at hand and reduction of uncertainty;

– affective or motivational relevance, i-e relations between intents, goals and motivations of a user and retrieved texts; this is inferred from satisfaction, success, accomplishment of the user's goals.

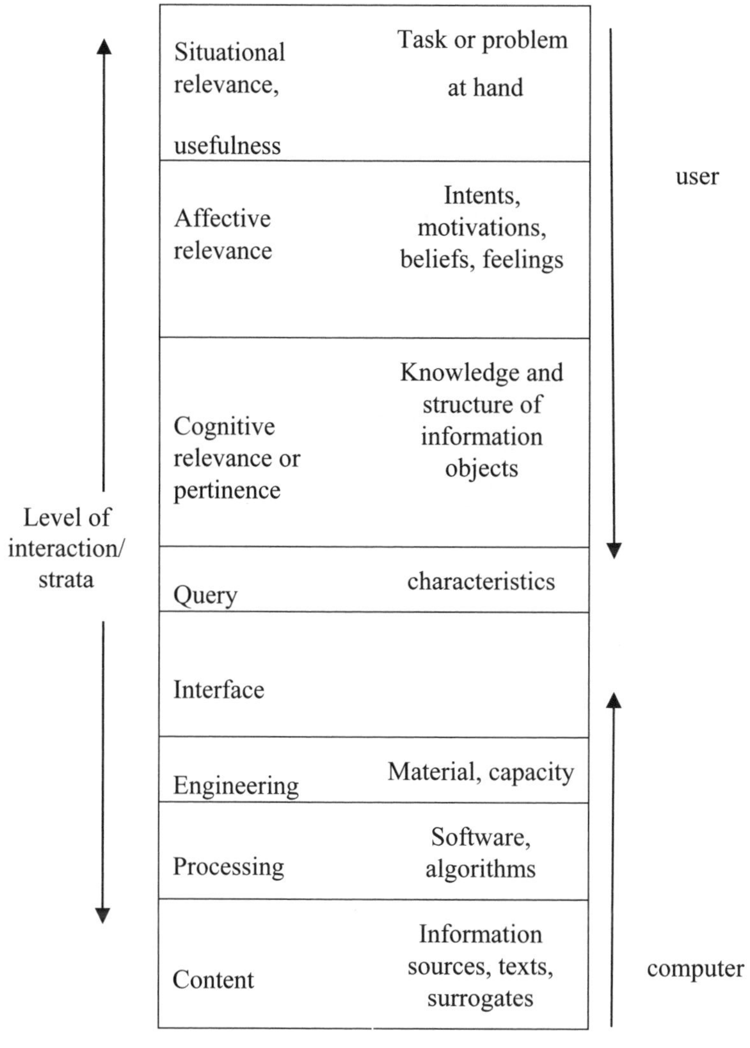

Figure 6.1. *Saracevic's system of strata (1997)*

Tefko Saracevic emphasizes interdependence in this system of relevances[4] – in the sense that each kind of relevance affects the others – and pleads for all to be taken into account in the conception of IRS.

The stratified model enables to distinguish different levels that are involved in the users' relevance judgments. For the author, it is a starting point to better model users of an IRS and to improve the system feedbacks following its querying.

Nevertheless, such a linear representation does not take into consideration all the possibilities of relations that are established between the different strata. Tefko Saracevic reexamines this model in a recent double publication [SAR 07a, SAR 07b] and refines on a certain number of points the teachings brought by more recent researches.

6.3.2. *The model revisited by Cosijn and Ingwersen*

Erica Cosijn and Peter Ingwersen [COS 00] endeavor to synthesize the various dimensions of the concept of relevance. Starting from Tefko Saracevic's stratified model, they suggest the term of sociocognitive relevance to name the relation between a situation, a task at hand, a problem to solve in a given sociocultural context and the information objects, as they are perceived by one or more cognitive agents. This vision of relevance includes the system, a group of users or individual agents and their socio-organizational environment at the same time. The example of sociocognitive relevance they give is the process of review by peers for scientific publications which comes to a classification of publications on which the reviewers agree. In such a process, different cultural factors can influence the evaluators. Cosijn and Ingwersen classify sociocognitive relevance as a kind of subjective relevance determined by a participant in interaction with other members in a community. This inter-subjectivity could be shown through statistically objective and measurable features. According to the authors, situational relevance should be distinguished from sociocognitive relevance because the former is purely subjective. These two kinds of relevance mainly differ through attributes that are intent, inference and interaction. Their paper discusses the subjective or non-subjective nature of different kinds of relevance.

Erica Cosijn and Peter Ingwersen characterize cognitive relevance or pertinence by novelty, degree of informativeness, preferences and quality of information objects relative to the user's information need at a given moment. They care about the difference between affective relevance and motivational relevance. By relying on John Searle (1984), they differentiate two levels of intentionality. The first level is

4. Tefko Saracevic borrowed this expression of "systems of relevances" from Schütz.

an intrinsic intentional phenomenon, made up of beliefs and, we could say, internal representations of individuals. The second level corresponds to an intentionality derived from the preceding level and which includes objectives, roles and expectations of the user.

For these authors, affective relevance is personal and therefore very subjective. It is linked to the individual's point of view and concerns the emotional responses at any aspect of the document. According to them however, even if it has effects on the other types of relevance, affective relevance cannot be classified in a clear way as a separate category because it behaves in a totally different way. Not all types of relevance can be totally measurable: we can have an operational variable but do not really know what its association with the underlying theoretical variable is. For example, the authors write, it can be difficult to experimentally distinguish cognitive relevance or pertinence from situational relevance, unless trying to measure the learning effect achieved during a retrieval session.

While acknowledging the importance of context for the comprehension of the concept of relevance, Erica Cosijn and Peter Ingwersen do not really define the notion but just give some examples of it. They evoke the context of information retrieval algorithm tests, for example that of Text REtrieval Conferences. For these authors, the context includes the given situation and/or the underlying organizational strategy of the user's environment but is not enough to distinguish the different kinds of relevance.

6.3.3. *Mizzaro's model (1998)*

In 1998 Stefano Mizzaro [MIZ 98], from a consequent review of literature on the subject, suggested a four-dimensional model of information retrieval: information resources, representation of the user's need for information (the "user's problem" in Mizzarro's terms), time and the contextual or situational "components". It is useful to look at this model that clarifies a certain number of points and was then refined [GAB 99] in detail.

First, the information resources that the IRS user can access are of different kinds:

– the set of documents (DS) that, together, can satisfy his/her need;

– the document itself (D), i.e. the physical entity found by the user, or a full information object a user can access after his query;

– metadata (MD), i.e. structured data about the document that concern its bibliographic description as well as indications or suggestions made by humans – as in the case of LOM (learning object metadata), which specifies the level of study to which the object is related);

– the surrogate of the document (S), i.e. for example, a bibliographical description or a snippet displayed in the search engines results.

Stefano Mizzaro suggests classifying these different information objects in the following partial order:

$$S \leq MD \leq D \leq SD$$

in relation to the capacity to answer the user's information need. For example, the note of a document can include a summary that lets the user decide that the document may be interesting in response to his/her demand, but only the reading of the full document proper will, or not, bring the desired information.

The second dimension is the representation of the user's information problem. It includes:

– Real information need (RIN) – Robert Taylor mentioned some "visceral" need in the sense that the user is not really conscious about it – it is an abstraction of an ideal need that includes the complete amount of information the person should have about his/her situation and his/her need so that information can solve it the appropriate way. To include the real information need in the model is important: an expert, for example, should be able to help the user to understand that the need for the information he/she perceives does not correspond to reality.

– The perceived or conscious need (PIN), in a more or less correct and often imprecise; it is an implicit representation of the problematic situation and of different possible ways to satisfy the need.

– The request (EIN), i.e. the expressed information need in "natural" language.

– And the query (FIN), or the formalized information need in a form that can be processed by the IRS.

These different elements can be ordered in the following way:

$$FIN \leq EIN \leq PIN \leq RIN,$$

according to the completeness of their description and the "potential expressiveness" of real need. For example, an individual can have an erroneous representation of what he/she needs to look for. He/she can be conscious of needing information on such an aspect of the subject but not on another that is nevertheless important to process it well. As a result, his/her need for information as he/she perceives it does not correspond to the real need for information. If he/she does not master the vocabulary linked to the subject nor the retrieval language of the IRS he/she uses, his/her queries will be poorly formulated. According to the nature of the need and the level of expertise of the user, both on the subject and in the domain of information retrieval, the expression is a more or less rough misrepresentation of it.

The third dimension of the model is time: during the information retrieval process, the user learns and his/her need for information is modified. A document that did not seem pertinent to him/her at the beginning of his/her query can appear very pertinent to him/her when he becomes aware of the elements that enable him/her to appreciate the tenure of it or to understand it. Some information needs are dynamic; they evolve as soon as the user learns new things about the subject. This is often translated by successive reformulations of the request and the query. Stefano Mizzaro will then suppress this dimension of the model because it cannot be structured like the other dimensions (but also, according to the author, because it complicates the graphical representation of the model). Nevertheless, some researchers will study this dimension by analyzing time not as a continuous variable, but like the discontinuous stages or intervals of time. It is the case, for example, of an exploratory study by Arthur R. Taylor *et al.* [TAY 07] who model time according to the stages of Carol Kuhlthau's ISP model (information retrieval process) [KUH 93].

The last dimension suggested by Mizzaro is more complex and heterogeneous; he calls it the "components" [of the problem] which gather:

– the thematic subject (or "topic") (To) which interests the user (a part of which can remain implicit) and on which his/her query is focused;

– the task (or "topic & task") (To + Ta), i.e. the activity for which the user needs this information;

– user attributes (or a "topic, task and user attributes") (To + Ta + UA), which take the place of the notion of context suggested in the first version of the model. In the first version of the model, context was defined in a very vague way, including every thing that is linked neither to the subject nor to the task but influenced the way in which the individual searches for and evaluates the results. Stefano Mizzaro classed the documents that the user already knows, for example, those he/she is not able of understanding, or even the time and money he/she has for his/her retrieval, in this dimension. In the second version of the model, the user attributes also include his/her degree of expertise in the domain and his preferences.

These elements can be partially organized in the following way:

$$\text{To} \leq \text{To} \leq \text{Ta} \leq \text{To} + \text{Ta} + \text{UA}$$

depending on the number of variables taken into account to facilitate information retrieval in context. The notion of context in the model is rather a non-category that enables us to include all the parameters not coming under the other classes and to reason under the hypothesis of a closed world.

This model considers information retrieval as a process of problem solving where we can distinguish the pertinence linked to information objects, pertinence linked to the user's representation of the problem and pertinence related to the knowledge of and on the user in context. It also emphasizes the evolution of information need in time. Finally, it turns out to be very interesting to explore and characterize the different trends in scientific research on IRSs.

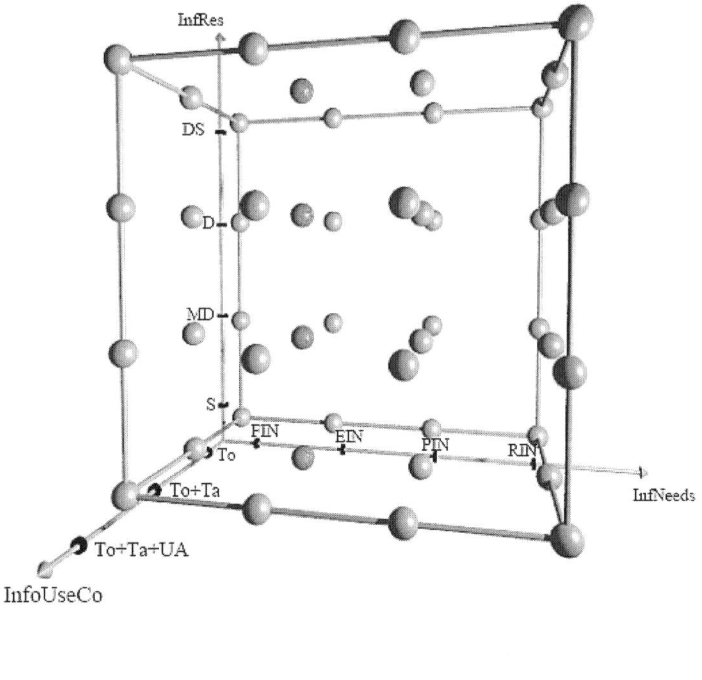

Figure 6.2. *Mizzarro's three-dimensional model according to [GAB 99]*

6.3.4. *The five dimensions of Wang and Soergel's cognitive model*

Relying on the research in psychology dealing with the decision-making processes, Peiling Wang and Dagobert Soergel [WAN 98] question the nature of the value attributed to documents by individuals in a document search situation. From a longitudinal qualitative study focusing on a sample of 25 participants (11 teachers and 14 graduate students), they analyze the way in which academics decide whether or not to use the documents in their search labor. They ascertain five categories of values assigned to the documents found:

– the epistemological value, which concerns the domain of knowledge on which documents and requests are focused; according to the authors, this one conditions all the others but cannot alone explain the choice of a document;

– the functional value of a document for the ongoing task; the document can serve as a theoretical basis, an empirical aid, a methodological guide or simply enable a good citation;

– the conditional value, i.e. the fact that the document could be able to have an epistemological and functional value, but not necessarily for the ongoing task;

– the social value, attributed through the notoriety and authority of the author, the journal, or the organization for which the author works in the field;

– the emotional value, i.e. the capacity of the document to stimulate feelings in a positive or negative way. For example, some participants of the study manifest affective judgments towards certain authors. These feelings incite them, or do not incite them, to use their writings, or to delay their use.

The authors then analyze the criteria used by people observed while selecting documents during a search. Among the criteria they raise, subject relevance (topicality) is the most frequently evoked in the explicitation of relevance judgments. It can have an epistemological value (the subject of the text matches the subject dealt with), functional (the methodology used in the text corresponds to what the individual is looking for) or conditional. The second most cited criterion is the kind of outline (theoretical/empirical) and the level of expertise of the text expected by the audience (in a university or in school, academic or professional). The academic discipline of the author of a text also plays a role, perhaps because it can predict the capacity of the reader to understand the contents. Other sociocognitive criteria are shown to intervene in relevance judgments: the author's authority, his/her reputation in the domain but also the consideration of the authorities in charge of publishing or organizations that supported the research.

The authors therefore distinguish different types of knowledge that influence participants' relevance judgments: their expertise in the subject domain, their knowledge of people, publications and organizations in the field. They suggest a list of clues that an IRS could provide about the documents to help users in their process of selecting documents.

The interest of this publication is to adopt an original approach to analyzing users' relevance judgments: more than focusing on problem solving, it brings forward the point of view on decision-making. It also shows the importance of sociocognitive factors in users' relevance judgments, at least for a particular public, academics. Finally, it also notes the emotional value expressed in relation to documents: individuals do not only base their judgments of documents that are suggested to them on merely rational criteria.

6.3.5. *Summary*

We can see that the concept of relevance was detailed using inspirations from different theories: Tefko Saracevic relies on Schütz's phenomenology and Dan Sperber and Deirdre Wilson's relevance theory in linguistic pragmatics. Peiling Wang and Dagobert Soergel are inspired by the theory of the decision to analyze the rationality of users' choices. These authors take different propositions from there to refine the modeling of IRS users. Stefano Mizzaro for his part designs a model that summarizes the researches in information retrieval and attempts to specify a generic model of an IRS.

Despite all this researches, many questions still remain open and discussed in the field. Among them, is relevance a totally objective phenomenon or will some of its aspects forever remain in the domain of subjectivity? What parameters should IRS consider to satisfy, at best, the user and why?

If relevance is the phenomenon that enables us to make sense of, understand and learn from information, should IRSs be conceived as systems of learning? Should they seek to reduce as quickly as possible the uncertainty of the user who is querying them on the subject or allow him/her to deepen his/her need, even diagnose the badly asked questions, in the way in which some now identify orthographical errors? Or is it simply a matter of conceiving the tools to which we turn punctually to satisfy an immediate need, like a phone book is consulted to find a telephone number? We can see that the field is open to different families of systems according to the way IRS designers model the user.

6.4. Criteria affecting relevance judgments

Analyzing the way individuals' relevance judgments are formed was another way for scientists to approach the concept. These studies showed that the criteria used by individuals are very numerous and, in addition, change during a retrieval session. Carol L. Barry and Linda Schamber [BAR 98] both proceeded to empirical studies on this question. Attempting to compare the results obtained in their respective studies, carried out in different contexts, they find mostly coherent categories of criteria. The main ones are:

– the extent, degree of deepening and the specificity of information;

– its accurateness, its validity;

– its clarity;

– its degree of updating, the fact that information is recent;

– its tangible character, if information includes data or concrete facts;

– the quality or reputation of the source;

– accessibility or usability;

– the availability of information or of the source of information the verification, the fact that the information can be can be supported by several documents or sources;

– the emotion induced by the information.

Other criteria remain specific to one or the other study, showing well the effect of context and of the retrieval situation on judgements that the users make on information.

Amanda Spink, Howard Greisdorf and Judy Bateman [SPI 98] sought to determine different regions of relevance. They suggest a 3D model of relevance judgments: kind of manifestation of relevance according to those determined by Tefko Saracevic, level of relevance estimated (they choose four levels: very relevant, partially relevant, partially not relevant, not relevant) and time. They show that users have more difficulty in judging relevant documents at the beginning of their retrieval, therefore keeping partially relevant documents.

The more knowledge and focus on a problem users have, the better their position to pronounce clear-cut judgments. Pertti Vakkari [VAK 00a; VAK 00b] shows that users identify more documents as relevant at the beginning of retrieval and fewer at the end. They explain this phenomenon through the acquisition of knowledge on the part of the users. For Howard Greisdorf [GRE 03], users' relevance judgments on information found during their searches evolve by levels, beginning with subject relevance (topicality), then cognitive relevance (or pertinence), the meaning they can give the information found to usefulness. Shirlee-Ann Knight and Janice Burn [KNI 05] identify the criteria necessary for evaluation of online information. Relying on other studies that focus on information quality, they identify numerous criteria of which a large number support the observations of Carol Barry and Linda Schamber.

Among the criteria they grasp, a larger number of them are linked to information usefulness. They also stress the influence of IRS on users' judgments.

Soo Young Rieh [RIE 02], about the behavior of seekers of online information, distinguishes predictive judgments made from elements of information proposed by IRS to represent documents in search results, and the evaluative judgments that focus on the document itself. She notes that individuals do not give the same importance to the various criteria of relevance at these two stages; the relative importance attributed to each varying depending on the situation.

The criteria on which individuals' relevance judgments rely seem to depend on a certain number of factors, notably the individual's experience in IRS use and his/her knowledge in the subject domain, on which he/she perform an information search. According to Peiling Wang and Dagobert Soergel [WAN 98], the criteria tend to become more and more exigent as the retrieval session progresses. System interface also plays a role especially in the order in which the results are presented [SPI 98]. Finally, even if some documents are judged relevant by an information researcher, they will not all be really used.

All these studies enrich the knowledge of criteria that play on the relevance judgments and, above all, the way in which they intervene during the retrieval process. They also suggest functionalities with which IRS should be equipped to help users in their information searches. Finally, some of them engage in being cautious when panels are established to judge information in Cranfield-type sessions with the goal of evaluating the efficiency and performances of IRS.

6.5. Communication and relevance

6.5.1. *Impact of Sperber and Wilson's theory*

Dan Sperber and Deirdre Wilson's relevance theory [SPE 86] developed in linguistic pragmatics, inspired many researchers who attempted to draw conclusions from it in information science. By considering information retrieval as a dialog between an individual and a system that is susceptible to provide it for him/her, this theory indeed brings interesting elements. Recently, Howard D. White suggested a new interpretation of this theory [WHI 07a; 07b]. He suggests that numerous studies characterize users' information behavior as being guided by the law of least effort. Furthermore, Dan Sperber and Deirdre Wilson attribute an important role to the effort in relevance. Two axioms of their theory serve as a basis for this parallel:

– a hypothesis is relevant in a context to the extent to which it produces positive cognitive effects in this context;

– a hypothesis is relevant in a context to the extent to which the effort necessary to deal with it in this context is weak.

White is inspired by Andrew Goatly's proposition (in *The Language of Metaphors,* 1997) which defines relevance by the cognitive effects ratio/processing effort. Using bibliometry, he interprets the famous tf*idf formula as an application of this principle. In this originating formula, the tf (term frequency) parameter represents the frequency of a term in the document. The idf (inverse document frequecy) parameter represents the inverse frequency of the term in the collection, and therefore the informational specificity of the term in relation to this collection. White assimilates the tf coefficient to the positive cognitive effect (the more frequent the term in the document, the more the document will have positive cognitive effects) and the idf coefficient to the processing effort: the more frequent the term in a collection, the greater the processing effort will be. Relying on other formula developped in bibliometry, he shows that by interpreting the sagittal diagrams obtained by projecting the tf*idf values to class documents of a collection in relation to a term enables to envisage the presentations of results at added value.

He also develops the notion of creative relevance: relevance relations created by individuals do not focus only on the fact that documents and queries include common (topical) terms. He lists:

– analogical relevance when individuals implement reasonings by analogy, by making the parallel between two different concepts;

– causal relevance, when they identify a causal relation between two concepts, taking up an example developed in the medical domain (such a sickness provokes such a blood deficiency; such a product plays on the same blood deficiency therefore this product should be able to act on the sickness);

– methodological relevance when the individual has an interest in a methodology rather than in the subject approached in the document;

– convincing relevance, when examples (even if example does not have strength of evidence) or data enable to reinforce or to weaken an assertion;

– poetic relevance, when a metaphor or an allusion helps to make the point in question;

– terminological relevance, when literary works comment in a metalinguistic way on the way the language is used in other literary works.

He comes back to the subjective or objective feature of relevance, arguing that the supposed subjectivity of relevance judgments is only due to the fact that individuals do not have the time to clarify the reasons why they judge such a document as relevant. According to him, there would be no subjective relevance, and relevance is always inferred from objective elements. The subjective character of relevance is linked to the creativity of individuals who do not necessarily reason in a rational way. However, users can have false initial knowledge or incorrect modes of reasoning.

Many studies carried out in real situations showed the importance of the criteria of novelty of information so that this information should be considered as relevant by the individual. Dan Sperber and Dierdre Wilson's theory also enables the interpretation of this phenomenon: a document that is already known by the individual does not necessitate the processing effort, but these "positive cognitive effects" are also useless, except if the individual interprets it in a new way by relating it to elements he/she did not know in his/her previous reading.

Even if some researchers contest that the thesis developed by Dan Sperber and Dierdre Wilson is a theory, because it is suggested in the form of axioms essentially supported on more or less imaginary dialog examples, none doubt that it stimulated reflections and help the comprehension of the phenomenon of relevance to go ahead.

6.5.2. *Emergent modeling*

Jim Ottaviani [OTT 94] also relied on Dan Sperber and Dierdre Wilson's relevance theory and the concept of significance by Marvin Minski (1986): a document is relevant if it makes a difference, if it has a discernible effect on the thoughts and behavior of the individual. He compared the process of information retrieval to a chaotic phenomenon, in the sense of Mendelbrot's chaos theory, and suggested a fractal model that enables to define clusters of relevant documents. His proposition, as far as we know, has led to many developments. Its interest was to stipulate that, for a similar query, several clusters of relevant documents could be constructed. But nothing enables us to state that the pattern to construct clusters is regular.

Christophe Brouard and Jian-Yun Nie [BRU 04], in their research on information filtering, suggest a new concept, that of resonance. They rely on Grossberg's adaptive theory of resonance (1976), following theories about situated cognition (CLE 1997) which was used to model different cognitive processes, from perception to categorization. This theory is based on the following principle: when a cognitive system interacts with its environment, it captures the signals that come from this environment but it also projects signals on it (we can make the analogy with the attention paid by an individual to an object at a given moment), depending on internal representations. Only the signals that are also activated in return by the internal representations propagate again, being amplified or extended, in the same way as an echo. The system thus enters a state of resonance. Such a process would enable us to select information. The stimulus which entered in resonance will be taken into account for learning. Other signals will not be taken into account or will have a different treatment. It is therefore necessary to apply internal knowledge to new stimuli so that they can be taken into account. And a new stimulus will only be taken into account if it corresponds well to an internal representation. The concept of resonance seems to well account the way these relevance interactions are produced. Therefore, neurosciences can also contribute to a better understanding of these mechanisms and help to determine the elements that underlie the phenomenon of resonance.

The resonance process can be assimilated to a certain extent to a process of acquisition and synthesis of knowledge: a piece of relevant information would be a piece of information that enables us to improve our knowledge but more widely to better understand a question. Therefore, a piece of information is relevant even if it does not focus directly on the subject at hand in a search, but brings elements facilitating our reasoning. The concept of relevance can also be linked to the phenomenon of attention: in order for us to judge a piece of information as relevant, some elements must hold our attention. The attention we pay to information is the first condition in order for us to take the time to evaluate its relevance.

6.6. Conclusion

Works on relevance have long had as their objective the improvement of the functioning of IRSs for users. A relevance theory in information sciences could be able to finish reconciling the two distinct scientific fields that work on such questions: research on information retrieval that seek to improve algorithms and research on informational behavior in human sciences.

Whereas many descriptive models have been suggested up to this point, a theory could be able to go beyond this: to be not only descriptive but also explicative and predictive about what we can or cannot expect from the automation of information processing. It could enable to conceive efficient IRSs, really adapted to users' needs, but also to better structure research in human sciences. The subjective or objective character of relevance has long held an important place in the debates among researchers. Rather than setting the issue in these terms, it would be better to pursue so that to find which elements could be objectified.

As noted by Tefko Saracevic [SAR 07b], most empirical research on the behavior of IRS users is made on student samples, the participants of which are not necessarily qualified judges or representative of the general population. Due to financial constrains, researchers are often obliged to conduct their studies on only these populations. Of course, despite the generalization of use of IRSs by the wider public[5], we cannot suppose that users are sufficiently "qualified" to determine which is the "right" information within the information that is suggested to them. Nevertheless, the success of commercial search engines attests that the need for such tools exists. Prospering thanks to marketing and advertising, these search engines do not have as a first objective to supply the best information at a given moment. They aimto distribute their advertising in the least "disturbing" way possible and to facilitate acceptance by the internet surfer by making advertising "relevant". Scientists should mobilize cultural stakeholders more, those who consider information to be a common good, to make alternative propositions and to participate in substantial works in this domain.

6.7. Bibliography

[BAR 94] C. L. BARRY, "User-defined relevance criteria: An exploratory study", *Journal of the American Society for Information Science*, vol. 45 no. 3, p. 149-159, 1994.

[BAR 98] C. L. BARRY, L. SCHAMBER, "Users' criteria for relevance evaluation: a cross study comparison", *Information Processing and Management*, vol. 24 nos. 2/3, p. 219-236, 1998.

[BAT 89] M.J. BATES, "The design of browsing and berry-picking techniques for the online search interface", *Online Review*, vol. 13, p. 407-424, 1989.

[BRO 04] C. BROUARD, J.-Y. NIE, "Relevance as resonance: a new theoretical perspective and a practical utilization in information filtering", *Information Processing and Management*, vol. 40, p. 1-19, 2004.

[CHI 07] Y. CHIARAMELLA, P. MULHEM, "La recherche d'information. De la documentation automatique à la recherche d'information en contexte", *Document Numérique* , vol. 10 no. 1, p. 11-38, 2007.

[COS 00] E. COSIJN, P. INGWERSEN, "Dimensions of relevance", *Information Processing and Management*, vol. 36 no. 4, p. 533-550, 2000.

[GAB 99] S. GABRIELLI, S. MIZZARO, "Negociating a multidimensional framework for relevance space", in: DRAPER et al. (eds), *Proceedings of Mira 99: Evaluating Interactive Information Retrieval*, p. 1-15, Glasgow, Scotland, 1999.

[GRE 95] R. GREEN, "Topical relevance relationships. I: Why topic matching fails", *Journal of the American Society for Information Science*, vol. 46 no. 9, p. 646-653, 1995.

[GRE 03] H. GREISDORF, "Relevance thresholds: a multi-stage predictive model of how users evaluate information", *Information Processing and Management*, vol. 39, p. 403-423, 2003.

---

5. By wider public we mean the people who did not receive documentary or information retrieval consequent training.

[HAR 92] S.P. HARTER, "Psychological relevance and information science", *Journal of the American Society for Information Science*, vol. 43 no. 9, p. 602-615, 1992.

[KNI 05] S-A. KNIGHT, J. BURN, "Developing a framework for assessing information quality on the World Wide Web", *Informing Science Journal*, vol. 8, p. 159-172, 2005. Available at: http://www.inform.nu/Articles/Vol8/v8p159-172Knig.pdf, accessed September 26, 2009.

[KUL 93] C.C. KUHLTHAU, *Seeking Meaning: A Process Approach to Library and Information Services*, Ablex Publishing Corp, Norwood, N.J., 1993.

[MIZ 98] S. MIZZARO, "How many relevances in information retrieval?", *Interacting with Computers*, vol. 10, p. 303-320, 1998.

[OTT 94] J. OTTAVIANI, "The fractal dimension of relevance: a hypothesis", *Journal of the American Society for Information Science*, vol. 45 no. 4, p. 263-272, 1994.

[RIE 02] S. RIEH, "Judgement of information quality and cognitive authority in the web", *Journal of the American Society for Information Science and Technology*, vol. 53 no. 2, p. 145-161, 2002.

[SAR 96] T. SARACEVIC, "Relevance reconsidered – information science: integration in perspective", *Proceedings of the Second Conference on Conception of Library and Information Science,* p. 201-218, 1996.

[SAR 97] T. SARACEVIC, "The stratified model of information retrieval interaction: Extension and applications", *Proceedings of the American Society for Information Science meeting*, vol. 34, p. 313-327, 1997.

[SAR 07a] T. SARACEVIC, "Relevance: a review of the literature and a framework for thinking on the notion in Information Science. Part II:Nature and manifestations of relevance", *Journal of the American Society for Information Science and Technology*, vol. 58, no.13, p. 1915-1933, 2007.

[SAR 07b] T. SARACEVIC, "Relevance: a review of the literature and a framework for thinking on the notion in information science. Part III: Behavior and effects of relevance", *Journal of the American Society for Information Science and Technology*, vol. 58, no. 13, p. 2126-2144, 2007.

[SPE 86] SPERBER D., WILSON D., *Relevance: Communication and Cognition*, Blackwell, Oxford , 1986.

[SPI 98] SPINK A., GREISDORF H., BATEMAN J., "From highly relevant to not relevant: examining different regions of relevance ", *Information Processing & Management*, vol. 34, no.5, p. 599-621, 1998.

[TAY 07] TAYLOR A. R., COOL C., BELKIN N. J., AMADIO W. J., "Relationships between categories of relevance criteria and stage in task completion", *Information Processing & Management*, vol. 43, p. 1071-1084, 2007.

[WAN 98] WANG P., SOERGEL D., "A Cognitive Model of Document Use during a research project. Study I. Document Selection", *Journal of the American Society for Information Science*, vol. 49, no.2, p. 115-153, 1998.

[WHI 07A] WHITE H. D., "Combining bibliometrics, information retrieval, and relevance theory, part 1: first examples of a synthesis", *Journal of the American Society for Information Science and Technology*, vol. 58, no. 44, p. 536-559, 2007.

[WHI 07B] WHITE H. D., "Combining bibliometrics, information retrieval, and relevance theory, Part 2: Some implications for information science", *Journal of the American Society for Information Science and Technology*, vol. 58, no. 4, p. 583-605, 2007.

[XU 06] XU Y., CHEN Z., "Relevance judgment: What do information users consider beyond topicality?", *Journal of the American Society for Information Science and Technology*, vol. 57, no. 7, p. 961-973, 2006.

Chapter 7

Electronic Information Access Devices: Crossed Approaches and New Boundaries

7.1. Introduction

The study of information retrieval systems and, more generally, information access systems is a vast domain of research at the crossroads of several disciplines, in particular information science, cognitive psychology, linguistics, computer science and artificial intelligence. The number and diversity of studies currently focusing on Internet searching give valuable insights regarding the importance of this activity, which has become a large-scale socio-economic, political and cultural phenomenon. Therefore, although over the decades, academic studies have essentially focused on the professional uses of information access systems, they are now more concerned with the question of the everyday use of these systems by a "wider public".

The aim of this chapter is to show that the joint evolution of information retrieval systems and their uses lead us to reconsider the theoretical and methodological frameworks in order to grasp new, observable information practices. On the one hand, online information retrieval (IR) systems are designed with new searching and browsing functionalities and deal with different digital collections (textual, music and video corpora, bibliographic records, etc.). IR systems tend to change very rapidly and become more and more integrated in wider devices. On the other hand, the advent of the Internet has created a diversity of small digital interconnected

---

Chapter written by Stéphane CHAUDIRON and Madjid IHADJADENE.

worlds, allowing millions of users to produce, navigate and search for information. These users have various backgrounds with different levels of ability and knowledge. Searching for information today is no longer the privilege of information professionals and scientists but has also become that of scholars, consumers, the general public, tourists, etc. Ordinary people have become end-users. The growing place of digital environments brings major changes to IR systems, on users and on information practices. Users now have to face a variety of IR systems and one major issue for researchers is to understand how they really use these technical devices, how they adapt themselves to the technical constraints, what kind of knowledge they use during search sessions, etc.

In the first section of the chapter, we highlight the rapid evolution of "electronic information access systems" and discuss some basic concepts used in the different user-oriented approaches. This first section is a terminological questioning which will not produce final statements but draw attention to the conceptual instability of the terms according to the various fields and disciplines they come from. As this chapter was originally published in France, for both the library and information science researchers and media studies scientists, we have paid special attention to the works conducted in the field of information and communication technologies (ICT). The goal of the chapter is therefore an attempt to fill the gap between the ICT community and the information-seeking behavior of the general community.

In the second section, we provide an overview of user-oriented studies that are essential to understand the different contexts of use of electronic information access systems. In particular, we point out the fact that these studies come from different disciplines, such as information science, communication science, sociology, psychology or marketing, and consist of complementary views on the same subject. With different goals and methodologies, they all want to capture the "users' behavior" at different levels, including search tasks and strategies, personal information infrastructure, cognitive or social-organizational contexts.

7.2. Conceptual clarifications

7.2.1. *Information access devices: a composite object*

Almost 60 years have passed since the first historical occurrence of the term "information retrieval" by Calvin Moers in 1948 [MOE 48], which designates the process of automatic indexation and retrieval of information, to the current variety of information access tools. In the recent past, the online industry has experienced considerable changes, namely with the increase of text and multimedia-oriented databases.

"Information retrieval" was initially defined by Frederick W. Lancaster [LAN 79] as:

> "the process of searching a collection of documents with the goal of identifying documents that relate to a particular topic"[1].

If this definition clearly distinguished documentary retrieval (or information retrieval) from fact retrieval, it made a regrettable confusion between "document" and "information", which unfortunately still lingers. The term "information retrieval" itself is problematic, as Frederick W. Lancaster and Amy J. Warner later pointed out [LAN 93]:

> "clearly, information retrieval is not a particularly satisfactory term to describe the type of activity to which it is usually applied. An information retrieval system does not retrieve information. Indeed, information is intangible"[2].

Jacques Maniez [MAN 04] suggests considering information retrieval systems (IRSs) as a subset of "object retrieval systems" which broadly include any kind of request for any kind of information, tool, service, product of consumption, etc. In Maniez's opinion, the particularity of IRSs comes from the imprecise character of the notion of "topic", which has been used in document processing to define the relevance of adequacy between a document and a query. To avoid the ambiguity of the English term "information retrieval", it has been suggested the French term "retrouvage d'information" is used, but the latter has never been adopted.

In addition to this previous ambiguity, the two English terms, "information seeking" on one hand and "information searching" on the other hand have both been translated in French by the expression "*recherche d'information*". Even if 'to seek' and 'to search' are effectively translated by "*chercher*" in French, the two expressions refer to two different contexts, which the French translation does not take into consideration.

The term "information seeking" is used to designate the context in which a user finds him/herself at the time of choosing the sources of information he/she judges to be relevant to respond to his/her information need. The source may be a library and he/she will then choose to browse the catalog, or to go through the shelves or even ask the librarian; he/she can also choose to ask colleagues or acquaintances or even decide to use a search engine on the web or consult a specialized portal. On the contrary, "information searching" explicitly designates the context of retrieval in an

---

1. LANCASTER F. W., *Information Retrieval Systems*, 1979, p. 11.
2. LANCASTER F. W. and WARNER A. J., *Information Retrieval Today*, 1993, p. 11.

IRS and even more precisely the context of formulation of the query. At this stage of the "retrieval" process, the system has been identified and the user is engaged in the task of elaborating the query while taking into account the functional specificities of the system used (choice of appropriate keywords, respect of syntactic constraints, etc).

To avoid all ambiguity, we prefer to designate the term "information seeking" in the global context of searching and the specific context linked to the use of an IRS by "information retrieval". This distinction permits us to consider wider information practices, such as navigating the web and finding useful, relevant documents, without having researched them. This way of accessing information has been referred to as "serendipity" for a few years now and designates a mode of "retrieval" of information that is not guided by the goal.

These new information practices were developed with the explosion of the web from the middle of the 1990s which, with its billions of pages, represented a new challenge for information retrieval. The introduction of the Internet has indeed drastically modified the world of automatic document processing by increasing the number of information resources available to people in their everyday lives. The expansion and variety of information access systems (online catalogs, digital libraries, search engines, portals, etc.) has lead to a multiplication and a diversification of users and a growing heterogeneousness of information. This double evolution has not, however, modified the fundamental objective of information retrieval: locating relevant information with maximum precision.

Even if the widespread use of online search engines could let us think that they are the only tools for information access, it is important to emphasize the diversity of electronic information access systems and their complementary nature:

– online databases,

– CD-Roms,

– open access catalogs,

– digital libraries,

– question/answer systems,

– syndication and aggregation tools,

– filtering and alerting tools,

– collaborative search tools, etc.

Similarly, places like libraries, information centers or museums also play a major role regarding information access. These places cannot be considered as "systems" in the sense of IRS but constitute information sources and knowledge repositories. In these places, communication processes take place between users and these sources and repositories. As a result, the expression "information access device" seems to be more appropriate if we want to include all aspects of the information access process. Indeed, the expression refers to all kinds of places, systems, objects of mediation, technical or not, permitting to identify, locate, gather, collect and eventually process all types of information. As indicated by [GUY 06], it also refers to the existing relation between stakeholders (designers and users) and objects (information and tools) across an interface (which can eventually be a place) that enables them to meet and thus creates a system of representations.

Among these information access devices, we are more particularly interested in those that enable access to electronic information *via* retrieval, navigation, reading, consultation, annotation interfaces, etc. Various criteria help to characterize different types of information access systems:

– the nature of recorded objects (texts, images, sounds, videos, etc),

– data collection (size, thematic coverage, etc),

– the representation of information (logical and physical structure of stored information, diversity of formats),

– the access process (recourse to an intermediary or not, retrieval logic, etc),

– the modes of access to information (by formulation of queries, by navigation),

– the retrieval performance,

– the role of the information broker and of the non-technical environment,

– users (type, context of use, information need, etc.),

– personalization of functions,

– consideration of collaborative practices.

This list is not exhaustive but indicates the extreme diversity of systems and modes of access. Thus, beyond information retrieval, new information practices take place. Exceeding their status of simple receptors, users however play an active role in the production, classification, evaluation of information, notably across online annotation systems, tagging and social referencing.

Similarly, with the emergence of new modes of interaction with the document combining for example reading, annotating and writing, the search function certainly remains an important function is but no longer the only function. A practical application of this can be seen in *InkSeine,* which allows us to take electronic notes, launch searches on words and expressions, and attach the information found to the document. Furthermore we can even note that the function of "information retrieval" is increasingly directly integrated in information systems, CMS, ERP, at the level of software infrastructures (Oracle, SAP, IBM, etc.). Consequently, IRSs are just a subset of information access systems which are themselves a subgroup of information devices.

These changes show the necessity of studying electronic information access devices by taking into consideration many aspects: social, symbolic, economical, ethical, political, organizational and cultural dimensions. In the same way, we need to pay special attention to the role of the user, as well as to the professional *versus* private (or everyday information) practices, to the individuals *versus* collective practices, and finally to the problems of mediation at stake with these devices.

7.2.2. *Some terminological questions*

Studying electronic information access devices brings us to examine a twofold terminological problem. First, according to their scientific origin, researchers dealing with search engines, digital libraries, question-answer systems, etc. use a very diverse and polysemic terminology. Most of the terms such as "appropriation", "use" or "practice" are used to refer to different theoretical frameworks and realities. Secondly, as these terms have been translated from French into English, in the following sections we will discuss these words in the context of the concepts themselves in order to provide a clear theoretical background.

7.2.2.1. *The polysemic notion of "use"*

The first term in need of clarification is "use" which has two different meanings in French: "usage" and "utilization". For Yves-François Le Coadic [LEC 04]:

> "*Use* […] has a more general meaning. *Utilization* is synonymous with *practical use*. It is the action, the way of making something serve a specific end".

The term "utilization" refers to the interaction between a person and a computer and to the way an individual uses a device according to his/her own skills, cognitive style, habits, etc. The "utilization" of a device denotes the way a particular user in his/her own singularity discovers, grasps and manipulates a technical device. We do not postulate here that this user is freeing him/herself from his/her environment (private, professional, social, symbolic etc) our purpose is to underline that the studies dedicated to individual users focus on the interactive dimension. This is for example the case for studies carried out in the framework of cognitive ergonomics and psycho-cognition.

In parallel with these observations, the term "use" has a wider meaning. According to Philippe Breton and Serge Proulx [BRE 06], it is used in a sociological perspective to describe the social framework that surrounds the interactions between a user and a device. As specified by Remy Rieffel [RIE 05], the first works focusing on "user-oriented" aspects of information and communication technologies (ICT) appeared in 1980, in which researchers speak of "users" and not "utilizers". We notice a modification of perspective and a shift of theoretical framework. Works on the user no longer focus only on the cognitive dimension of the person-system interaction but on the social and symbolic dimensions. Should we consider here that studies on uses do not take into account the cognitive dimension? We do not think that the two approaches are exclusive even if it must be stated that studies within the sociology of uses very rarely consider the technical dimension of use.

Thus, even if they share the same research objects, different scientific communities coexist with diverse theoretical and methodological frameworks. Let us cite two examples illustrating this difference. In 2003, we studied the way a group of students operated the newly offered functionalities of classification and categorization of the *Exalead* search engine [IHA 03]. This work focused on a panel of 12 students divided up according to their level of expertise in cognitive psychology and their knowledge on the utilization of search engines. In this approach, we did not take into account contextual elements such as age, gender or socio-professional category. Similar research, but conducted in the field of sociology of uses, would have implied:

– to extend the scope of observation to the private and professional practices of search engines,

– to observe these practices in relation with other information access devices,

– to take into account the collective and social dimensions.

It is our belief that uses cannot be considered independently from interactions between individuals (who are historically, socially and cognitively situated) and devices. These interactions are organized within the framework of a "communication contract" resulting from the ergonomic features of the device (position of texts and images on the screen, size and type of characters, etc.) on one hand and the reading habits of the user on the other hand. As a result, uses are viewed as the expression of a process made of complex interactions relating an individual and a device, which may or may not be a technical artifact (a printed book for example). Another characteristic of the dimension of use is its stability or at least its relative stability, diachronic and synchronic at the same time. Diachronic since the use is anchored in a socio-technical reference framework (see Patrice Flichy [FLI 95]) and synchronic because it is collectively observable. We will thus speak of the uses of the Internet (see [GUI 01]) or the uses of the Public Library of the Pompidou Center or the uses of the Cité des Sciences et de l'Industrie (see [LEM 01]). This ties up with Jacques Perriault's statement [PER 89] according to which use is a "stabilized utilization of an object, tool, to obtain an effect".

We will conclude on the distinction between "utilization" and "use" by quoting again Jacques Perriault, who distinguishes three elements regarding "use":

> "first comes the project. It refers to the anticipation of what the user is going to do with the apparatus; this anticipation is more or less clear, more or less accepted, which will often be modified during the use. Second comes the apparatus proper, the instrument. The third element is the function assigned to it. There is not always a bi-univocal relation between instruments and functions"[3].

These three elements, i.e. the project, the device and the assigned function(s), clearly underscore the difference between "use" and "utilization", while insisting on taking into account the technical dimension in the study of uses. Finally, underlining the various forms of use of a similar device highlights the different types of "appropriation" of the device.

7.2.2.2. *The notion of "appropriation"*

The term "appropriation" needs to be thoroughly clarified. In English, following the definition given in the New Oxford Dictionary of English:

> "appropriation" refers to "the action of taking something for one's own use, typically without the owner's permission".

The term "appropriation" in French, and more specifically in the field of innovation theory, is defined as the capacity for an individual to negotiate the protocol of utilization as it was expressed by the designers of the device. It refers in particular to the user's freedom to adopt or to refuse to utilize certain functions, to choose those that seem best suitable to perform a task, to the possibility to assign other functions to the device than the ones offered. In the most extreme case, "appropriation" may lead to a total diversion of the device and its use as it has been initially designed.

---

3. PERRIAULT J., *La Logique de l'Usage*, 1989, p. 205.

The process of appropriation can lead either to alienation or liberation. Jean-Luc Michel[4] [MIC 92] differentiates between "technical appropriation, which is reductive" and "technological and formal appropriation which contains the seeds of liberation".

To illustrate this distinction, Jean-Luc Michel gives the example of the technical appropriation of the typewriter which is not very liberating and may cause a new alienation. He also gives the example of the technological appropriation of a word-processing software which, in some cases, may reassess the organization of work and the relations with the hierarchy. The distinction established by the author is in accord with the two classical meanings of the term "appropriation". On one hand, it makes reference to the concept of "adaptation"; it is a matter of "making something proper for a precise goal", to "conform" to a device or to a situation. On the other hand, the definition refers to taking something for our own use, usually without permission, to make something our own "property".

This last explanation is at the heart of the exertions of numerous researchers who, inspired by the works of Michel de Certeau [CER 90], insist on the capacity of users to bypass the imperatives in the device to "appropriate" it.

In this sense the modes of appropriation determine the functions of real use. As Josiane Jouët points out [JOU 00], "appropriation is a process, it is the act of creating a person's sense of self"[5].

7.2.2.3. *Distinction between behavior, use and practice*

Although the distinction between behavior, use and practice is not always clearly established in social sciences and even though numerous researchers fail to make it, it is our belief that some elements should be specified.

The term "behavior" is more frequently used in English-speaking countries than in France and may be found in the expression "information behavior" which designates the situation in which a user is implicated in a process of information access. For Tom Wilson [WIL 00], information behavior covers all of human behavior in relation to its sources and information channels. This includes active and passive information retrieval and the use of information.

It is probably because of its "behaviorist" connotation in French that "information behavior" is often translated in French as "*pratiques informationnelles*". As a matter of fact, the American Society for Information Science and Technology recently edited a book entitled *Theories of Information*

4. MICHEL J.-L., *La Distanciation*, 1992, p. 319-320.

5. JOUËT J., *Retour Critique sur la Sociologie des Usages*, 2000, p. 502.

Behavior [FIS 05], which presents over 70 different models of information behaviors and practices.

The term "behavior" is also used in microeconomics, and specifically in marketing, to characterize the attitudes of consumers, particularly during the information searching process. For Michael Solomon [SOL 99], consumer behavior:

> "is the study of the process involved when individuals or groups select, purchase, use or dispose of products, services, ideas, or experiences to satisfy needs or desires."[6]

For Josiane Jouët [JOU 93] the notion of "practice" is more comprehensive than the notion of "use" because it includes the utilization of techniques as well as the behaviors, attitudes and representations of those who have recourse to them. Unlike her, however, we do not believe the two terms are embedded. In our opinion, they are two different and complementary approaches to the same reality. We suggest keeping the term "use" to designate works focusing on devices, technical or otherwise, and their interactions with users. We will therefore speak about the uses of a search engine, the Internet, a digital or multimedia library to designate the way in which the device is used, taking into consideration the socio-professional, cultural, political, economical, etc, frameworks. The use of technical devices refers to the different professional and private contexts.

On the other hand, the term "practice" will serve to characterize the approaches centered on what we call the "composite behavior" that can be observed in the different information, cultural, journalistic, etc, spheres. The studies concerning practices, such as "information practices", imply they are centered on human aspects (whether individual or collective) in order to be able to analyze their behavior, habits, representations and attitudes. Analyzing "practices" therefore requires us to consider human action as a complex process resulting from many aspects: the individual's knowledge, abilities and cognitive skills that can be used to act, create a habitus, etc. (Habitus is a term used in Bourdieu's theory of practice [BOU 90] to roughly designate the relatively stable system of dispositions by which individuals integrate their experiences and evaluate the importance of different choices.)

The concept of "information practice" is therefore used to consider the ways people effectively interact with devices and artifacts, formal and informal information sources, needs, habits, etc, in producing, sharing, processing and researching information. Information practice may be understood as a set of socially

6. M. Solomon, G. Bamossy, S. Askegaard, *Consumer Behavior – A European Perspective*, 1999, p. 34.

and culturally established ways to identify, seek, use, share, communicate and produce available information.

Information practices are embedded in both work and personal contexts. Even if most of the studies focus its use at work, information practices also include daily information access and retrieval to solve everyday problems (such as accessing the *Yellow Pages*, train schedules or medical information on the Internet, etc).

In English, this domain is referred to as ELIS (everyday life information seeking) and has been developed since the middle of the 1990s by several researchers including which Reijo Savolainen [SAV 95, SAV 08].

7.3. Trends in information access studies

The first studies related to information access devices, and more precisely to IRSs, date from the 1950s. They successively focused on the technical approach then the user's cognitive, affective, communication, etc dimensions. However, they rarely took the socio-economical environments (the cultural and linguistic stakes, digital gap, payment for referencing websites, online advertising, etc) into account, which are now decisive factors in the use of Internet search engines.

Other aspects also need to be considered in any study on the use of information access devices:

– ethical aspects (such as the traceability of users,the e-reputation management, preservation and marketing of personal data),

– political aspects (such as the censorship in indexation of sites by engines, restricted access to the Internet in some countries),

– legal aspects (such as the respect for privacy, capability of search engines to track users, illegal access to protected digital contents, etc).

All of these aspects are now strictly related to the global information access environment because they influence and depend on the users' information behavior. Many approaches exist for studying information access systems that may be classified according to the role they give the user and his/her environment. In the following pages, we present an overview of the five approaches that have played a dominant role in the comprehension of information access process in the past and, in some cases, still do so.

7.3.1. *System-oriented approach*

The first studies related to information access devices focused on the functional analysis of systems (indexation, matching, formulation and reformulation of queries, structuring and organizing of data and information, etc), with the goal of improving their global performance. Most of these works were conducted from an evaluation perspective (comparative and/or progressive evaluation) and refer to the now well-known system-oriented approach, or to what David Ellis [ELL 92] also calls the physical paradigm.

In this approach, emphasis is put on the evaluation of the way the systems function and assumes a linear model of the information retrieval process. This retrieval process has been described by David Ellis [ELL 84] and Tefko Saracevic [SAR 96]. This approach deals with the technological aspects, particularly with the performance of research algorithms. In particular, in the past and even now efforts have focused on the matching process. All the works developed in order to improve the performance of systems are based on a triple hypothesis. First, the hypothesis that the documents retrieved by the system are supposed to satisfy the user's information need. Second, the hypothesis that the better the terms match between a query and a document, the more likely the document is to be relevant to the user. Finally, the last hypothesis is that user wants to retrieve all relevant documents in the database and no irrelevant documents.

In this approach, the efficiency of a system is measured by using recall and precision metrics (and some other measures such as the F-measure) and the major efforts of developers have been towards improving these metrics. For over 40 years, therefore, the system-oriented approach has constituted the dominant paradigm in the information retrieval field. The latter was elaborated for the evaluation campaign of indexation systems conducted in Cranfield (in the UK) by Cyril Cleverdon in 1957 and 1967. Although it was initiated in the 60s, this approach is still an important model in information retrieval, particularly with TREC[7] (Text REtrieval Conferences) evaluation campaigns and the TREC-like campaigns.

In the United States, since 1992, these campaigns have been financed by the Defense Advanced Research Projects Agency and organized by the National Institute of Science and Technology. Over the years, and despite criticism, the TREC methodology has become the reference methodology and has been generalized throughout the continents. Let us just mention the NTCIR Japanese program[8] or the European Cross-Language Evaluation Form (CLEF)[9] program.

---

7. http://trec.nist.gov accessed October 25, 2009
8. http://research.nii.ac.jp/ntcir/, accessed September 26, 2009.
9. http://www.clef-campaign.org, accessed September 26, 2009.

The increasing number of participants and the widespread adoption of the TREC methodology testify to the interest in this approach. In addition, the wide media coverage of TREC conferences and non-restrictive policy for distributing the tests corpora and evaluating software largely contribute to reinforcing the role of TREC in the community. But besides its indisputable interest, the TREC methodology raises some questions concerning both protocol and metrics, as well as some theoretical questions. In [CHA 04a] and [CHA 04b] there is a detailed presentation of the theoretical and methodological limits regarding this approach. Let us just remind readers that the main criticisms focus on:

– the evaluation protocol (mainly the building of test collections and theoretical backgrounds of the metrics modeling users' satisfaction),

– the absence of the user in the evaluation process (in particular, his/her interaction with the system),

– the problem of the representation of an information need that is too mechanical (queries are imperfect representations of information needs),

– the much simplified modeling of information practices (the mode of access to information, such as serendipity, is not taken into account), and finally

– the simplification of the notion of "relevance".

Since 1968, researchers like Robert Taylor [TAY 68] have showed that the notion of information need was much more complex than the definition commonly accepted by IRS designers, and that different levels of information need existed. Following these ideas, the issues of "information need" and "query formulation" became important as does the necessity to incorporate the user as a major element in the information retrieval process.

On the other side of the system-oriented evaluation, the user-oriented evaluation considers that attention must be paid to users' real expectations in respect to the system he/she operates and his/her environment. Although the initial interest in the user was an attempt to incorporate some behavioral characteristics to improve the performance of the systems, it gradually became a separate research domain whose specific issues were, and still are, to better understand the users' information practices.

In the "user-oriented approach", we identify four major trends that we will roughly present: the cognitive and psychological approaches, library and information science approaches, management science approaches and marketing science approaches.

7.3.2. *Models based on cognitive and psychological approaches*

In cognitive psychology, information searching is considered a secondary task serving the purpose of a more strategic activity (decision-making, problem solving, teaching, etc) [DEN 06]. In this approach, the term "information search" does not refer to the global definition of "information seeking" but is used to refer to the task of information identifying and gathering, textual exploration, content extraction and analysis, etc.

There have been several attempts to characterize hypermedia and web access in cognitive terms. Existing theories, such as information foraging [PIR 07] and construction-integration [KIN 98], and models, such as ESP [ROU 98] and CoLiDeS [KIT 00], are concerned with general cognitive processes that take place when reading a hypermedia/web document.

Proposed by Peter Pirolli, the information foraging theory assumes, for example, that people have strategies for maximizing information gain and minimizing the cost (effort) associated with that gain. Based on the text comprehension theory of Walter Kintsch [KIN 98], the CoLiDeS model (Comprehension-based Linked model of Deliberate Search) explains how users parse and understand the content and meaning of a webpage when selecting which action to perform next. Jean-François Rouet and André Tricot [ROU 98] developed a cyclic model of cognitive steps (the ESP model), which relies on the hypothesis that every information retrieval process is based on three basic stages: evaluation, selection and processing (i.e. ESP). Three cognitive management mechanisms represent the interaction between the ESP phases: planning, control and regulation.

From a methodological point of view, on most occasions the psycho-cognitive approaches in information retrieval have considered the user as an isolated individual, neglecting his/her social and cultural dimension.

One limitation of these models is the relatively narrow conceptualization and modeling of the information seeking concept.

7.3.3. *Library and information science models*

According to Donald Case [CAS 02], "the history of research on information-related human behavior demonstrates that the topic has remained salient for almost a century". Donald Case [CAS 02], Karen Fisher [FIS 05] and Iris Xie [XIE 08] among others have provided a comprehensive overview of the many models used in studying information behavior and practices.

According to [FIS 05], more than 70 models (or proposals considered as such) have been suggested over the last three decades that take into consideration users' information behavior including tasks, activities, affective, social and even cognitive dimensions.

Researchers, such as Robert Taylor [TAY 68], were interested in the notion of information need, which would subsequently be studied by Nicholas Belkin in his ASK model [BEL 80] and Brenda Dervin [DER 92] in the sense making model. These models were then enriched by Carol Khulthau [KHU 93], who included the affective dimension of information retrieval. By the end of the 70s, other researchers, such as Marcia Bates were interested in the decomposition of users' research strategies in an initially pedagogical perspective in their search tactics model.

In the 1990s, Marcia Bates [BAT 89] proposed the berry picking model, which can be considered to be one of the first approaches suggesting the inclusion of navigation in the information retrieval process. Following this model, David Ellis [ELL 97] and Gloria Leckie [LEC 96] suggested more detailed models describing the different stages of an information seeking process.

The cognitive approach to information seeking in LIS was introduced by De Mey's [DEM 80] and was popularized by different conceptual frameworks, such as Nicholas Belkin's ASK framework [BEL 80], Bryce Allen's analysis of cognitive skills, processes and styles [ALL 91] and finally Peter Ingwersen's poly-representation model [ING 96]. Peter Ingwersen and Kalervo Järvelin [ING 05], for example, pointed out the necessity of switching from an individual to a holistic cognitive viewpoint. They presented a cognitive framework for information seeking and retrieval, representing relations of information objects, information technology systems, interfaces and cognitive participants in context (their organizational, social and cultural context). These perspectives are different from the psycho-cognitive approaches described above insofar as they try to enlarge the cognitive dimension of the user to other contextual and social aspects.

Another trend that does not consider the user as an isolated individual confronted with a device but which takes into account his/her social, cultural, and linguistic context, focuses on the interpersonal and social forces between individuals during the information process. This trend is illustrated by Tom Wilson's 1996 model [WIL 96], Brenda Dervin's sense-making model [DER 92], Elfreda Chatman [CHA 99], and more recently Reijo Savolainen's everyday life model [SAV 95].

To illustrate this trend, we will discuss Tom Wilson's model [WIL 96] which, to take into consideration certain particular aspects of behavior, relies on works originating from other disciplines. The central point of the model is made up of two activating mechanisms corresponding to the “lacks” that occur between the initial situation (or the individual in his/her specific context) and information retrieval. Tom Wilson suggests the presence of diverse sources of motivation for information retrieval:

– “stress/coping theory”, which offers the chance of explaining why some needs do not necessarily imply the implementation of an effective retrieval strategy,

– the “risk/reward theory”, which helps us to understand why some sources of information are used and others not, and

– the social learning theory, which introduces the self-efficacy concept (i.e. a person can constantly adapt his/her behavior to meet the expected result).

In Tom Wilson’s opinion, information seeking is part of the human communication processes. He suggests we take into account the contextual factors that modify information behavior; such as:

– the general social environment: historical, geographical and politico-economic context,

– the demographic context: impact of demographic variables that are age, sex, socio-professional category, level of education and socio-linguistic characteristics,

– the social position of the user,

– the micro-sociological or organizational context,

– the physical and material context.

Consequently, Tom Wilson puts forward the multidimensional aspect of the informative process by drawing attention on the user and his/her context.

7.3.4. *Models from management science*

Another field is the study of information behavior within organizations (company, institution, etc) from the management sciences viewpoint. According to Anne Fiedler, Patricia B. Lash, Roman M. Wong and Tarja Tiainen [FIE 06], these studies take place in two contexts: during organizational entry (the socialization phase of a new incomer) and for managerial decision-making.

Organizational socialization is the process through which individuals acquire knowledge about the context of their work and adjust to it [ASH 07]. The process of socialization has often been operationalized as either socialization tactics (formalized means of socializing individuals) or newcomer proactive behavior (individual-driven or an informal means of “self-socializing”).

Research has shown that newcomers in organizations vary their tactics according to the type of information they are trying to obtain [GRI 00]. They use various strategies for information acquisition. Researchers have identified three information seeking behavior types: monitoring, observing by seeking signals that can be derived from an event or the behavior of others, inquiring (asking people for information) and consulting written materials. Vernon Miller and Frederic Jablin's model [MIL 91] focuses on newcomers' pro-active search for information in order to reduce the uncertainty associated with organizational socialization. On her part, Elisabeth Morrison [MOR 93] investigated several types of information that newcomers seek: referent, social, feedback, technical and normative information as it relates to the behavioral and attitudinal expectations of the organization.

In the domain of strategic scanning and business intelligence, the question of information access is also a concern, specifically for decision makers. Different models scan the information processes, such as Francis Aguilar's strategic scanning process [AGU 76] or Richard Daft's chief scanning behavior [DAF 88]. Other models in information management, in particular the one suggested by Robert Taylor and then revisited by Howard Rosenbaum ([CHO 00]), aim to articulate information-seeking and decision-making processes. To illustrate this trend, we present the environment scanning model suggested by Chun Wei Choo [CHO 00] and the informational ecology model of Thomas Davenport [DAV 97], which are similar to the informational models presented in the previous section.

Chun Wei Choo places emphasis on the individual and the group at the same time. This is the reason why he speaks of information processing within the organization. He proposes an integrated model (human information seeking: an integrated model), which contains three components: information need, information seeking and information use.

Thomas Davenport [DAV 97] on the other hand proposes an informational ecology model that distinguishes six components in the information environment of organizations:

– the definition of an information strategy,

– information governance,

– information culture and behavior,

– the information professionals' network,

– information processes, and

– architecture of information.

For these two authors, strategic business management requires us to consider information not as an object, but more as the result of a subjective construction; at this level, the cognitive, affective and situational factors play a decisive role.

7.3.5. *Models from marketing*

We conclude this overview by considering the marketing approach that researchers of consumer behavior have long been studying – how consumers search for information about products. They claim that information search behavior is the prerequisite of decision making [KOT 00]. The advent of the Internet and the proliferation of online stores have given rise to a number of studies that look at the consumer's intention to make online purchases. Researchers use the term "information search" more often than "information seeking". The information search process can either be an internal information search, which denotes information retrieval from long-term memory, or an external information search, which indicates the active information searching using outside information sources [ENG 95]. Other researchers insist on the two-fold dimensions of the commercial information searching: a pragmatic dimension in order to make the best choice, and a leisure dimension that refers to pleasure and satisfaction [BAB 94].

Consumer-oriented research specifically examines the effects of psychological characteristics, demographics, perceptions of the risks and benefits, and shopping motivation with respect to the users' choice of information sources.

Songpol Kulviwat, Chiquan Guo and Napatsawan Engchanil [KUL 04] suggested a conceptual model that allows us to study different determinants of information retrieval on the Internet. According to these authors, it is necessary to take into consideration the various components (usability, efficiency, risk perception, consumer satisfaction, user knowledge and level of education) to explain these behaviors.

7.4. Conclusion

In this chapter, we have tried to show that "information access" is similar to a "boundary object". Various researchers from different disciplines have been studying information search, information seeking and information acquisition from numerous perspectives, including consumer behavior, cognitive psychology, communication research, library and information science, management, marketing and computer science. We have tried to point out that the problem with this broadening of scope is terminological instability.

Following the first criticisms addressed in the 1980s to the techno-centered approach of the evaluation of electronic information access devices, a large diversity of models destined to understand information practices was suggested.

First of all, this diversity enabled us to consider new dimensions in the analysis of practices and structuring of a research community. Nevertheless, the very large number of these models end in such a profusion that it is legitimate to question the status of modeling in this domain, and more generally in social sciences.

Other questions may be also addressed. One such question deals with the difficulty in comparing the various models. They do not operate at the same levels of analysis. Some of them, such as the cognitive models, are interested in the micro-level (characteristics of the user, cognitive styles, level of expertise, teaching, tactics, tasks, etc) whereas others consider the social and cultural dimensions and may be viewed as macro-level models.

A second question addresses the "mechanical" character of some of those models; the widespread use of diagrams to make us realize that dynamic and multidimensional information processes do not really explain the sophistication and complexity of information practices. Why do people do what they do and when they do so? Whatever the visual appearance of these diagrams, the models suggested most often boil down to sequences of actions or steps that oversimplify the reality of human action.

We may also doubt the explicative and predictive power of the models and their ability to efficiently represent the information process. Even if their attempts to take into account the dynamics of information access, the diverse abilities, styles and skills are noticeable, the models seem rigid. Whereas the researchers' observations show that information behaviors and practices are multidimensional, the proposed models seem to be incapable of grasping the real practices of users.

Consequently, the operational character of the models is not really established. Theoretically, modeling should allow us to identify the variables that intervene in behavior, the role they play, and their balance. Yet in reality this is rarely the case.

Finally, many methodological questions are also asked. In particular, a large methodological variability exists that directly influences the results of data analysis and poses interpretation problems. The method chosen to collect data influences the analysis of users. The choice of method is therefore not neutral and depends on the objectives of analysis, which are more or less explicit.

Faced with these deep evolutions, no isolated approach can pretend to "exhaust" the study of information access. Only "crossed approaches" allow us to work towards a better understanding of information practices and the uses of electronic information access devices.

7.5. Bibliography

[AGU 76] F.-J. AGUILAR, *Scanning the Business Environment*, MacMillan, New York, 1967.

[ALL 91] B. Allen, "Cognitive research in information science: Implications for design", *Annual Review of Information Science and Technology*, Martha E. WILLIAMS (ed.), vol. 26, p. 3-37, 1991.

[ASH 07] B. E. ASHFORTH, D. M. SLUSS, A. M. SAKS, "Socialization Tactics, Proactive Behavior, and Newcomer Learning: Integrating Socialization Models", *Journal of Vocational Behavior*, no. 70, 2007, p. 447-462.

[BAB 94] B.J. BABIN, W.R. DARDEN, M. GRIFFIN, "Work and fun: measuring hedonic and utilitarian shopping value", *Journal of Consumer Research*, vol. 20, no. 4, p. 127-140, 1994.

[BAT 89] M.J. BATES, "The design of browsing and berry picking techniques for the online search interface", *Online Review*, vol. 13, p 407-424, 1989.

[BEL 80] N.J. BELKIN, "Autonomous states of knowledge as a basis for information retrieval", *The Canadian Journal of Information Science*, vol. 5, p. 133-43, 1980.

[BOU 90] P. BOURDIEU, *The Logic of Practice*, Polity Press, Cambridge, 1990.

[BRE 06] P. BRETON, S. PROULX, *L'Explosion de la Communication. Introduction aux Théories et aux Pratiques de la Communication*, La Découverte, Paris, 2006.

[CAS 02] D. CASE, *Looking for Information: A Survey of Research on Information Seeking, Needs, and Behavior*, New York: Academic Press/Elsevier Science, 2002.

[CER 90] M. CERTEAU DE, *L'Invention du Quotidien. Tome 1 – Les Arts de Faire*, Gallimard, 1990.

[CHA 99] E. A. CHATMAN, "A theory of life in the round", *Journal of the American Society for Information Science*, vol. 50, no 3, p. 207-217, 1999.

[CHA 04a] S. CHAUDIRON, "L'évaluation des systèmes de recherche d'informations", in: M. Ihadjadene (ed), *Les Systèmes de Recherche d'Informations: Modèles Conceptuels*, Hermès, Paris, 2004.

[CHA 04b] S. CHAUDIRON, "La place de l'usager dans l'évaluation des systèmes de recherche d'informations", in: S. CHAUDIRON (ed), *Evaluation des Systèmes de Traitement de l'Information,* Hermès, Paris, 2004.

[CHO 00] C. CHOO, B. DETLOR, D. TURBULL, *Web Work: Information Seeking and Knowledge Work on the World Wide Web*, Kluwer Academic publishers, Norwell (MA), 2000.

[DAF 88] R. L. DAFT., J. SORMUNE, O. PARKS, "Chief executive scanning, environmental characteristics and company performance: an empirical study", *Strategic Management Journal*, vol. 9, p.123-139, 1988.

[DAV 97] T. H. DAVENPORT, *Information Ecology: Mastering the Information and Knowledge Environmen*, Oxford University Press, New York, 1997.

[DEM 80] M. DE MEY, "The relevance of the cognitive paradigm for information science", *Theory and Application of Information Research*, Ole Harbo (ed.), London, Mansell, p. 48-61, 1980.

[DEN 06] C. DEDENCKER, E. KOLMAYER, *Eléments de Psychologie Cognitive pour les Sciences de l'Information*, The ENSSIB Press, Villeurbanne, 2006.

[DER 92] B. DERVIN, "From the mind's eye of the user: The sense-making qualitative-quantitative methodology", in: D.J. GLAZIER , R.R. POWELL (eds), *Qualitative Research in Information Management*, Libraries Unlimited, Englewood. p. 61-84, 1992.

[ELL 84] D. ELLIS, "Theory and explanation in information retrieval research", *Journal of Information Science*, vol. 8, p. 25-38, 1984.

[ELL 92] D. ELLIS, "The physical and cognitive paradigm in information retrieval research", *Journal of Documentation*, vol. 48, no. 1, p. 45-64, 1992.

[ELL 97] D. ELLIS, M. HAUGAN, "Modelling the information seeking patterns of engineers and research scientists in an industrial environment", *Journal of Documentation*, vol. 53, no. 4, p. 384-403, 1997.

[ENG 95] J. F. ENGEL, R. D. BLACKWELL, P. W. MINIARD, *Consumer Behavior*, Hindsale, The Dryden Press, 1995.

[FIE 06] A. M. FIEDLER, P. B. LASH, R. M. WONG, T. TIAINEN, "The impact of individual employee difference on information seeking in today's information rich information-seeking behaviors environment", Paper presented at the *International Consortium for Electronic Business (ICEB) conference*, 2006. Available at: http://www.ebrc.fi/kuvat/Fiedler_Lash_Wong_Tiainen.pdf, accessed October 25 2009

[FIS 05] K. FISHER, S. ERDELEZ, L. MCKECHNIE (eds), *Theories of Information Behavior*, ASIST, Information Today Inc., 2005.

[FLI 95] P. FLICHY, *L'innovation Technique. Récents Développements en Sciences Sociales. Vers une Nouvelle Théorie de l'Innovation*, La Découverte, Paris, 1995.

[GRI 00] A. GRIFFIN, A. COLELLA, S. GOPARAJU, "Newcomer and organizational socialization tactics: An interactionist perspective", *Human Resources Management Review*, vol. 10, no 4, p. 453-474, 2000.

[GUI 01] E. GUICHARD (ed.), *Comprendre les Usages de l'Internet*, Editions Rue d'Ulm, Paris, 2001.

[GUY 06] B. GUYOT, *Dynamiques Informationnelles dans les Organisations*, Hermès, Paris, 2006.

[IHA 03] M. IHADJADENE, S. CHAUDIRON, D. MARTINS "The effect of individual differences on searching the web", *Proceedings of the 66th Annual Meeting of the American Society for Information Science and Technology*, p. 240-246, 2003.

[ING 96] INGWERSEN, P. "Cognitive perspectives of information-retrieval interaction - elements of a cognitive IR theory", *Journal of Documentation*, vol. 52, no. 1, p. 3-50, 1996.

[ING 05] INGWERSEN P., JARVELIN K., *The Turn: Integration of Information Seeking and Retrieval in Context*, Springer Verlag, New York, 2005.

[JOU 00] J. JOUET, "Retour critique sur la sociologie des usages", *Communiquer à l'ère des Réseaux*, Réseaux vol 100, Hermès, Paris, 2000, p. 489-521.

[JOU 93] J. JOUET, "Pratiques de communication et figures de la médiation", *Réseaux*, vol. 60, Hermès, Paris, 1993, p. 99-120.

[KIN 98] W. KINTSCH, *Comprehension: A paradigm for cognition*, New York, Cambridge University Press, 1998.

[KIT 00] M. KITAJIMA M. H. BLACKMON, P. POLSON, "A Comprehension-based Model of Web Navigation and Its Application to Web Usability Analysis", in S. McDonald, Y. Waern & G. Cockton (eds.), *People and Computers XIV - Usability or Else!* (Proceedings of HCI 2000), Springer, p. 357-37, 2000.

[KOT 00] P. KOTLE, P. FILIATRAULT, R. TURNER, *Marketing Management*, Edition Gaëtan Morin, Montréal, 2000.

[KUL 93] C. KHULTHAU, *Seeking Meaning: a Process Approach to Library and Information Services*, Ablex Pub. Corp., Norwood, 1993.

[KUL 04] S. KULVIWAT, C. GU., N. ENGCHANIL, "Determinants of online information search: a critical review and assessment", *Internet Research*, vol. 14, no. 3, p. 245-253, 2004.

[LAN 79] F. W. LANCASTER, *Information Retrieval Systems: Characteristics, Testing and Evaluation*, John Wiley, New York, 1979.

[LAN 93] F. W. LANCASTEr, A. J. WARNER, *Information Retrieval Today*, Information Ressources Press, 1993.

[LEC 96] G. J. LECKIE, K. E. PETTIGREW, C. SYLVAIN, "Modeling the information seeking of professionals: a general model derived from research on engineers, health care professionals, and lawyers", *Library Quarterly*, vol. 66, no. 2, p. 161-193, 1996.

[LEC 04] Y.-F. LE COADIC, *Usages et Usagers de l'Information*, Coll. 128, Armand Colin, Paris, 2004.

[LEM 01] J. LE MAREC, "L'analyse des usages en construction: quelques points de méthode", in: E. Guichard (ed), *Comprendre les Usages de l'Internet*, Editions Rue d'Ulm, Paris, 2001, p. 146-155.

[MAN 04] J. MANIEZ, *Actualités des Langages Documentaires*, ADBS, Paris, 2004.

[MIC 92] J.-L. MICHEL, *La Distanciation. Essai sur la Société Médiatique*, L'Harmattan, Paris, 1992.

[MIL 91] V. D. MILLER, F. M. Jablin, "Information seeking during organizational entry: influences, tactics, and a model of the process", *Academy of Management Review*, vol. 16, no. 1, p. 92-120, 1991.

[MOE 48] C. MOERS, Application of random codes to the gathering of statistical information, Masters thesis, MIT, 1948.

[MOR 93] E. W. Morrison, "Longitudinal study of the effects of information seeking on newcomer socialization", *Journal of Applied Psychology*, vol. 78, no. 2, p. 173-183, 1993.

[PER 89] J. PERRIAULT, *La Logique de l'Usage. Essai sur les Machines à Communiquer*, Flammarion, Paris, 1989.

[PIR 07] P. PIROLLI, *Information Foraging Theory: Adaptive Interaction with Information*, New York, Oxford University Press, 2007.

[RIE 05] R. RIEFFEL, *Sociologie des Médias*, Ellipses Marketing, Paris, 2005.

[ROU 98] J.-F. ROUET, A. TRICOT, "Chercher de l'information dans un hypertexte: vers un modèle des processus cognitifs", in: A. Tricot, J.-F. Rouet (eds), *Les Hypermédias: Approches Cognitives et Ergonomiques*, Hermès, Paris, 1998, p. 57-74.

[SAR 96] T. SARACEVIC, "Modeling interaction in information retrieval (IR): A review and proposal", *Proceedings of the Annual Meeting of the American Society for Information Science*, vol. 33, p. 3-9, 1996.

[SAV 95] R. SAVOLAINEN, "Everyday life information seeking: approaching information seeking in the context of way of life", *Library & Information Science Research*, vol. 17, no. 3, p. 259-294, 1995.

[SAV 08] R. SAVOLAINEN, *Everyday Information Practices: A Social Phenomenological Perspective,* The Scarecrow Press, 2008.

[SOL 99] M. SOLOMON, G. BAMOSSY, S. ASKEGAARD, *Consumer Behavior – A European Perspective*, 4th ed., Prentice Hall Europe, 1999.

[TAY 68] R. TAYLOR, "Question negotiation and information seeking in libraries", *College and Research Libraries*, vol. 29, p. 178-194, 1968.

[WIL 96] T.D WILSON., *Information Behavior: an Interdisciplinary Perspective. A Report to the British Library Research and Innovation Centre*, London, British Library Research and Innovation Centre, 1996. Available at: http://informationr.net/tdw/publ/infbehav/chap7.html, accessed September 26, 2009.

[WIL 00] T.D WILSON, "Human information behavior", *Informing Science*, vol. 3, no. 2, p. 49-55, 2000.

[XIE 08] I. Xie, *Interactive information retrieval in digital environments*, Hershey, IGI Pub, 2008.

Chapter 8

Relevant Information in Economic Intelligence

8.1. Introduction

Information retrieval always depends on the knowledge we have of the information sought and their final uses. Based on the content-based search principle, the knowledge we have on information sought will be translated and used for specifying information needs, often in the form of search equation.

This principle applies no matter the search agent (a human being or a search robot) and no matter the source of information (formal source – Internet, database, etc – or informal source – human networks for example). The principle does not permit directly specifying the final uses of information sought because these uses are not taken into consideration in the description of documents. Furthermore it is the knowledge of the final use of information that enables the evaluation of its relevance.

In this chapter we will provide a summary of the way in which the concept of relevance is studied up to today and we will present the concept of economic intelligence to better grasp the complexity of the concept of relevance in this framework. As we think that the problems involved with the relevance information cannot be limited to search equations, we will present approaches originating from

---

Chapter written by Amos DAVID.

research studies in progress on the relevance of information in economic intelligence. These approaches concern new approaches for the representation of documents as well as new functionalities of information retrieval systems.

8.2. Current approaches of information relevance

Interest in information relevance is not new because it was largely dealt with in the study of information retrieval systems (IRS), particularly in the domain of documentation. As shown in Figure 8.1 – the rate of relevance, recollection and noise – are among the commonly used measures for measuring the efficiency of the IRS. They refer to the concept of relevance of documents, where the term "document" signifies the container as well as the contents, a document containing information. The knowledge on what we are looking for focuses on the container as well as on the contents.

relevance ratio:

$$\frac{\text{(number of relevant documents found)}}{\text{(number of documents found)}}$$

recall ratio:

$$\frac{\text{(number of relevant documents found)}}{\text{(number of existing relevant documents)}}$$

noise ratio:

$$\frac{\text{(number of non-relevant documents found)}}{\text{(number of documents found)}}$$

Figure 8.1. *Examples of IRS performance ratios*

In these ratios, the measure of the efficiency of IRS concerns the difference between documents found (relevant or non-relevant) and existing documents (relevant or non-relevant). This is why the proposals to make the IRS more efficient based on these indicators are focused on the process of mapping the user's query and the documents. A strong assumption on which these propositions are founded is that the user's query expresses his/her informational need.

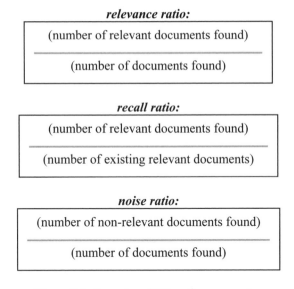

Thus we find approaches to improve the mapping and formulation of queries – vectoral search, relevance feedback, fuzzy search, statistics, linguistics, etc., which are based on query and document descriptions.

Historically, the first IRSs were documentary systems and databases. In the domain of documentation, the users' objective was to find where a document is located in a document resource center or simply to find out whether the document exists. Thus, the description of documents is focused on the indexation of documents (the properties of documents, their localization and the information contained in the documents, notably by keywords).

However, the technological advancement, which not only makes it possible to obtain descriptive information on the documents but also to have access to the contents of documents, introduced evolution of the objective. The user's objective is now not only to find the location of documents but also to gain access to the whole contents of these documents and be able to carry out analyses on the informational contents. It is this last evolution which establishes the convergence of the needs on databases and the IRS in the field of documentation. The technological evolution, in particular the Internet, allows the widening of the documentary sources where the care to index is no longer as controlled as in the documentary bases of the document resource centers.

Regarding databases, they were designed from well-identified data and were often well structured. The access needs were identified and the access interfaces adapted to these needs. Furthermore, the types of use of results obtained on the databases also advanced the following the technological evolution, in particular the progress that concerns the capacity of storage, which in turn permits the integration of heterogeneous and voluminous data. Hence, the organizations can manage internal as well as external data. The needs are no longer limited to simple accesses but to the analysis of the results obtained. The most current example is the need to cross-analyze information.

Thus the need to analyze information in the domain of documentation as in the organizations is evloving towards the analysis of results. But we must note that the analyses can only be made if the indicators for these analyses were well-identified. And that is what shows the limit of the approaches of relevance that are based uniquely on the contents.

For a very long time librarians have known that a similar query formulated by two different people does not necessarily correspond to a similar need, and that a query formulated by the same person at different moments does not necessarily mean a similar need. These observations show that relevance, even in the field of documentation, cannot be limited to query and document descriptions, but concern the users and the final use of results. To sum up, we see that relevance must integrate the user, information and uses of this information. These three elements make up the basic elements of any economic intelligence (EI) project.

In EI, where the main objective concerns strategic decision taking, the relevance of information will only be measured as a function of its contribution to solving the decision problem. To better grasp the specificity of the concept of relevance in EI, we give some definitions of EI as well as problems associated with it in the following section.

8.3. Economic intelligence

Many definitions were suggested for EI, of which the following are two of them [CAR 03].

It is a set of coordinated search actions, processing and distribution of useful information for exploitation by economic actors. These actions are legally carried out with the necessary protection guarantee for protecting the organization's patrimony [MAR 94].

It is the process of collection, processing and distribution of information with the aim of reducing the level on uncertainty in strategic decision making [REV 98]. The concepts found in all EI definitions are: decision-maker, decision problem, information and protection of the material and immaterial heritage.

To better understand the problems associated with EI, the concept can be considered as a process, composed of the following phases:

a) identification of a decision-problem;

b) translation of a decision-problem into an information retrieval problem;

c) identification of relevant sources of information;

d) collection of relevant information;

e) the collected information for the extraction of decision making;

f) interpretation of tables;

g) decision making.

The following problems can be identified from this process:

1. Problems linked to the decision-making process that cover phases (a, f, and g), of which the participants are mainly the decision-makers. Here, the interest focuses

on the comprehension of the decision-problem by the decision-maker as well as by the person who will be in charge of the information retrieval to solve the decision-problem.

2. Problems linked to the process of information collection that cover phases (b, c, d, e) of which the participants are the watchers, organization personnel, and information systems developers. Here, the interest relates to necessary competences to achieve the research activities of information to solve the decisional problem.

3. Problems linked to the protection of information heritage that cover all the phases, of which the participants are the decision-makers, watchers, organization personnel and the information systems developers. Here, the interest focuses on the knowledge of precautions to take in order to safeguard the material and immaterial heritages of the organization.

4. Problems linked to the use of information as a positive or negative weapon of influence, of which the participants are mainly decision-makers and watchers. Here, interest focuses on the fact that a decision often has consequences on the external environment of the organization and the decision-problem often originates in the observation of external phenomena of the organization. It is necessary be competences in influential techniques in order to identify the decision-problems or to facilitate the implementation of decisions taken.

In EI we see that information relevance can only be measured in relation to its contribution to solving the decision-problem. A piece of relevant information is therefore not necessarily the one that best responds to other types of expression of information need, such as the oral interview or questionnaires.

8.4. Relevance indicators in EI

We present in the following sections two key indicators that permit the measuring of relevance of information in EI – the knowledge of the decision-problem and its translation in information retrieval problems. Actually, all the other phases of the process depend on this knowledge and competence.

8.4.1. *Knowledge of the decision-problem*

The first indicator concerns the knowledge of the decision-problem by the decision-maker (the one who formulates the problem) as well as by the one who will be in charge of information retrieval to solve it – called the watcher.

Any EI project, i.e. information retrieval to be used for strategic decision taking, begins with the identification of the decision-problem. This stage is the responsibility of the decision maker [DAV 01]. The complexity of this phase is presented in [BOU 04] because the transformation of a stake into a decision-problem is not always rational. Yet it is the level of expressivity of this knowledge on which all the other phases of the process depend.

As the retrieval of information necessary to solve this problem is often sub-contracted to a third party, the precise specification of the decision problem is indispensible. Furthermore another fundamental problem is attached to the complexity – the problem of trust between the decision-maker and the one in charge of information retrieval. Indeed, most limits of the success of an EI project sub-contracted to consultants are manifested by this problem. What can be given to the subcontractor while protecting the intellectual heritage of the organization? Does the decision-maker feel like saying everything or can he/she say everything?

Thus it is indispensible to have the definition of the decision-problem as explicit as possible in order to be able to measure the relevance of information gathered for its resolution.

A model of specification of a decision-problem was proposed by [BOU 04] in his thesis in order to facilitate the activities of the one in charge of information retrieval – the watcher – and to help the decision-maker to better understand his/her decision-problem. This model suggests a representation of a decision-problem by:

– information on the decision-maker;

– the stake associated with the problem, defined by the object of the stake, the signal and the associated hypotheses;

– information on the internal and external environment of the organization.

The watcher's activities begin with the transformation of this problem into information retrieval problems.

A model for the specification of a problem of the watcher's information retrieval was suggested by [KIS 07] and completed by the specification model of expressions of an information need of [GOR 06].

8.4.2. *Knowledge of the information problem*

As we can see, already for the specification of the decision-problem and its translation into an information retrieval problem, three theses were produced to try to understand how to model them. That shows the complexity of the relevance of information in EI. The results of these studies are used for the specification of functional requirements of information retrieval. For example, in the framework of their information retrieval projects for organizations, Master's students in EI at Nancy 2 University in France, employ this methodology for better understanding the decisional problems in order to better determine the relevance of collected information. As expected, however, students encountered difficulties in determining the true objective of the demands because some of the decision-makers do not want to reveal their strategies because they do not have enough confidence in the students. Nevertheless, decision-makers cannot contest the information supplied if they correspond to the specification of the functional requirements, itself, is based on what the decision-maker agreed to contribute as specification of his/her decision-problem.

The phase of information retrieval implies the identification of relevant sources of information. The experiences of the watcher, translated into competences, are going to be necessary for this phase. The main problem of this phase is to know how to identify relevant sources from the specification of the decision-problem. Actually, the sources of information strongly condition the relevance of information.

For the piloting of an organization, two types of information are usually used: the information from open sources and the information from information bases previously filtered, structured and formatted. These two categories of sources of information and the problems associated are presented in the two following sections.

8.4.2.1. *Open sources*

In the framework of information systems that exploit open sources, the provision of information is at the initiative of the provider. The users use the available information for some and often varied needs. The objectives of the providers and users are not necessarily the same. Thus, there is a high probability that the information deposited does not correspond exactly to that which users need. This is why it is necessary to first identify the relevant sources and then extract the relevant information. The lack of correspondence between the objective of the provider and the objective of the user explains in large part the difficulty of information systems that exploit the open sources for obtaining relevant information.

The functionalities of a IRS that exploits this type of source are essentially of the exploration type, because there is a need to first discover what the sources offer as well as potentials of use of information contained. The exploration can be expressed by hypertext navigations or by alert systems. It is also possible to carry out full-text searches by specifying the keywords that we wish to have in the proposed documents. It is rather rare to be able to specify attributes of the documents in which we wish to see the keywords as values, because the documents are not structure in the form of attribute-values. For example, a search engine like Google does not permit searching for an article specifically by name of author, title, year of publication, etc. Of course, it is possible to specify the values of these attributes but the engine will search for the values in the whole document because documents are not structured as value-attributes.

For an information retrieval for a decision taking project, we must therefore hope that the information proposed by the open sources will correspond in form and in content to the decision-problem.

In order to get around the gap between the proposed information and the decision-problem, annotation tools are suggested more and more in order to be able to re-qualify (or restructure) the information from open sources in relation to a decision-problem. Despite the enormous progress of classification tools and synthesis of information indexed as potentially relevant by linguistic methods, statistical or other methods, the problem of correspondence between the decision-problem to be solved and the information suggested persists.

8.4.2.2. *Preformatted information bases*

Instead of using the information freely deposited by voluntary depositors, some information bases are made up of information that was previously selected, sorted treated to structure and format them. This initial information can come from open sources. The difference here is that information will have been selected because of its final usefulness. Thus, the contents and structuring of information, are thought and established according to final uses.

In IRS that exploit this type of source of information, taking into account the fact that information is structured, expressions of requirement in information are made more precise. The user will be able to specify the values associated with the information attributes.

Nevertheless, there are still two problems. The first problem concerns the fact that retrieval is always based on content-based principle. Without a minimum knowledge of what we are looking for, it is not possible to find the information. For example, at least the value of one of the attributes of documents available must be specified. The second problem concerns the fact that the attributes of documents do not take into account some possible uses. One of the causes of this phenomenon is that the designer of the base probably ignored some uses. But we must know that even if the designer integrated the exhaustiveness of the uses listed at the moment of the development of the system, it is possible that the environment of the organization entertains new uses (or new needs). Thus, the problem of the evolution of information structures is posed and constitutes a scientific research object [AFO 07].

The functionalities that are found in the systems of this category are the functionalities of multicriteria research and the synthesis of information by cross-analyzing the attributes. These systems are very useful for bibliographic type applications, permitting bibliometric studies. For example, these systems permit the verification of the evolutions of works on some concepts, knowing who works on what concept, knowing who works with whom, etc.

In order for this type of system to be usage oriented, there is a need to have two levels of information filtering:

– The first filtering concerns the extraction of information from open sources (heterogeneous in form and in content). The result is generally a unique base that will be used by an information system of the second category, containing structured and formatted information. This base corresponds to a warehouse of information.

– The second filtering concerns the partitioning of the information base into more specialized bases. These derived bases make up the data marts. The specialization can be based on the roles of the end-users of the system.

Like the bibliographic bases, it is possible for the user to undergo multidimensional analyses, i.e. the cross-analysis of information.

8.5. Towards integrated functionalities in IRS

We showed that information retrieval activities are presented in forms of diverse functionalities on the IRS – exploration, multicriteria search, multicriteria analyses and annotation. These functionalities are not often available simultaneously.

As it is a question of using the information system to help with the resolution of a decisional problem, the SITE research team of the Lorrain Laboratory of Computer Science and its Applications suggested a functional model to facilitate the process of solving a decision-problem using IRS. Since information depends on the final uses and that according to the user, the functionalities suggested are user-oriented. Thus, the relevance of information will no longer be based only on the expression of search equations but based on the end use of the information and the type of activity.

The functionalities are based on studies in cognitive psychology. They permit the participants of the EI process (the decision-maker, the watcher and the personnel of the organization) to evolve in the four cognitive phases encountered in a problem-solving process. All the functionalities should be available on an information system for EI. The proposed EQuA^{2}te model is based on the four phases: exploration, query, analysis and annotation, with the functionalities presented below:

– *To explore the data warehouse, i.e. to navigate in the data*; the hypertext system well illustrates this functionality. For an information system applied to the EI, it will be a matter of navigation by attributes of system data. For example, by clicking on an attribute of the documents, the system will give all the values of the attribute, a form of list or index. And from this list, the user will be able to obtain the whole of a document or the information. We note that this functionality can help the watcher, as well as the decision-maker, to better understand the decision-problem.

– *To query the data warehouse, i.e. to search using the content-based principle, in the form of multicriteria searches.* The documentary systems and most search engines use this approach for information retrieval. The major inconvenience is that the degree of relevance of information depends on the level of knowledge of the use on the information the user is looking for as well as on their competence specifying the values of the attributes.

– *To analyze all the system data to produce distributions, tendencies, etc emerge.* The quality of the analysis will obviously depend on the degree of transforming the decision-problem into indicators. Analyses will not be possible for the attributes that are not integrated into the system.

– *To annotate the solutions suggested for contextualizing them according to personal criteria.* This functionality makes it possible to adapt the system by the information contents to individual characteristics.

To further illustrate the concept of relevance for EI, we present in the following section another possible way to grasp the watcher's process as it is currently practiced.

8.6. Watching process and EI

Any information retrieval activity is doomed to fail if the context of use of this information is not well specified before beginning the search. In the information and communication sciences domain, the effort has, up to today, been devoted to watch systems, i.e. tools that facilitate the tasks of gathering of information, whether in a momentary or recurrent way. The schema adopted to this day for the use of watch tools for decision-problem solving is illustrated in Figure 8.2.

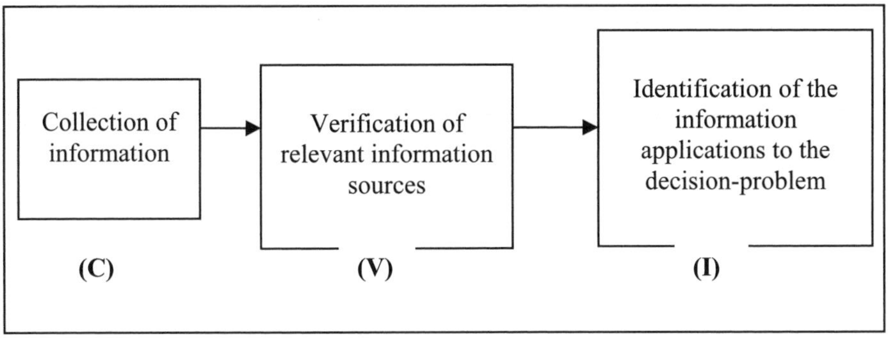

Figure 8.2. *Strategic watch tools for EI in CVI schema*

Collection of information is made by the formulation of research equations on the information collection tools search. Furthermore, as the information retrieval tools function using the content-based principle, the less we know the context of use the less relevant the responses will be. Unfortunately, even if we know the context of use, the information system is capable of providing inadequate means of expression.

We think that it is indispensable to properly understand the decision-problem in order to be able to determine the relevance of information that will be necessary for its resolution.

We suggest that the stages in the schema in Figure 8.2 be reversed, which will become the schema in Figure 8.3.

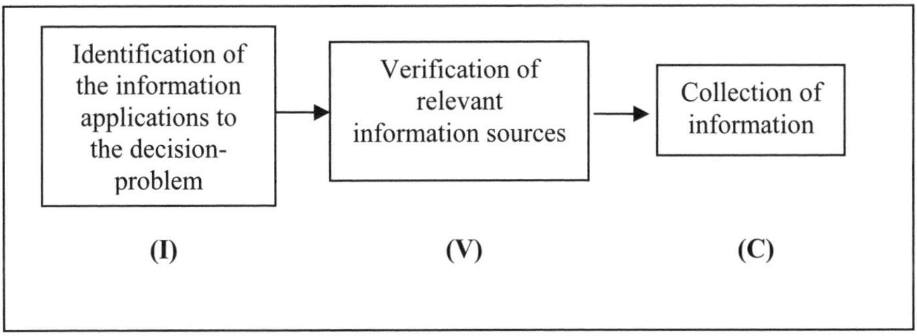

Figure 8.3. *Watch tools for EI in IVC schema*

Thus, instead of verifying the sources of information, their relevance and their potential uses after having gathered them, we suggest beginning by defining the decision-problem as explicitly as possible.

We think that all these efforts of modeling and integration of functionalities can be further exploited by mutualizing the competences of participants of the EI process. This is why the SITE research team works on the concept of collaborative information retrieval. This approach is founded on the principle of knowledge sharing.

8.7. Towards collaborative information retrieval

To better illustrate our proposals, we will present the types of knowledge that are necessary for collaboration and how to implement the collaborations. The four first sections present the different types of knowledge implemented in a process of information retrieval.

8.7.1. *Information base of the domain*

Let us recall the great principles of databases on which information systems rely: the conception of a database must guarantee the integrity of the data and reduce redundancies. However, these principles are called into question because of the integration of the criteria of evolution of the environment. For example, the user can feel the need to integrate new attributes that had not been identified during the process conception or that are introduced as a result of the evolution of the environment. Also, new types of exploitation might appear, notably the need to historicize information. This means that we can no longer delete information but make them evolve by archiving.

The data warehouse approaches enable the integration of the need to historicize data but do not solve the problem of evolution of information. In fact this last problem is due to the fact that the methodology of conception is linked only to the needs identified at the time of conception. Furthermore, these needs evolve according to the evolution of the environment and the users' needs. This phenomenon is more pronounced in the EI context: we live in an increasingly evolutionary world. The possibility of taking into account the evolution of the requirements in information even after the design is studies in the research field of annotation [ROB 07]. This methodology enables users to integrate new attributes and new values [AFO 07].

The information base of the domain of application contains the factual information of the domain. We can take as an example a bibliographic database that contains bibliographic references of a scientific domain. When a bibliographic database is designed, we specify the list of attributes to represent a scientific publication: title, author, date of publication, list of keywords, etc. The documentary base contains these attributes and the values associated for each publication.

8.7.2. *Domain knowledge base*

Although the information base represents factual information, the knowledge base of the domain represents the knowledge (or concepts) of the domain of application independently of the facts noticed. For example, we can use a thesaurus to represent the concepts used as keywords or the structure of a research laboratory.

The information base of the domain and the knowledge base of the domain are directly linked to the domain of application. This means that indispensable to take into account not only of the knowledge of the domain but also of the knowledge on the users.

8.7.3. *User's experiences*

The utility to memorize the experiments is not longer shown. Three main reasons for memorizing experiences are:

– to find a solution already obtained for a similar problem in order to accelerate the solution;

– to use experiences to avoid past errors;

– to memorize experiences in order to share them with other people.

Some experiences are easy to represent and store. For example, the storage of Internet sites visited can be easily done by bookmarking them by using attributes of the description of this page. Thus the navigators currently enable searching in bookmarks (the case of solutions/experiences of solutions) by specifying values for the attributes.

A first type of collaborative information retrieval is to share these bookmarks with collaborators.

Some problems are posed for the representation of experiences. Some experiences are very difficult to represent. Taking the example of webpage bookmarks, we notice that only the final page is stored. It is more difficult to represent how we arrive at this site. If the site was located through navigation by following hypertext links, the user will have difficulty in indicating all the links followed until the result, and still more difficultly showing the criteria that guided him/her in this course. Furthermore these last experiences (the reasons of following a course by hypertext links) are very useful for another user who would be confronted to a similar problem.

In the same way, the use of a search engine presents the same types of difficulty: why the search equation? What criteria are used to choose the site from amonst hundreds of thousands? etc.

Two approaches of solution are suggested for the acquisition of knowledge on the experiences of a user in information retrieval.

8.7.3.1. *Implicit approach*

By this approach, all the activities of the user are represented (texts selected, sites visualized, search equations) [KIS 07]. This approach has the advantage of liberating the user of the task of recording his/her activities. The major inconvenience concerns the incapacity to represent the reasons why these activities.

8.7.3.2. *Explicit approach*

This approach combines the implicit approach by completing it with the specification of reasons of these activities by the user him/herself. This approach allows a better understanding of the reasons that brought the user to undergo the operations. Nevertheless, it remains an important problem that concerns the diversity of reasons that can bring a user to undergo similar activities – the large volume of information generated and the difficulty for an optimal exploitation of the large volume of information.

We have chosen to use the approach of data warehouses for the representation and the management of these different types of knowledge. Some results were tested in the frameworks of European projects and others in progress for the exploitation of bibliographic bases.

8.7.4. *Knowledge of decision-problems*

One of the experiences that can be stored in an EI process focuses on decision-problems. Even if we know that two decision-problems are never identical, these decision-problems can share common some elements. It is on this aspect of the decision-problem that Najoua Bouaka's thesis [BOU 04] focuses: how to explain (or describe) the decision-problem of the decision-maker.

We can understand that the more refined the description of an object, the greater the degree of similarity with another object. Thus Najoua Bouaka suggests representing a decision-problem by parameters that will be more adapted for the comparison of two decision-problems. According to her, a decision-problem can be represented by the description of the stake (the object of the environment, the level of the signal of the object and the hypotheses associated in the form of gains and losses). Other parameters include:

– the identity of a decision-maker;

– his function in the organization and some psychological attributes;

– the description of the internal environment of the organization;

– the description of the external environment of the organization to better understand the origin of the decision-problem; and

– to better evaluate the extent of a decision.

As we indicated before, the value of a piece of information cannot be dissociated from its contribution to the resolution of a decision-problem. Thus, the relevance of a piece of information can be better evaluated with the good comprehension of the decision-problem.

We suggest in the framework of our studies representing and storing the decision-problems. The basis of decision-problems can be shared by a group of decision-makers or by a group of organizations that are in collaboration and which have enough confidence between them. Even if two decision-problems are never identical, the information that a decision-problem generates can serve to partially solve another. Thus through the sharing experiences in the formulation of the decision-problems, we contribute to solving problems linked to the decision-problems and to the process of information retrieval.

8.7.5. *Knowledge of the information problem*

Some propositions were put forward for the transformation of the decision-problem into information retrieval problems by Philippe Kislin [KIS 07]. Philippe Kislin proposes to represent knowledge which guided the transformation of a decision-problem into information retrieval problems. He also suggests representing information retrieval activities of this identified information retrieval problems as well as the solutions obtained in order to associate them to the decision-problem. We can also cite the thesis of Stéphane Goria on the specification of information retrieval problems in the context of task delegation [GOR 06].

Thus, not only do we have a collection of decision-problems, but we also have the associated information retrieval problems as well as the final information obtained.

This approach allows the development of a case based reasoning system starting with decision-problems to get the associated solutions.

It should be noted that knowledge sharing between the decision-maker and the watcher represent a form of collaborative work.

It should be noted also that the concept of individual competence includes training, know-how, abstract knowledge and practical knowledge. Let us also recall that experience does not imply competence. For example, the memorization of information retrieval results on the Internet does not show the competence of the user for the methods of information retrieval by search engines.

Nevertheless, a user's competence level can be measured by his/her experiences in the domain concerned. Thus, if we have an information retrieval problem, we can estimate the competence of an individual for solving such a problem by examining the history of his/her activities on this type of problem, i.e. to evaluate the importance of experience of the individual to solve the same or similar problems.

In our framework of study, we are interested in the capitalization (memorization and sharing) of competences of watcher (or individuals) in transforming the decision-problem into information retrieval problems. This competence will be measured in relation to the contribution of solutions suggested for the solving of decision-problems – in other words, the competences required to find relevant information.

8.7.6. *Collaboration diagrams*

The modes of collaboration that we present in this section and the next are presented from the technical angle.

Collaboration in the framework of our study is no longer only by the man-machine interaction but more by the man-machine-man interaction. The man-machine interaction emphasizes the transfer of all knowledge into the computer and a user is alone faced with the computer. In man-machine-man interaction, the interaction is between two (or more) users but through the intermediary of the computer.

In this configuration, some knowledge is held by users and others by the computer. This new form of interaction brings an extra advantage, which is to be able to share competences that are difficult, or impossible, to represent on a computer.

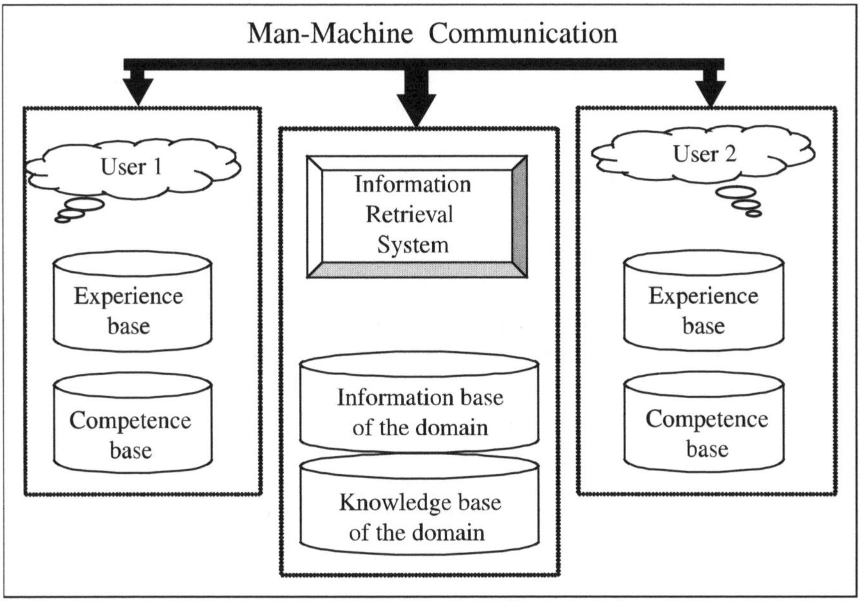

Figure 8.4. *Collaboration diagram: distributed knowledge*

The modes of collaboration (or the mode of interaction) can be considered from a strictly technical point of view or a mixed point of view: cognitive and technical. From the cognitive and technical point of view, we can identify two modes of interaction: the observation mode and the collaborative mode.

The implementation of environments for these two types of mode of interaction can be represented by the two diagrams in Figure 8.4 and Figure 8.5. In Figure 8.4, the bases of experience and competence of collaborators are delocalized on the collaborators' sites. This type of configuration is often used in situations that need protection of knowledge.

Thus a collaborator will only transfer what he/she judges to be non-harmful. We find, as an example of application of this type of configuration, the annotation projects of documentary resources. Annotations on documents are locally memorized. On the other hand the annotated documents and the knowledge bases to facilitate the access to these documents are centralized.

The second diagram (see Figure 8.5) is used when the trust is total. All the competences and experiences of collaborators are centralized. The control of access on this knowledge is implemented by software tools. The advantages of this type of organization are:

– the reduction of knowledge duplication. A piece of shared knowledge does not need to be duplicated in collaborators' environments;

– the exploitation and global analysis of competences are easier in a centralized environment;

– the acquisition and the transfer of knowledge by the collaborators is simplified.

In terms of interaction, we can note three types of mode: autonomous mode, observation mode, and collaborative mode. We are not interested in the autonomous mode within the framework of this study because there is no direct collaboration even though there could be sharing of competence.

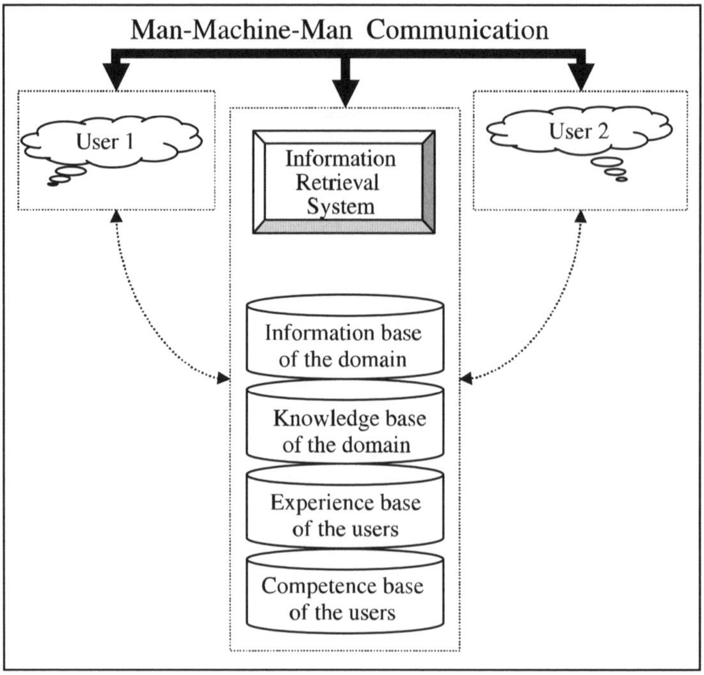

Figure 8.5. *Collaboration diagram: centralized and shared knowledge*

We present very briefly the observation mode and the collaborative mode in the next two sections.

8.7.6.1. *Observation mode*

In observation mode, one of the collaborators undergoes the operations and the other collaborators can only observe the first carry out the operations. It is a passive mode of collaboration that can be observed, for example, in lecture teaching. In the same way, in a document resource center librarians collect the users' demands, process them and deliver the results to the user without the latter having to intervene in the process by the librarian.

8.7.6.2. *Collaborative mode*

In the collaborative mode, two (or more) collaborators carry out the information retrieval activities at the same time. The collaborators have a similar objectives and they work towards solving the problem. In this study, it is a matter of information retrieval problems, defining a decision-problem, of the transformation of the decision-problem into information retrieval problems. In the two modes of collaboration, the notion of the collaborators' status is very important. We can note the status of the decision-maker, specialist in information retrieval, specialist in the domain of study, etc. In this way the collaborators' contributions can be analyzed and exploited according to their status. In the same way, access or exploitation controls will be elaborated according to the collaborators' different types of status.

8.8. Conclusion

We have shown the complexity of the notion of relevance in the framework of an EI project. The complexity is as much a problem linked to the individuals as to the group concerned by the project. This is why we conclude this complexity by the properties/faculties of bee colonies – to locate, indicate, gather, construct, organize and protect:

– *To locate (to localize and validate)*: the bees have a formidable faculty to locate flowers that can supply nectar. It is therefore not a matter of just locating a plant but to identify the useful plants. This ability corresponds to a faculty that is expected when participating in an EI process. Not only must the person be able identify information, he/she must be able to judge the relevance or usefulness of a piece of information. The activity of a watcher is based mainly on this type of faculty.

– *To indicate (common communication language)*: bees are capable of indicating the direction and distance of the location of a plant where nectar is to be found. This type of faculty is indispensable for the participants in an EI process because they must be able to indicate in as exact a way as possible where good information is found. For this, the participants must have communication competences adapted for transmitting these types of indication (or knowledge).

– *To gather (to utilize the existing objects)*: bees do not just indicate the location and direction of a plant, but they also gather nectar for their society. For this they have natural tools to do it. They gather nectar for a common use of the colony but they unconsciously contribute to the pollinization of plants. Compared to the faculty expected of a participation the EI process, the participant must have tools for gathering information. These tools are not necessarily natural but people have the faculty to develop tools adapted to his/her need: in this case, the tools for information collection can fill this role.

– *To construct (to fabricate the non-existing object)*: another admirable skill of bees concerns the faculty of construction. Bees make hives with an almost perfect precision. We therefore notice that they are capable of fabricating a non-existent object for the needs of the colony. In the same way, we expect participants of the EI process to be able to fabricate objects needed for running the socio-economic organization.

– *To organize (role sharing, sense of belonging)*: the organizational structure of a colony of bees is almost perfect. Each member of the colony knows its role and the hierarchies are perfectly respected. We also notice a form of role adaptation according to age, which we can associate with a form of role attribution as a function of experience. In the same way, we expect a socio-economic organization to be able to distribute roles to its collaborators according to the needs of the organization, taking into consideration its members' experiences.

– *To protect (to defend oneself with adapted weapons – sting, heat by vibration, etc)*[1]: the giant Asian hornets feed on Hymenopterans amongst others, and often attack bee hives. European melliferous bees (often raised by apiculturists in Asia) cannot defend themselves against this predator. Indeed their sting has no effect on these hornets. On the other hand the Japanese variety of melliferous bees, whose sting also has no effect, have developed an effective defense strategy against this predator: they make the hornets die of heat by sticking together on top of the hornets in groups of several hundreds of bees for one hornet. The bees surrounding the hornet in this way produce heat by contraction of wing muscles, making the surrounding temperature rise to about 47°C, thus causing the death of the hornet (hornets die when the temperature passes 45°C, however bees can resist higher temperatures). This faculty shows the necessity of having a community approach to the defense of the heritage of the organization, notably in an EI process. The defense strategies must be adapted to environments and to those who are seeking to disrupt the good running of the organization.

---

1. http://taiwannature.canalblog.com/archives/2005/05/index.html, accessed September 27, 2009.

To sum up, bees have a perfect knowledge of the environment, the members of the colony have a project and a stake in common (the survival and continuity of the species). They have a perfect sense of belonging and the competences of each member are directed towards the accomplishment of these objectives, and more particularly through sense, of collaborative work.

In order for the information systems to be effective for EI, they have to be use-oriented, user oriented and, in order to facilitate the collaborative retrieval of information, they must have the necessary ability to measure relevance of information.

8.9. Bibliography

[AFO 07] AFOLABI B., La conception et l'adaptation de la structure d'un système d'intelligence économique par l'observation des comportements de l'utilisateur, doctorate thesis, University of Nancy 2, March 2007.

[BIR 00] BIRD S., DAY D., GAROFOLO J., HENDERSON J., LAPRUN C., LIBENNAN M., "ATLAS: A flexible and extensible architecture for linguistic annotation", *Proceedings of the Second International Conference on Language Resources and Evaluation*, p. 1699-1706, 2000.

[BOU 04] BOUAKA N., Développement d'un modèle pour l'explicitation d'un problème décisionnel: un outil d'aide à la décision dans un contexte d'intelligence économique, doctorate thesis, University of Nancy 2, 2004.

[BRI 04] BRINGAY S., BARRY C., CHARLET J., "Les documents et les annotations du dossier patient hospitalier", *Information-Interaction-Intelligence*, vol. 4, no. 1, 2004.

[CAD 00] CADIZ U., GUPTA A., GRUDIN J., *Using Web Annotations for Asynchronous Collaboration Around Documents, CSCW'OO*, Microsoft Research, Collaboration & Multimedia Group, Philadelphia, 2000.

[CAR 03] CARAYON B., *Intelligence Economique, Compétitivité et Cohésion Sociale*, La Documentation Française, Paris, 2003.

[CAR 04] CARTER S., CHURCHILL E., DENOUE L., HELFMAN J., NELSON L., *Digital Graffiti: Public Annotation of Multimedia Content*, Vienna, Austria, CHI 2004.

[CAS 96] CASSALLAS-GUTIERREZ R., Objets historiques et annotations pour les environnements logiciels, doctorate thesis, Joseph Fourier Grenoble 1 University, May 1996.

[CHO 04] CHOU W., DAHL D., JOHNSTON M., PIERACCINI R., RAGETT D., "EMMA: extensible MultiModal Annotation markup language", W3C REC WD-emma-20050916, September 2005.

[DAV 05] DAVIS J., HUTTENLOCHER D., "Shared annotation for cooperative learning", 1995. *Shared Annotation for Cooperative Learning*, Prog of CSCL'95, pp. 84-88.

[DAV 06] DAVID A., "La recherche collaborative d'information dans un contexte d'Intelligence Economique", *Le Système d'Information de l'Entreprise*, Algérie Télécom, Alger, Algeria, 2006.

[DAV 01] DAVID A., THIERY O., "Prise en compte du profil de l'utilisateur dans un système d'information stratégique", *Congrès VSST'01*, Barcelona, October 2001.

[DEN 05] DENOUE L., VIGNOLLET L., "An annotation tool for Web browsers and its applications to information retrieval", *Proceedings of RIA 0200*, April 2000.

[DIE 01] DIENG-KUNTZ R., CORBY O., GANDON F., GIBOIN A., GOLEBIOWSKA J., MATTA N., RIBIERE M., *Méthodes et Outils pour la Gestion des Connaissances: une Approche Pluridisciplinaire du Knowledge Management* (second edition), Dunod, Paris, 2001.

[GOR 05] GORIA S., Proposition d'une démarche d'aide à l'expression des problèmes de recherche d'informations dans un contexte d'intelligence territoriale, doctorate thesis, University of Nancy 2, 2005.

[HAN 03] HANDSCHUH S., STAAB S., "Annotation for the semantic Web", *Frontiers in Artificial Intelligence and Application*, vol. 96, p. 46-60, 2003.

[KNAU 07] KNAUF A., Caractérisation des rôles du coordinateur-animateur: émergence d'un acteur nécessaire à la mise en pratique d'un dispositif régional d'intelligence économique, doctorate thesis, University of Nancy 2, October 2007.

[KIS 07] KISLIN P., Modélisation du problème informationnel du veilleur dans la démarche d'intelligence économique, doctorate thesis, University of Nancy 2, November 2007.

[MAR 94] MARTRE H. *et al.*, *Intelligence Économique et Stratégie des Entreprises*, La Documentation Française, Paris, 1994.

[RAZ 03] RAZMERITA L., Modèle utilisateur et modélisation utilisateur dans les systèmes de gestion des connaissances: une approche fondée sur les ontologies, doctorate thesis, University of Toulouse 3, 2003.

[REV 98] REVELLI C., *Intelligence Stratégique sur Internet*, Dunod, Paris, 1998.

[ROB 07] ROBERT C., L'annotation pour la recherche d'informations dans le contexte d'intelligence économique, doctorate thesis, University Nancy 2, February 2007.

[SAL 00] SALLES M., "Problématique de la conception de méthodes pour la définition de systèmes d'Intelligence Economique", *Revue d'Intelligence Economique*, no. 6-7, Association Française pour le Développement de l'Intelligence Economique, October 2000.

Chapter 9

Representations of Digital Documents in Automatic Text Analysis: a Pluridisciplinary Problem

9.1. Introduction

The substitution of paper support by digital support has reduced the possibilities of access, research, gathering, treatment, sharing and use of electronic documents. This is the case whether from a cultural [RAC 07][1], educational [PAP 04] or economic (economic intelligence, client relations management, civil security, knowledge management competence management, etc) point of view.

This socio-economic demand for a better exploitation of knowledge contained in collections of documents in electronic format [ZAN 05], as well as the progress undergone in the domain of language processing [GRI 06b], caused the emergence of a new field of research aimed at improving information retrieval in collections of documents by the modeling of their contents.

Chapter written by Luc GRIVEL.

1. Three years after Google's announcement of the digitization of millions of works, the French National Library (BNF) announced for March 2008 a new version of its online library, Gallica2. Accessible to all, it includes several dozens of hundreds of thousands of digitized titles. (Interview with Bruno Racine, president of the BNF, *Libération,* 2-3 February 2008.)

Two scientific specialties are particularly concerned with this objective: linguistics, in its automatic language processing (ALP) orientation (linked to the computer science discipline) and information science.

It is no accident these specialties have been brought together. The communities of these two specialties have long made use of bodies of documents for, for example, the construction of terminologies, the construction of thesauruses, the construction of ontologies, the construction of social models, by analysis of the production and communication activity of the publications, notably scientific ones, as well as their use.

The researchers of these two specialties have such a strong habit of collaboration that this common interest for the treatment and analysis of corpora of documents has led to fruitful research that is situated in the combination of methods and concepts defined and used by them.

It is this field of research that we are going to try to characterize according to three dimensions:

– *the socio-economic dimension*: the space in which the socio-economic stakeholders evolve;

– *the documentary dimension*: the space in which the collections of documents are constructed and organized;

– *the cognitive dimension*: the space in which the reader analyses, assimilates, criticizes and finally brings out the meaning of the discourses held in document collections, briefly, and constructs a new representation of the information.

Section 9.2 illustrates these three dimensions of the activity of information analysis. It describes the types of resources that would be available to mobilize and the types of treatment to be carried out to respond to a question that necessitates including a collection of documents and the modeling of their contents by techniques of text searching.

Section 9.3 presents some topics of reflection for research on this theme in information sciences. We will rely notably on the works of the pluridisciplinary thematic network baptized "Document and contents: creation, indexation, navigation"[2], which, from 2002 to 2004 gathered together several hundreds of researchers originating from 26 laboratories, to work on two main objectives:

2. Under the responsibility of Salaün (ENSSIB), this network launched eight programs of reflection (specific actions) in two years, which gave place to several reports available on the ESSIB website (http://rtp-doc.enssib.fr), accessed on September 27, 2009.

– to analyze documents, mediations and their relation with the human activity and its limits;

– to question the tools to be constructed, the modalities of their construction and the consequences of their use.

The examples and their analysis, according to the three dimensions cited above, are taken from our own works concerning the analysis of information buried in a collection[3] of digital textual documents. This work was produced in the framework of devices giving access to multiple sources of information (economic, scientific, technical, judicial, etc.) and integrating tools relying on search techniques and models of representation of the contents of documents.

9.2. Limits of the classic information retrieval scheme: an example in the pharmaceutical sector

9.2.1. *The socio-economic dimension and its impact in the process of information retrieval*

The pharmaceutical sector is characterized by extremely high research and development costs. The figure most often cited is of 802 million US dollars per medication[4] [DIM 03]. In projects at this scale, making good choices for deciding whether or not to pursue a path, to be well situated in relation to the market, choosing a partner, are all essential things. The documentation produced is overabundant because it covers all the phases of a necessarily very long process of development.

In this context, let us take the example of a pharmacologist[5] who is seeking to identify new treatments concerning atherosclerosis on behalf of a big company within the pharmaceutical sector, and let us describe his/her cognitive process.

He/she must find therapeutic targets, a protein or a gene, which would mark the development of atherosclerosis. These targets must be recent, because it is a matter of finding targets that have not yet been extensively studied. Then it will be a matter of finding all of the sicknesses associated with this target and choosing a sickness

3. Collection means here a group of documents gathered by a person in view of achieving a specific, conceptualized, finalized task.

4. According to the journal *Prescrire* vol. 23, no. 144, p. 782-787 2004, this cost was estimated by an institute mostly financed by pharmaceutical firms, from confidential data supplied by the latter. It is in fact a matter of a cost "failures included, financial costs included, and pre-taxes". The cost really paid out is seemingly inferior by half.

5. Here we are describing a research strategy for information retrieval conceived by Mathieu Plantefol, pharmacologist, former researcher of the Pasteur Institute, now a Temis consultant.

that is found in the therapeutic field of the company where this pharmacologist works. Then he/she will have to search, among the recent molecules, those that have a functional grouping with an effect on the therapeutic target and which are associated with this sickness.

He/she will therefore be in a position to write a synthetic report of the tendencies and results relative to the new, potentially interesting molecules for his/her business.

The next stage will then consist of giving prominence to the position of societies that are competing in relation to these new molecules (R&D investments, acquisition of patents, establishment of partnership with a research laboratory, etc). This information will permit him/her to establish recommendations, for example to advocate deeper, more extensive investigations on the molecule.

Now let us look at what this means from the point of view of the documentary space where the analysis of information will be carried out.

9.2.2. *The documentary dimension*

What are the types of sources where our pharmacologist can hope to find the answer? Implicitly, this information supposes that the answer will be found in the document.

Here, let us posit that there is no recent document of synthesis on this subject. It is therefore necessary for him/her to develop a strategy of information retrieval that mobilizes different types of information to be retrieved, as we described above.

In the first place, we must identify the databases likely to contain elements of response. In the domain of scientific information, according to past agreements between editors and producers of bibliographic databases, it is becoming easier than ever to directly access the full text of patents as well as scientific articles via these databases:

– banks of bibliographic notes covering scientific and medical literature;

– banks of notices of patents (European, American, Japanese, and worldwide) in the chemistry domain;

– banks of nucleic or protein sequences banks of molecular structures, banks of genes, etc.

How could our pharmacist retrieve all the useful information for identifying a chemical compound that could be able to have an positive effect on the treatment of a disease?

Even by limiting him/herself to building a base that would concern atherosclerosis, the volumes remain very important. Here are two examples of results of research carried out on 19 July 2007:

– a retrieval of "atherosclerosis" in PubMed (Medline[6]), without restrictions of date of publication, nor language, brings up 52,702 documents;

– a retrieval of "atherosclerosis" in espacenet Worldwide, in the same conditions, produces 7,402 documents.

Because of the volume of documents concerned, several hundred thousand to millions of documents, the results are not directly exploitable by an analyst who would want to extract relevant information from this set of documents.

The classic documentary tools, like the thesaurus, are poorly adapted for the full text.

Actually, in the present case it is a matter of identifying:

– genes or proteins (for example anti-apoptosis protein);

– cells (for example langerhans cell);

– diseases (for example tumor cells);

– processes (for example G → S transition);

– therapeutic treatments (for example UV-irradiated HL60 cells);

– medication (for example quinidine);

– tissues (for example total bone marrow);

– etc.;

as well as specific relations between these entities:

– activation (apoptosis is induced by depsipeptide),

– inhibition (the suppression of cell growth),

– regulation (depsipeptide-mediated apoptosis),

– etc.

6. Medline (16 million references in 2007) covers about 5,000 biomedical journals in all domains: biochemistry, biology, clinical medicine, economics, ethics, odontology, pharmacology, psychiatry, public health, toxicology and veterinary medicine.

A thesaurus like the MESH cannot cover this requirement. By definition, the lists of descriptors are closed and the semantic relations of a thesaurus are limited to two roles:

– to settle the linguistic problems (synonymy and homography);

– to suggest to the indexer other descriptors susceptible to being used to characterize the contents of the document (enriching relations).

The use of a thesaurus for indexing usually provides a limited number of words (a maximum of about 10) for characterizing the content of a document. This indexation is efficient enough to permit document retrieval according to a general topic, but not for giving precise access to specific information in the documents. As a matter of fact, the vocabulary of a thesaurus is generally not very evolutive and not necessarily sufficiently precise. It is not well adapted to retrieve unseen information, as is often the case in a knowledge discovery task.

The limits of the classic scheme of information retrieval popularized by Google – formulation of a request in the form of keywords or in a natural language, then return of an ordered list of documents – with or without a thesaurus, are attained.

The classic approaches of automatic indexation do not permit the taking into account of dependences between constituents (inter- and intraphrases) of texts to be analyzed. They consider the text as a bag of words, at best reducing it to its constituents (nouns, adjectives, verbs) or to terms, even complex (noun phrase, prepositional phrase).

These dependencies between constituents have a semantic role. To ignore it is to lose a large part of the intention of the act of communication conveyed by the text.

Therefore we now move on to consider discourse.

9.2.3. *The cognitive dimension and the space of discourse in the context of an automatic analysis of texts*

The discourse space is the space where the act of narration is carried out [CHA 78].

In the present case, articles are written in a specialty language, correct from a grammatical point of view and from a point of view of that vocabulary is relatively limited. The information retrieved is expressed in a sentence, some lines at most:

– *protein-A is a mediator of cell cycle arrest*;

– *protein-induced cell death*;

– etc.

In the context of an automatic text analysis, three objectives[7] are aimed at:

– Selecting the meaning of words or more precisely lemmas (semantic disambiguation). In the present example, names of molecules, treatments, diseases, etc are sought. Names of molecules are "entities" that are referenced in the text, for example H2O (water) ethylenediammonium diacetate (EDDA). Even if it is possible to draw up at a moment t a list of molecule names, these lists will always be incomplete at a moment t+1. Nevertheless, these entities have a micro-syntax that belongs to them and which permits them to be located in the texts. Thus, chemists use a nomenclature for the description of molecules that are organic components: the nomenclature of IUPAC[8]. It defines a certain number of arbitrary rules which, applied to each molecule, will give it its name. A disease name is part of a specialty language, usually less polysemic, than a nominal word group extracted on the base of linguistic rules [FAB 97].

– To understand the meaning of the sentence that comes from the comprehension of relations between words. It needs the identification of arguments of each predicate and their semantic role (for example, the action of a protein on a gene), which is supposed to describe the possible semantic relations between concepts.

– To give meaning to utterances by seeking who the interlocutors are, by taking into account the circumstances in which the predicate is uttered (for example, the purchase of pharmaceutical company X by company Y in 2005).

---

7. The two first items come from the semantic analysis. The third from pragmatic analysis [LAL 05].

8. In the International Union of Pure and Applied Chemistry (IUPAC) nomenclature, the name of a compound, is based on the number of carbon atoms linked together in the carbonaceous chain. This is the first characteristic used to form the IUPAC name. The second characteristic results from the following observation: different organic compounds containing the same grouping (also called functional grouping) react chemically in the same way. These compounds are grouped by family, which gives the second characteristic the IUPAC nomenclature.

9.3. Themes of reflection

9.3.1. *Revisiting the documentary space*

What does the example presented show us? With the Internet, the extraordinary disequilibrium between the volume of the available documentation potentially offered to our consumption and our real human capacities of consumption is only accentuated [GAR 01]. But is there such a thing as being "too-full" of information[9]? Would it not be better to speak of the difficulty in making informational and terminological resources correspond to a finalized activity?

What are the constraints that weigh on this approach?

In the framework of economic intelligence, it is the confrontation of the strategic project[10] of the business to the analysis of the competing framework that gives the keys for the definition of types of useful information (before the gathering) and, for the analysis of the discourse (after the treatment of the collection of documents by text search tools).

The competing framework of a business is made up of forces that impact on the participants of its sector of activity. Any business exists in a state of permanent negotiation with its competitors, bankers, suppliers, clients, personnel and shareholders. Each one, according to its positioning, undergoes and creates constraints that weigh on the others to attain its objectives [POR 79].

In an systemic vision of the environment of businesses, the behavior of each element (participant) of the system can influence the behavior of the whole. No element (participant), however, can have an effect on the whole without being affected by it itself (retroaction principle). For a business, to have an intelligence of its economic environment is to be able to model itself as a system with its participants and their objectives (supposed), their interdependent relations, and their processes of interaction.

---

9. The information does not exist as such if it is not actively received [MEY 85].There must be a "view focused" on the document for there to be information [JEA 00]. From this point of view, information is a point of arrival of documentary activity [CHA 03].

10. That is to say who engages in the future of the business, whether it is a matter of developing a new product or a new proceeding, of becoming established in a new country, of creating or changing its distribution network, of delocalizing a production, of purchasing parts of a company, of buying or selling a factory, etc. Without information on the project, without strategic vision, the watchman will face the impossibility of precisely defining his/her research plan.

How do we take into consideration and manage different types of knowledge, not only those that come from the terminology of a domain, but also those that come from the socio-economic context, in adequacy with users' demands?

Documentary space plays a central role in this question, like a mediation space between the authors of documents and readers/analysts.

We hypothesize that in the context of gigantic documentary wholes, the process of information cannot be reduced to the author-reader relation via documents. It crosses the mediation of tools capable of proposing models of representation of the information contained in these wholes, which go beyond classic approaches[11].

In the framework of economic intelligence, the type and nature of information to be retrieved necessitates the gathering and organization of large quantities of documents coming from varied and heterogenous sources of information, whether this is from the point of view of their:

– domain: financial, commercial, technical, scientific;

– structure: very structured, little or not structured;

– language: multilingualism;

– format of support: XML, Word, html, PDF, etc.;

– size: documents to be analyzed are of variable size (several tens of pages for the full text of a license, some sentences in a summary of a notice).

This heterogeneity implies that, after the gathering, any human analysis will have to be generally preceded by the reformatting and organization operations of the documentary space, etc.

A document can comprise numerous text zones playing different roles (title, summary, body, introduction, etc.). According to the type of document, according to the application and according to the objective aimed at, the documentary unit will be the sentence, in others the paragraph, in others still the summary, the title, the acknowledgements, etc.

Reformatting must take into account the structure of documents that are to be examined, in order to provide the possibility of classing or indexing parts of specific documents and applying various strategies of selection of terms as a function of objectives pursued.

---

11. Like, for example, those based on the use of a thesaurus of which we showed the limits in section 9.2.

The detection of parts of a document offering a certain coherence or autonomy (thematic) makes it possible to supply, in response to a question asked, the segments of texts relative to this question. This notion of autonomy is important if we offer to facilitate access at a finer level of the document, where the useful information is found.

Consequently, the notion of bibliographic notice[12] is in the process of evolving. We can make the link here with one of the objectives of the semantic web: to make web resources more easily accessible by man/woman as well as by machine, thanks to the semantic representation of their contents. This objective brought the W3C consortium to suggest norms for the description of relations between resources, RDF (resource description framework), the description of ontologies (classes of objects), etc. [CHA 03].

How do we enrich digital contents with metadata? How do we go beyond retrieval or access to the digital document and for the proposal to transform digital libraries into sites suggesting new services, permitting users to collaborate in the production of new learning?

In addition to the classic metadata (title, author, date, source, contributor, etc) we can create some metadata of specific analyses: temporal, spatial, geographic metadata, metadata relative to the discursive data, etc.

How do we generate metadata? It is here that text search techniques can intervene.

9.3.2. *Revisiting methods of contents modeling*

Text mining, in its widest definition, groups together techniques permitting the achievement of an automatic analysis of the contents of digital textual documents. On a functional front, text mining can be defined, for example, by the capacity to extract informational segments judged important in the text, or the capacity to visualize a document or a grouping of documents in the form of a graph, by revealing correlations between words, sentences, documents from a large mass of documents. Text mining combines methods and techniques stemming from infometry, computer linguistics (text analysis and information extraction), data analysis (factorial analysis, classification, etc) and artificial intelligence (teaching techniques, inference rules) [FEL 06, GRI 06a, HEA 99, ZAN 05].

---

12. A bibliographic notice is structures, divided into elementary units in a hierarchy, with multiple cross-references (bibliography, notes, links between authors and affiliation, etc.) which can be used for generating links.

9.3.2.1. *Linguistic approach*

Language technologies supply the ways of extracting useful information according to different points of view of reading [GRI 01, JAC 03, MIN 02]. That will consist of, for example:

– selecting key sentences, or identifying elements of structure in the document (thematic advertisement, definition, conclusion, citation), by being based on the presence of linguistic markings (connectors such as "therefore", expressions such as "it is necessary", "it is useful");

– identifying a "facturation problem" in a client e-mail, by exploiting *ad hoc* dictionaries on the domain, linguistic signs (co-presence of some terms);

– extracting predicates (resolution of a problem by an invention, fusion of company A with company B) from an utterance, by defining extraction rules;

– etc.

In order to detect novelties, a watchman generally relied on the documents or the most recent parts of documents (the "delta" between the two groupings of documents corresponding to two successive gathering operations). In this case, the time of the enunciation, that of the narrator, identifies with the socio-historic time of related events, and is not very far from the reader's time, which facilitates interpretation. On the other hand, in the framework of a retrospective analysis, the gap between the reader's time and the narrator's time supposes on the part of the reader to make the effort of reconstructing the universe in which the author wrote to be able to situate statements in their context of production. It is also the case for "memoirs"[13] of a business, as stressed by [AS 95]. The name of a company and its situation within a group can have changed, which produces the question of reliability of resources to associate with the tools of analysis, as we will see later.

There is therefore a context of enunciation (by the author) and a context of interpretation (by the reader).

How do we take into account the context of interpretation?

Among recent research on the subject, we cite an approach developed within the S3IS laboratory at Marne-La-Vallée. This approach hypothesizes that in a situation of analysis, the interpretant calls to mind his/her knowledge, his/her memory asset, in order to progress from certin units of meaning to other units of meaning, and then carry out in this way a possible interpretation of the statement.

---

13. Documents written *a posteriori* by those that lived the socio-historic period studied.

In a strategic scanning context. [SCH 05] proposes taking into account the knowledge associated with the context of interpretation by translating them into a sort of memoir thesaurus. More precisely, it is a matter of the MEVA (event memory of updating) memory approach described by Christian Krumeich: associations of context to a memory descriptor. For example, to speak of "RNAi (ribonucleic acid interferent) infection" in medicine implies an applied therapeutic strategy to the mouse model, and no doubt alludes to a search concerning the most serious hepatitis [SCH 05].

In the same spirit, in the framework of use of a watch tool of the Paris National Higher Chemistry School (*Ecole Nationale Supérieure de Chimie*), [SAV 07] describes the collaboration between an expert (a scientist in the chemical domain) and a librarian (with good watch skills for using the watch tool) to formalize the forms or patterns to extract from the corpus.

The extraction systems developed by software editors Temis, Clearforest, Inxight, SPSS, etc., suggest a language based on rules, which most often rely on the outputs of a morphosyntactic analyzer to carry out the semantic and pragmatic analysis of the sentences of a text. In this framework, the definition of extraction (patterns) rules rest on a syntactico-semantic description of elementary syntactic dependences between the relevant syntagmes for the domain studied [GRI 01].

In all the cases, the process of information extraction comprises two stages [AUS 03]:

– a stage of construction of linguistic resources;

– a stage of use of these resources to analyze the contents of texts, to index them, to find them or retrieve information, whose results can be reinjected to update the rules, in them.

Sure, the linguistic problems are complex and only partially solved; the global comprehension of a document is still an object of research. But the level of existing solutions to extract information is sufficient to be usable by people engaged in a process of research and analysis of information to the ends of aiding the decision, and to permit the knowledge produced by authors to engender "new" knowledge for the readers.

Nevertheless, on the methodological front, numerous questions remain unanswered [AUS 03]. In the case of the implementation of a process of teaching to facilitate the identification of these dependences, the results are strongly dependant on the teaching materials, which begs the question of the construction of the materials. How do we construct samples of sentences, documents or parts of documents representing the problem for solving without having means for locating them, if not manually? How do we measure this representativness? The cost of constitution of such corpora therefore remains elevated and slows the research in this domain.

A system of extraction of information is by nature calibrated for a domain of activity, a type of document given and a given socio-historic time. According to predicted use, the process of construction of the resource can vary. How, from a user's need, do we define the process and identify the techniques that are going to permit the construction of the right resource and make it evolve?

More generally, for all these methods based on a linguistic approach, the question of stability, specialization, construction and re-use of terminological resources is asked, because, obviously, the evaluation of the use of a resource for a watch activity will have an impact on the resource that will have to be adapted at this stage.

9.3.2.2. *Statistical approach*

This approach permits the organization of the documentary space by distinguishing, initially, the possibilities of regrouping of similar entities within an entity of a superior level (a class). Two approaches are possible:

– Supervised classification or categorization [SEB 05] consists of identifying the class of belonging of an object from certain descriptive features. This approach permits the automatic classing of documents in pre-existing classes. It necessitates the constitution and utilization of nomenclature tables, plans of relatively stable and durable classification topics such as, for example, the rubrics of a journal (society, sport, science, France, Europe, world, economics, politics, etc) to carry out the aggregations.

– The non-supervised classification of documents or clustering, i.e. the discovery of documents without *a priori* (the classes are not known in advance). As in any non-supervised approach, these methods suppose the choice of [MAN 05]:

- a representation of objects for classing (documents, keywords),
- a measure of similarity between objects,
- a classification algorithm (hierarchical or non-hierarchical).

Second, we can envisage the creation of cartographies of the whole of these classes by situating one in relation to the other. It is at this level that we can make the link with the methods of relational analysis of infometry. Infometry designates the whole of metric activities relative to the information [POL 95]. There are essentially two families of infometric methods [CAL 93] in existence:

– 1D methods, which count the publications that have such or such a characteristic, and which are most often based on the laws of hyperbolic distribution (Lotka, Zipf, Bradfprd), also called bibliometric or infometric laws [LEC 04]. They are what the analysis of information, that which the Pareto law (individuals-taxes) is to the economy, or the demographic statistics to the study of populations. These three laws help to determine the quantitative criteria, to select a representative grouping (from the point of view of data analysis) of authors, periodicals or keywords on which techniques of descriptive analysis or analysis of data can then be applied to produce guides that permit quantitative comparisons between characterized groupings of publications.

– Relational methods based on the existence of links between publications [CHE 06, SMA 97, 99] (citations, co-citations, authors, descriptors, etc.). They enable the structuring and mapping of domains covered by groupings of publications. These links can be deduced from the structure of documents and calculated with the help of statistical methods cited above. Thus, in the TELplus plan of the BNF[14], one of the first treatments tested will be based on the recognition of citations, permitting a linking of collections of internal as well as external documents (with collections of other organizations).

There also, on the methodological front, many questions remain unanswered.

Let us take the example of clustering and mapping techniques applied to texts [HUA 06, MAN 05].

What do they enable us to see, to interpret, exactly? I observe that what the clusters or maps suggest varies with the individuality of the observer and his/her representation. How can the reader-analyst articulate his/her representations with those supplied by tools of analysis?

This takes us to the watch, to the axes of surveillance and to the objectives and to the strategy of development of the enterprise and individual strategies of information analysts, to their subjectivity and their training for information analysis.

Maps and clusters, worked by a researcher, confronted with his/her conscious and unconscious representation of the world (or of the situation), can be a way of expressing his/her particular vision of reality.

What do we say about the sharing of this interpretation with others via a map produced by a system from a body of information, constructed with a certain intention? We should at this point approach the question of the use of these

---

14. Interview with Bruno Racine, president of the BNF, *Libération*, 2-3 February 2008.

representations in a sociological perspective (like the process of building of social relationships).

Many factors come into play [BON 08]:

– competencies and profiles of participants charged with the administration of these systems;

– end users, their aims and their objectives;

– available resources (dictionaries, catalogues of authorities, thesauruses, texts, etc);

– organizational factors belonging to the organization or its methods and tools that are used.

The competencies mobilized to run a system of gathering and to analyze their results are not the same. Professionals of the watch master the utilization of gathering and analysis of information tools. Generally originating from the world of documentation, they know well the value of information. Their culture of service permits them to ensure that the information arrives at the right person, at the right time, but they are often badly prepared to lead an in-depth analysis of the information gathered [BON 08]. The study led by [SAV 07] in a context of scientific research, accredits the idea that the optimization of the efficiency of the watch crosses a dual organization with one part professionals qualified in the utilization of watch tools at the heart of research teams, and the other part from networks of experts only qualified in the analysis of information collected.

9.4. Conclusion

The field of research which we presented tries to articulate three types of approaches:

– a systemic approach, relative to the social space;

– an approach by document, in which the organization in collections constitutes the documentary space;

– a linguistic and statistic approach, like a construction tool of representations relative to the space of the discourse.

The practical improvement of information processes only seems possible by progressing conjointly in all these directions.

Regarding the process of construction of these representations by techniques of semantic analysis of texts, we saw that it generally requires a phase of acquisition of knowledge. The acquisition of knowledge goes back to methodological questions concerning:

– the nature of the knowledge to be managed [AUS 03];

– the selection of sources, the building of corpora;

– the choice of techniques and tools;

– the adaptation of resources associated with tools of text analysis as a function of the sector of activity of the watchman;

– the ability to meet the needs (requests, questions) of users [CHA 04, LAI 06] linked to objectives of strategic scanning pursued [GRI 01, GRI 06b].

Whereas information crosses the mediation of documentary tools[15], it is to the reader/analyst that it comes back from searching for the principles, reasons for the actions of socio-economic participants, that the tools of analysis were able to reveal.

As recalled by [LEL 08], intelligence in the man-machine system is in the individual, and it is the individual who constructs sense in response to the reception of representations constructed by tools of analysis.

One of the characteristics of this research is to be interested in more than the technical or algorithmic aspects[16] of the treatment of language. This research is also aimed at reducing the gap between the users mental representations in his/her activity framework (including the intentions of the user) and what device integrating techniques of text mining offers, that is to say some means of selecting documents, various representations of the content of the documents (descriptors, extracts of sentences).

It is all about a field of applied research of a pluridisciplinary nature (information sciences, sociology of organizations, cognitive, linguistic and computer sciences). These lead to a valuing of documentary capital and the conception of terminological resources, methods of tools/systems of acquisition of knowledge, access, organization and analysis of documentary information to the service of the competitiveness of economic actors.

In other words, this research leads to an engineering of the knowledge for the intelligent management of information buried in digital documents.

15. From this point of view, search tools of texts are agents. They extract, remove, categorize, classify in a supervised or unsupervised way. Should they be incorporated into the systemic model? In my opinion no, because they are deprived of intent.

16. For example, the improvement of text analysis techniques, to architectural aspects of systems mobilising knowledge.

9.5. Bibliography

[AUS 03] AUSSENAC N., CONDAMINES A. (eds), “Corpus et terminologie”, *Rapport Final de l’Action Spécifique AS-34 - RTP DOC STIC CNRS*, July 2003.

[BON 08] BONNY P., GRIVEL L., “Leviers d’optimisation d’une démarche de veille et d’intelligence économique: quelques pistes pour améliorer l’efficacité de la veille dans les organisations” , 2008. *Journal of Global Management Research (JGMR)*, vol. 2, no. 3, p. 160-170, 2008.

[CAL 03] CALABRETTO S., LALLICH-BOIDIN G., SEDES F. (eds), “Les temps du document numérique”, *Rapport d’activités Final de l’Action Spécifique 95 - RTP DOC STIC CNRS*, April 2004.

[CAL 93] CALLON M., *La Scientométrie, Que Sais-je?,* PUF, Paris, 1993.

[CHA 03] CHARLET J., LAUBLET P., REYNAUD C. (eds), “Web sémantique”, *Rapport Final de l’Action Spécifique 32 RTP DOC STIC CNRS*, October 2003.

[CHA 78] CHATMAN S., *Story and Discourse: Narrative Structure in Fiction and Film*, Cornell University Press, Ithaca (NY), 1978.

[CHA 01] CHAUDIRON S., FLUHR C. (eds), “Filtrage et résumé automatique de l’information sur les réseaux”, *Actes du 3ème Congrès du Chapitre Français de l’ISKO*, University of Paris X, Nanterre, July 5 and 6 2001.

[CHA 04] CHAUDIRON S., “La place de l’usager dans l’évaluation des systèmes de traitement de l’information”, *L’Évaluation des Systèmes de Traitement de l’Information*, Hermès, Paris, 2004.

[CHE 06] CHEN C., “CiteSpace II: Detecting and visualizing emerging trends and transient patterns in scientific literature”, *Journal of the American Society for Information Science and Technology*, vol. 57, no. 3, p. 359-377, 2006.

[DAV 05] DAVID A. (eds), “Organisation des connaissances dans les systèmes d’informations orientés utilisation: contexte de veille et d’intelligence économique”*, Actes du colloque international de ISKO France, April 28-29 2005*, PUN, Nancy, 2005.

[DIM 03] DIMASI J. *et al.*, “The price of innovation: new estimates of drug development costs”, *Journal Haelth Economics*, vol. 22, p. 151-185, 2003.

[FAB 97] FABRE C., HABERT B., LABBE D., “La polysémie dans la langue générale et les discours spécialisés”, *Sémiotiques*, vol. 13, p. 15-31, 1997.

[FEL 06] FELDMANN R., SANGER J., *The Text Mining Handbook, Advanced Approaches in Analyzing Unstructured Data*, Cambridge University Press, Cambridge, 2006.

[GAR 01] GARDIN J.C., “Vers un remodelage des publications savantes: ses rapports avec les sciences de l’information”, *Troisième colloque du Chapitre Français de l’ISKO: Filtrage et Résumé Automatique de l’Information sur les Réseaux*, Paris, July 5-6 2001.

[GRI 97] GRISMAN R., “Information extraction: Techniques and challenges”, in: M.T. PAZIENZA (ed.), *Lecture Notes in Artificial Intelligence*, Rome, Information Extraction, Springer-Verlag, 1997.

[GRI 01] GRIVEL L., GUILLEMIN-LANNE S., LAUTIER C., MARI A., "La construction de composants de connaissance pour l'extraction et le filtrage de l'information sur les réseaux", *ISKO International Society for Knowledge Organization*, p. 197-208, 2001.

[GRI 05] GRIVEL L., "Customer feedbacks and opinion surveys analysis in the automotive industry", *Text Mining and its Applications To Intelligence, CRM And Knowledge Management (Advances in Management Information),* vol. 9, Management Information Systems, WIT Press, 2005.

[GRI 06a] GRIVEL L., "Outils de classification et de catégorisation pour la fouille de textes" , in: M. Harzallah, J. Charlet, N. Aussenac-Gilles (eds), *Colloque international de ISKO France – Pratiques et méthodes de classification du savoir à l'heure d'Internet*, vol. 3, p. 95-104, Universtity of Nantes, 26-30 June 2006.

[GRI 06b] GRIVEL L., "Comment faire face à l'explosion des volumes d'information ? Le *text mining* et ses applications à l'intelligence économique, la gestion de la relation client et la gestion de connaissances", *Recherche, Technologie & Société*, vol. 62, p. 12-14, 2006.

[HEA 06] HEARST M., "Clustering versus faceted categories for information exploration", *Communications of the ACM*, vol. 49, no. 4, 2006.

[HUA 06] HUANG Y., MITCHELL T., "Text clustering with extended user feedback", *Proceedings of the ACM SIGIR Conference*, p. 413 – 420, August 2006.

[JAC 03] JACQUEMIN C., BOURIGAULT D., "Term extraction and automatic indexing", in: R. MITKOV (ed.), *Handbook of Computational Linguistic*s, Oxford University Press, Oxford, 2003, p. 599-615.

[JEA 00] JEANNERET Y., *Y a-t-il Vraiment des Technologies de l'Information ?* University of Septentrion Press, Villeneuve d'Ascq, 2000.

[LAI 06] LAINE-CRUZEL S., *AMETIST: Appropriation, Mutualisation, Expérimentations des Technologies de l'Information Scientifique et Technique*, vol. 0, p. 11-22, 2006.

[LAL 05] LALLICH-BOIDIN G., MARET D., *Recherche d'Information et Traitement de la Langue: Fondements Linguistiques et Applications*, ENSSIB Press, 2005.

[LEC 04] LECOADIC Y., *La Science de l'Information*, Que Sais-je?, 3rd edition, PUF, Paris, 2004.

[LEL 04] LELEU-MERVIEL S., "Effets de la numérisation et de la mise en réseau sur le concept de document", *Revue i3 Information, Interaction, Intelligence*, vol. 4, no.1, p.121-140, 2004.

[MEY 1985] MEYRIAT J., "Information vs communication?", in: A.-M. LAULAN (ed.), *L'Espace Social de la Communication: Concepts et Théories*, Retz-CNRS, Paris, 1985, p.63-89.

[MAN 05] MANDREOLI F., MARTOGLIA R., TIBERIO T., "Text clustering as a mining task", Chapter 3 in: A. ZANASI (ed.), *Text Mining and its Applications To Intelligence, CRM and Knowledge Management*, vol. 9, Series: Management Information Systems, WIT Press, 2005.

[MIN 02] MINEL J.L., *Filtrage Sémantique. Du Résumé Automatique à la Fouille de Textes*, Hermès, Paris, 2002.

[PAP 08] PAPY F. (ed.), *Digital Libraries*, ISTE, London, John Wiley & Sons, New York, 2008.

[POL 95] POLANCO X., "Aux sources de la scientométrie", in: J.-M. Noyer, *SOLARIS*, vol. 2 *Les Sciences de l'Information: Bibliométrie, Scientométrie, Infométrie*, PUR, Rennes, 1995, p. 13-78.

[POR 79] PORTER M.E., "How competitive forces shape strategy", *Harvard Business Review*, March/April 1979.

[QUO 97] QUONIAM L., BALME F., ROSTAING H., GIRAUD E., DOU W., "Bibliometric law used for information retrieval", in: J.M. PERITZ, B.-C. EGGHE, L. GLANZEL (eds), *6th ISSI Conference*, Jerusalem, 1997.

[RAC 07] Press conference of Bruno Racine, president of the BNF, 13 November 2007. (available at: http://www.bnf.fr/pages/presse/dossiers/conf_racine_13nov07.pdf, accessed October 3, 2009.)

[SAV 07] SAVINA S., CAREIL J.M., GRIVEL L., "Améliorer la veille des chercheurs dans un contexte académique: les apports conjoints d'un outil de veille, de ressources humaines et documentaires d'une bibliothèque de recherche", *VSST 2007, Veille Stratégique Scientifique et Technologique*, Marrakech, October 21-25, 2007.

[SCH 05] SCHARBOCHI E., KRUMEISH C., MALLET V., LAURENT D., "L'approche mémorielle, une méthode pour la veille documentaire scientifique et technique. Application dans le domaine de la recherche en médecine régénérative", *Actes Conférence Ile Rousse*, 2005.

[SEB 05] SEBASTIANI F., "Text categorisation", Chapter 4 in: A. ZANASI (ed.), *Text Mining and its Applications To Intelligence, CRM and Knowledge Management*, vol. 9, Series: Management Information Systems, WIT Press, 2005.

[SMA 97] SMALL H., "Update on science mapping: creating large document spaces", *Scientometrics*, vol. 38, no. 2, p. 275-293, 1997.

[SMA 99] SMALL H., "Visualizing science by citation mapping", *Jasis* vol. 50, no. 9, p. 799-813, 1999.

[ZAN 05] ZANASI A. (ed.), *Text Mining and its Applications to Intelligence, CRM and Knowledge Management*, vol. 9, Series: Management Information Systems, WIT Press, 2005.

Chapter 10

Freedom of Information, Participative Democracy and Local Economy

10.1. Introduction

This chapter seeks to establish the relationship between freedom of information and economic, social and human development, by showing that democratic demands regarding information are very much like the necessity of local economic development.

Modern economic information theory represents an analysis tool for these links and the limitations imposed on freedom of expression by technological and economic constraints and the information strategies of participants.

Thus, on the theoretical front we can set up some propositions along the lines of participative democracy and freedom of information in the local development perspective.

The theories in motion also enable us to contribute to the current debate on "methodological individualism" *versus* "holism", two approaches that are often opposed in the social sciences.

Chapter written by Yves THÉPAUT.

10.2. Technological mutation and freedom of information

Contemporary technological mutation based on automation opens perspectives along the lines of freedom of information, but these potentials have reservations linked to globalization and economic liberalization.

10.2.1. *Automation and information revolution*

Automation appears to be the deciding factor in explanations of crucial contemporary phenomena. This is because of its multiple effects, which are combined to information properties.

First, automation transforms the classic company into a "mono technology" but "multiproduct" company. In this way, it equips the company with the capacity to elaborate a differentiated and varied production by introducing technological flexibility and the possibility of tailor-made production [COR 90].

Next, automation enabled the considerable growth of performances in electronics (Moore's law) simultaneously with the fall of the cost of electronic components (technology paradox). The considerable lowering of the cost of information treatment resulted from it. These technological progresses developed at the same time as telecommunications. Their cost reduction is linked to the deregulation and the competition movement in this sector, provoking a quasi-suppression of the cost of information transport. These effects led to the quasi-nullification of "information distance" and its cost [THE 02].

Moreover, automation ensures information literacy and its reproduction at low cost. Information is actually a collective good whose production cost is negligible (see section 10.2). For example, the copy of an information program costs practically nothing compared to its development. In addition, the progress realized regarding information digitization considerably reduces its distribution cost [SHA 99].

Automation combined with information also leads to a specific cost function, that is a high fixed cost and a low, even null, variable cost. For example, once the equipment has been installed and the software set up, a production unit of goods, such as electronic chips or CD-ROMS, behaves like an automaton and its functioning only needs a small quantity of direct labor confined in surveillance, maintenance and conditioning tasks [VOL 99].

Lastly, automation enables us to expand telecommunication networks and it facilitates economic globalization. The globalization process has thus been accelerated by the systematic introduction of networked technology in the management of firms [MIC 02].

10.2.2. *Potentialities and limits of technological mutation*

By equipping the company with great technological flexibility, automation enables the support and a variety of services related to data, voice and image transfer, to be multiplied. Automation, in synergy with information properties, thus opens new potentials for freedom of information and expression. But at the same time, the underlying mechanisms of information mutation, as well as the excess of economic liberalization, can considerably corrupt and reduce these potentials. Two essential phenomena interact: company concentration and the economic liberalization and globalization movement.

Concentration in the communication sector has always been viewed suspiciously because it causes a risk of decreasing the variety of media products. The French Media Observatory [OFM 05] underlines the fear of seeing logic at work in the media industry lead to a more accentuated concentration. This fear is justified because of the dominant techno-economic logic in this sector.

In network industries like audiovisual and telecommunications industries, the risks linked to concentration are actually worsened by economic mechanisms linked to the electronic revolution. Three phenomena interact.

First, the increase in the size of companies linked to the introduction of new technology. Networked technologies actually increase the "minimum efficient scale" of firms as a result of their important fixed costs and the economies of scale produced by it. In concrete terms, the scale of production that enables us to obtain the minimum unit cost of production is larger, which forces concentration [ANG 07].

Next is Metcalfe's law. The "use" that a "user" takes from his/her belonging to a network grows with the number of members of the network. In other words, large networks attract more users because the larger the network, the more interesting it is to be a part of it. The operators therefore have an in interest in increasing the size of their networks [SHA 99].

Lastly, the feedback effects linked to supply and demand. Professionals benefit from production externalities to the extent that the growing use felt by the user, which comes from the widening of the network, enables them to broaden their market and realize economies of scale. These feedback effects between professionals and users have a cumulative character, which can be positive or negative, such as in the case of the computer. It is a well-known phenomenon: all a system has to do is to take the lead for new users to join it since they benefit from more important externalities. This leads to a tendency to form monopolies or quasi-monopolies, as illustrated by the example of PC and Microsoft. The crucial element in this approach is that a distinctive feature of the feedback linked to demand is “to strengthen the strong and weaken the weak” [SHA 98]. These two aspects of feedback intervene in information sector industries and force the concentration of firms.

In fact, we notice an emphasizing of concentration in information technology and media industries [MEI 05]. This phenomenon can also be connected to economic globalization and deregulation processes.

10.2.3. *Freedom of information, liberalization and economic globalization*

Since the 1980s, concentration in the media sector has obeyed the logic of deregulation and globalization [MAT 03]. The context of globalization and opening to market competition lead to the reinforcement of “media groups” that acquired an international dimension while attributing a deciding importance in their strategic decisions to the financial sphere. This evolution was marked by the arrival of new participants coming from industries such as telecoms, building, armament, electricity or water industries, attracted by the prospect of gains and new markets. These large industrial groups have strategies that rely on essentially financial logic. They also favor instant returns by placing managers who aim for a high return on investment in directing positions. The objective of profit thus prevails over values like diversity and quality of information.

There are many examples of groupings of companies within the information sector, examples of absorption of media by industrial groups, and of setting up of multi-national conglomerates integrating media that illustrate disruptions which the media scene has experienced since the beginning of the 1990s [BRE 05, RAM 05].

The debate on risks encountered ensuing from concentration in the communication sector thus doubled in intensity with the development of large multimedia groups and the taking control of media companies by industrial groups that appropriate factors that grow the most, while causing their profits to circulate freely on the global front. It leads to a weakening of the competition, which threatens media independence and pluralism and, consequently, the functioning of democracy.

This concentration leads to a structural asymmetry of information from which information power and information dominance[1] originate. The power linked to information confronts other powers, in particular, economic, financial, and political powers, in a process of auto-reinforcement.

Press concentration thus contributes to power concentration. In this matter, the proposals of Serge Dassault – reported by Claire Moriset and Bernard Miège [MAR 05] – are revealing: "The press is an interesting world that enables a certain number of sound ideas, orientations, to pass, in order for the economy to be better managed".

In fact, economic liberalization and globalization furthered the relief of public stakeholders through multinational private organizations. These processes lead to a private oligopolistic regulation that makes up the new package that weighs on freedom of expression.

Globalization in interaction with economic liberalization thus transforms the conditions of exercising freedom of expression and freedom of information. These two processes consequently modify the potentialities of participative democracy, of which the electronic revolution is a carrier.

10.3. Freedom of information and participative democracy

10.3.1. *Globalization, regionalization and need for information*

The approach of the current phase of globalization in terms of "local globalization" deepens the current globalization analysis. It is no longer simply a matter of considering globalization as a progressive process of opening of local systems pre-constructed on the exterior and the international. It means, however, that local-global relations are internal to the territorial entities themselves, and that a territorial economy is characterized by local-global coherence relations making up the local globalization [RAL 00]. In this perspective, an essential place is given to decisions taken at the local level for which information plays a central role. This information does take into account the increase in information demand and the

---

1. The "information power" of a unit or a stakeholder is based on an unequal possession of information and is defined as the capacity this unit has to modify, through information, the behavior of other units, with the goal of obtaining a clear advantage. This advantage, called "*rente informationnelle*" (translator's emphasis) consists, for example, of obtaining an economic gain to become a more important part of the market, or of a political advantage such as the gaining of votes. Information power in organizations and networks is, in the perspective of organization analysis, qualified by "information dominance" to signify that it enables a "domination" linked to information to be exercised within the organization [THE 02].

political and administrative process of regionalization, which is accompanied by the transfer of decisions to local authorities.

Empirical data actually attest to the growing place of information in economic and social mechanisms [COH 00]. We notice an increase in needs and use of information by stakeholders, consumers, producers and citizens for their decision-making.

In modern economies and societies, citizens and consumers need information in order to make the best decisions. In economic and financial markets, consumers demand that they be informed before choosing their products and titles. Producers need information on markets and competitors, and on market orientation. In the political domain, citizens must also have information on party candidates and programs in order to make the right choices. Stakeholders have recourse to varied sources of information and more and more to the Internet (*Le Monde* newspaper, dated 19 August, 2005).

Another fundamental tendency of today is the more and more urgent requirement to make decisions that engage the mid- and long-term future, such as decisions related to the degradation of the environment at the local or global level, the growing revenue gap in a country or on the global scale, or still the digital gap, questions that are a concern of the political sphere. The growing need for information is explained by political decision makers according to interdependence and phenomena for mastering information becoming more and more complex. It is also driven by user-citizens who want to participate in public debate, taking part in decisions, and evaluating the results obtained.

Modern economic information theory enables us to analyze the opposing mechanisms and to display the synergies existing between information and networked information and communication technologies from a participative democratic perspective. It also proves the perverse effects linked to information properties and leads to concrete propositions of policies.

10.3.2. *Economic information theory and secret information strategies*

Modern economic information analysis considers that its intrinsic characteristics of indivisibility or non-rivalry, inappropriateness (or non-exclusion) and externalities production, give it the status of collective goods, while its asymmetry contributes to the explanation of its influence and power effects.

Non-rivalry, in "pure" theory, means that the use of information by an agent does not diminish the possibilities of use of the same information by other individuals.

Thus there are national information services. Non-exclusion of information use means that an agent cannot prevent another individual from using such a good, as from the time it is produced it is potentially at everybody's disposal.

Because of these two properties, information generates "externalities" that designate all direct economic relations between agents not giving place to an exchange across market mechanisms. The proximity of a high turnover network exercises, for example, a positive externality if an individual takes an advantage from it without having to pay for it directly.

These properties lead to outstanding phenomena that are beneficial and harmful at the same time [THE 07]. Two advantageous effects are well known:

1) *Low cost reproducibility of information.* The same piece of information can be reproduced indefinitely, at low, even null, cost. In theory, the marginal cost of a pure collective good is null as its consumption by an extra individual does not represent any cost. In fact, information is costly to produce, but less costly to reproduce. But at the same time, this advantage can lead to a sub-optimal situation as it appears below.

2) *Increasing returns of information.* The same piece of information, like a piece of scientific or technical information, can be used several times in a production cycle or simultaneously in different places, which is a source of considerable increasing returns: information, not destroying itself in usage (property of non-rivalry), can be reutilized as long as it does not become obsolete. This effect is preferred by the diffusion facility of the collective good, at low, even null costs. Thus, by preserving its accessibility to the entire community, the collective advantages are greater than the private advantages. In other words, the "social return", as the effects are reduced.

Three other effects linked to intrinsic properties of information lead to the "failure" of the market to achieve the optimum in the welfare economics perspective– *A sub-optimal production by the market sector.* To leave information production to the sole market sector can turn out to be counterproductive. In the canonical neoclassical model, the price of a good must be fixed at its marginal cost of production, this condition ensuring the realization of Paretian optimality. Furthermore, the marginal cost of a pure collective good is null (see above). The Paretian optimality would therefore command a null price for this good, even if its fixed costs would be important. In theory, the good therefore risks not being produced by the private initiative.

– *The free rider phenomenon.* As an agent cannot be excluded from consuming a pure collective good, individuals, taken one by one, are not interested in announcing the true value they attribute to this good, to not have to pay as a consequence. This way, from the time it is produced, it is entirely at their disposal, without having to pay for it, or only pay a small price, which is below its value. Recent research showed that individuals tend to undervalue information compared to other goods, especially material goods [SAK 05; SAK 07a; SAK 09]. Concrete solutions to these paradoxes can consist of the setting up of property laws that enable private appropriation of the "information" good. However, since this appropriation is only imperfect because of the character of the information collective good, we run the risk of finding ourselves in a situation in which the information becomes artificially rare and socially under-utilized. A case representative of this phenomenon, currently the object of debates, focuses on human gene patentability [HEL 98]. The recognition of market "failure" because of the presence of collective goods justifies the recourse to an allocation of an alternative resources mechanism. The solution often comes back to the need for the State to intervene. But the supplying of "collective goods" by public powers can also generate "public discontentment". These perverse effects, such as the opportunist behaviors of bureaucrats, lead neo-liberal economists to advocate limiting State intervention to a minimum. These critics rely in particular on the property of information asymmetry, which represents another case of market failure.

– *Strategies of* rente informationnelle *and secret strategies*. The asymmetry of information causes "opportunistic behavior" and power relations. Opportunism in the sense used by Williamson includes, in particular, "adverse selection" and "moral risk", two attitudes that sum up the concept of opportunism. In more general terms, opportunism implies the dissemination of incomplete or deformed information with the goal of "misleading, de-naturing, disguising, disconcerting or planting confusion" [WIL 94]. Opportunism has been shown to be positively associated with Machiavellianism [SAK 07c] and to individualism [SAK 07b]. The retention or manipulation of information, similar to the breach of engagements taken without the other party in the contractual relation knowing, are examples of opportunistic attitudes that bring an added advantage beyond the normal profit of the standard model of welfare economics, to the detriment of the less informed party.

Information asymmetry is can be analyzed in terms of information power and *rente informaitonnelle*: if we assume the perspective of power based on a dis-symmetric relation, information asymmetry is situated at the cause of "information power". Information power measured by *rente informationnelle*, as a definite advantage, such as the gain resulting from possessing information advantage, remains to be seen [SAL 94].

Rente informationnelle, like all income, represents a surplus and appears as an explicative element of observable behavior. Economic gain obtained is a price, profit, part, market, etc., advantage. This analysis enables us to understand the information strategies of production, capitation, dissimulation or diffusion of information with the aim of benefiting from this income in ways that are not only economic but may be social or political [SAK 02; SAK 07c].

10.3.3. *Profitable information and participative democracy*

In fact, information asymmetry between governments and those which politicians are delimited to serve thus confer to them, in place of discretionary power, the ability to apply policies that serve their own interests more than those of citizens. By multiplying information, political men and those in power can obtain advantages like electors' gains and a re-election, thus assuring that they are kept in power, thus preserving the economic or social advantage linked to the exercise of power.

This process supposes that political decision makers and governments are interested in disseminating certain information or, on the contrary, hiding it from others, i.e. to practice the secret, to escape public control. These "opportunistic" practices go against the interests of citizens and of democracy. Transparency in the actions and results of policies practiced is, thus, as a keystone of democratic processes, a demand that enables us to fight against the abuses of secrecy.

The challenge is to know, because of possible opportunistic behaviors, which institutions are going to supply this information of general interest. There are several ways of tackling this challenge:

– Public powers must first work in this sense. In this perspective they must:

- ensure the transparency of actions and of those in power, by producing, for example, economic and social guides such as price indicators, rate of unemployment, etc. in a way that supplies quality information to citizens;

- preserve freedom of expression and freedom of the press, which is threatened in the context of economic liberalization and globalization through an accentuation of the concentration threatening media pluralism and functioning of the democracy;

- promote the "quasi-markets" of information. Whereas information asymmetry justifies public intervention in the domain of general interest information, this information can also produce "public discontentment" to effects that are more important than the advantages of "public goods" because of possible opportunistic behavior [GRE 94]. A possible solution is therefore the recourse to "quasi-markets", the setting up of independent organizations functioning on public finances and of which the mission would be to supply quality and independent information [KAU 02, MER 03].

– For their part, citizens and non-governmental organizations also have to lead actions to supply such information and demand more transparency. This can be done by institutions such as the French Media Observatory (whose mission is "to defend the right to inform and free and pluralist information") [OFM 05] or the promotion of concepts like "media concentration governance" which predicts a transparency debt of the media *vis-à-vis* the society [MEI 05].

– A central place must be accorded to the freedom to inform through the press, as when freedom of the press is respected not only do those in power generally not abuse their power, but they better satisfy the elementary social needs of the people.

Amarta Sen [SEN 03] showed in this way that the countries enjoying freedom of the press did not experience famine as newspapers attract attention to the problem and people considered it intolerable that the government did not do anything to remedy the situation. Similarly, studies of the World Bank [BAN 05] showed that making the publication of pollution rates obligatory was an efficient mechanism by which to lower pollution levels.

This democratic demand of freedom of information rejoins the imperatives of economic, social and human development.

10.4. Freedom of information and local economy

10.4.1. *Information and freedom of information, factors of prosperity and economic and social development*

A piece of information, such as a piece of economic information or a production technology, represents a factor of production and productivity that is particularly efficient as we are in the presence of increasingly high returns. Information is in fact an autonomous factor of production, in the same way as capital and work, with multiplying effects. From this fact, we can see that information represents an essential growth and productivity factor in the present context.

In the same way, freedom of information and expression, by favoring information dissemination, is also a factor and a component of economic and social development. Understood in its general sense as the freedom of speech, writing, publication, freedom of expression includes, in particular, freedom of informing *via* the press, and more generally media such as the internet.

The freedom to inform and the freedom of information dissemination enable agents to seize the economic opportunities or to cause competition to play. Thus, Stigler [STIR 61] and Stiglitz [STIZ 02] demonstrate that the availability of information is a crucial determinant of the efficiency of markets, both economic and political. For Stigler, the activity of information research by a consumer enables him/her to buy cheaper goods. In the same way, the information supplied by the media is of a nature for improving the performance of the economic system and ensuring economic and social growth and development [BAN 05].

New potentialities ensue from properties of information and networked technologies as collective goods. They are located in multiple domains, like those of economic growth, spatial localization of companies, and local development. Information mutation thus operates a progressive sliding of motors of economic development, from material towards immaterial. Furthermore, information and the services strongly contained in information are goods whose marginal cost is always decreasing, even null. The law of "growing offer of information at constant price" that ensues from it means outstanding economic growth perspectives are opened by the use of information as a productive resource, even if this law is only valid for a given infrastructure or scale [THE 02]. By stylizing the facts, this law translates, for example, to the fact that an administration can respond, at constant cost, to a growing demand for information on a site as long as it is not saturated and the information is not obsolete. It is a matter of course of stylization, and therefore of approximation of facts as in practice. The birth of the site represents a cost, while benefiting economies of scale that are much higher than the capacity of the infrastructure is important.

Another significant characteristic of an economy based on information stems from rapid and important development of an associative and cooperative non market production of individual and social utilities, which must certainly win, for the economic viability of the system, with a marketing of a part of the goods and services produced. The example of the Internet signifies this change [BOM 07]. Thus we enter an economy of abundance and possible varieties, but in which are posed the questions of financing of the high initial investment, of the job and the sharing of riches produced.

10.4.2. *Local economic and social development*

Information asymmetry can also have beneficial effects for a group of people, by obtaining collective *rente informationnelle,* such as those retrieved by a territorial community, for example. It is a matter of a rivalry and competition perspective at the same time. The mechanism put forward is that of the exercise of power with the view of obtaining income.

Information policy led by some territorial communities is analyzed as a procedure of creation of richness crossing, obtaining an economic advantage thanks to the combination of information and information and communication technologies

[THE 02]. It is therefore a matter of a "collective *rente informationnelle*", retrieved in view of its sharing by the community concerned. This policy crosses cooperative strategies with private operators in accordance with competition rules, but it also crosses cooperation, or competition, dynamics with other territories by practicing a selective distribution of information.

Placed in a collective dynamic perspective, information policy on one hand creates for users advantageous conditions of access to private and public information services, such as administrative services or tele-teaching. On the other hand it renders the territories more attractive for companies that are set up there or are likely to become established there. Finally, it aims to create, with the goal of favoring local development, a competitive environment for economic and social stakeholders, by being based on externalities produced by information and information technologies.

According to the scale considered, it is a matter of making at the local, regional or national level, a competitive information advantage in the perspective of territorial competition and global competition. In this perspective, territories and local participants are placed in a situation of competition, to use Perroux's terminology (1973).

However, another political economy perspective must be considered. The dominant economic analysis is actually strongly marked by its axial object, competition, and from now on produces and examines non-cooperative games. One alternative consists of examining cooperative games situations. This opening of the analysis leads to an interest in the cooperation between countries and regions, and must today develop, because of the current globalization of society and the economy, a problem in terms of "global cooperation" at the world level.

10.4.3. *Information and freedom of information as global collective goods*

In the perspective of such a cooperation, a certain number of arguments can be put forward enabling us to transpose the problem of collective goods as information and freedom of information, at the global level:

– with the development of recent communication technologies, more and more immaterial flow, such as flows of information, escape all possibility of control at the geographical borders of states;

– in the economic field, global participants appear, such as the large multinational societies whose strategies and economic and financial powers enable rivalry with the state's;

– the r state finds its role weakened by globalization, in particular, when it comes to the control of movements of capital and teleservices activities;

– problems like pollution, natural catastrophes or epidemics exceed state boundaries;

– globalization unveils global stakes linked to the definition of the field of goods and services escaping to purely market exchange like knowledge;

– a political and civilian procedure estimates that questions of economic and social development come under decisions made at the global level.

In fact, neoliberal regulation progressively put in place since the 1980s is a regulation by imperfect markets that represent unstable conditions as demonstrated by economic theory and which cause structural and conjectural economic dysfunctions to appear nowadays. It is therefore necessary to find new frameworks of analysis and propositions.

One answer is based on the idea that the states cannot again become central operators of a new regulation of world economy [MIC 02]. Regulation agencies in charge of elaborating and causing universal norms to apply, for example, could be put in place. The domains of competences of these regulators correspond to the existence of global collective goods, such as anti-trust regulation, the global environment, the harmonization of work conditions, the control of speculative movement, intellectual and industrial property, global humanitarian aid, knowledge, etc.

The evolution of ideas in this direction is in line with the current globalization movement and takes on a capital importance for envisaging cooperation and solidarity at the global level. We assume that information of general interest, in the same way as the freedom to inform, covers the status of "global collective good", at the same level furthermore as other goods like knowledge, or still the security and economic, social and human development. We then enter a problem of global governance, in which freedom of information has a crucial place because of intrinsic characteristics of information. The taking into account of these properties of information at the theoretical level enables us to put forward propositions of concrete policies.

10.5. Conclusion

The preceding developments enable us to contribute to the current debate on "methodological individualism" *versus* "holism", two methods of analysis, often opposed, and lead to suggesting an integrated approach.

In social sciences, methodological individualism is intended to go from the individual (the part) to society (the whole), economic and social phenomena being explained exclusively from individual behavior. In economics, this mode of analysis is central in the neoclassic theory which is situated at the base of the liberal economic model and the foundation of competitive capitalism. The standard version of this theory, dominant today in economic thought, develops the problem of rational choices and stipulates the neutrality of economic agents, i.e. the absence of the individual power of agents "atomized" within the economy. The rational individual, or *Homo œconomicus*, is selfish (he/she only takes into account his/her own interest), maximizing (he/she maximizes his/her profit or his/her use) and makes an autonomous unit of decision (his/her behavior is not determined by social constraints). Guided by the principle of rationality, individuals search for their personal interest and achieve an optimal situation in a competitive system, under the hypothesis of perfect information. To strive towards this ideal, we must turn back to economic liberalism, a model of organization that leads to general economic equilibrium and thus brings proof of market optimality and the superiority of the capitalist system. These results explain why liberal economists refer to the competitive market.

Holism, the system of global explanation, adopts the procedure that first assumes the whole (a given society) then analyses how to insert therein the decision of individuals or parties. According to this method, it is possible to lead theoretical and empirical analyses from global entities (social groups, for example) to which are attributed specific properties, individual behaviors being inscribed in an institutional framework (social organization, belonging to a social category, etc), the study of which is at least as important as that of individuals.

By mobilizing the "principal-agent" model, economic information theory is based on a method of analysis situated between methodological individualism and holism. This model actually examines, in the framework of contracts theory, the bilateral relations between a "principal" and an "agent" placed in information asymmetry, with some individuals having an information advantage. This configuration represents a particular form of organization in which the two fascinating parts of the contract are always equipped with absolute rationality, but no longer have the same information as the standard model. Economic agents adopt, from then on, research or manipulation of information strategies and thus cover the status of participants, the opposite of the neutrality principle. This renewing of the neoclassic theory thus introduces dimensions that are similar to the holistic approach.

Actually, in the configurations under information asymmetries, some individuals have, only, information to which others do not directly have access. The essential problem is from now on that of the revelation to other agents of private information held by informed agents. The mode of revelation of information advantage leads to two principle mechanisms: "moral risk" [ARR 63] and "adverse selection" [AKE 07].

In the presence of these two behavioral mechanisms, imbalances appear. To overcome these market failures, incentive mechanisms are implemented to reveal hidden information and to thwart "opportunistic behaviors" linked to information asymmetry. The analysis of strategic implications of information asymmetries progressed thanks to advances of incitation theory and, more generally, of contract theory. The latter, of neoclassic inspiration, was revealed to essentially explain the existence of behavioral mechanisms and institutions that do not find a place in the models with perfect information and neutrality of agents.

Contract theory also presents the advantage of introducing the phenomenon of power in neoclassical theory. The different approaches of contracts actually agree at the minimum on an implication of the possession of an information advantage: economic agents that hold this advantage tend to use to their profit by extracting from it a "*rente informationnelle*" defined as the differential gain procured by an information advantage [SAL 94]. It is a matter of a considerable overhang compared to the power status in the model of general equilibrium. But this theory remains of limited reach to take into account the power attached to information in the economy as it essentially mobilizes the micro-economic calculation and confines itself to the framework of bilateral relations, by retaining always the principle of "absolute rationality" or "substantive".

This principle was however challenged, from the 1940s, by Simon who forges the notion of "limited rationality". This notion expresses the idea that the economic agent, confronted with partial knowledge and equipped with restricted cognitive capacities to deal with information in an accurate way, cannot lead a program of maximization of its utility, as envisaged by the premise of "unlimited" or "substantive rationality". He is happy with a certain level of "satisfaction" and when applied achieves routine and sequential decision making procedures, from where the expression "procedural rationality" comes.

Simon's ideas [SIM 45] originate from fruitful theoretical developments that take into account information costs and no longer make, from the calculation of maximization, the foundation of action against agents. Thus, the neo-institutional theory, of which Williamson is the leader, was constructed from 1975 on the basis of the theory of "transaction costs" – costs linked to the exchange and ensuing from the limited rationality of "opportunistic behaviors". For its part, the conventions theory was developed from 1985 through recognizing the contributions of the neoclassicist and by introducing non-market forms of coordination to guide individuals' decisions. For its part, evolutionist theory takes as reference the work of Richard Nelson and Sidney Winter [NEL 82] and shows the role played by routines and teaching, therefore by the transmission and transformation of information and knowledge in the evolution of companies and productive sectors.

The economic heterodox theory also recognizes the existence of global power phenomena linked to information in organizations and networks. An attempt to model this power was undertaken notably following Perroux's theory of domination [PER 73], which deals with information like a typical form of power. The notion of "economic domination" was deepened by authors like Lantner [LAN 74], who forged formalized concepts of "dominance, dependence, economic interdependences". Elaborated in the prolonging of these analyses, the notion of "information dominance" [THE 02] designates the information power within an organization or a network of exchanges and is translated by obtaining a *rente informationelle*.

To these structural approaches today echo many socioeconomic works that return to the flavor of the day questions relating to power, authority and influence [FRI 01]. These are asked for example by the study of the dynamic of virtual communities, transformation of modes of consumption, mutations of salary relation and, more generally, in the study of the dynamic of collective action [WAT 04].

In fact, the contributions of modern economic information theory renew the standard neoclassical theory while surpassing it through the taking into account of the existence of conventions, institutions, teachings and routines, whose representations come under the holistic method. Here, agents have behaviors of individual interest research, but their rationality is limited and their strategies are inscribed in an institutional framework whose emergence is explained by their limited capacities of information treatment and their insertion in an environment of imperfection of information and uncertainty.

10.6. Bibliography

[AKE 70] AKERLOF G., "The market for "lemons": quality uncertainty and the market mechanism", *The Quarterly Journal of Economics*, vol. 84, no. 3, p. 488-500, 1970.

[ANG 07] ANGELER J.-P., *Economie des Industries de Réseau,* PUG, Grenoble, 2007.

[ARR 63] ARROW K.-J., "Uncertainty and the welfare economics of medical care", *American Economic Review*, vol. 53, no. 5, p. 941-973, 1963.

[BAN 05] BANQUE MONDIALE, *Le Droit d'Informer. Le Rôle des Médias dans le Développement Économique*, 2nd edition, De Boeck University, Brussels, 2005.

[BRE 05] BRÉMOND J., "Lagardère, Bouygues, Dassault, Vivendi, Bertelsmann et quelques autres", in: *Observatoire Français des Médias (OFM), Sur la Concentration dans les médias*, Liris Editions, Paris, 2005.

[COH 98] COHEN D., DEBONNEUIL M., *Nouvelle Économie*, report of the Conseil d'Analyse Economique, La Documentation Française, Paris, 1998.

[COR 90] CORIAT B., *L'Atelier et le Robot*, Christian Bourgois, Paris, 1990.

[FRI 01] FRIEDKIN N.E., "Norm formation in social influence network", *Social Networks*, vol. 23, p. 167-189, 2001.

[GRE 94] GREFFE X., *Economie des politiques publiques,* Dalloz, Paris, 1994.

[HEL 98] HELLER M., EISENBERG R., "Can patents deter innovation? The anticommons in biomedical research", *Science*, vol. 280, p. 698-701, 1998.

[KAU 02] KAUL I., GRUNBERG I., STERN M., "La définition des biens publics mondiaux", *Les biens publics mondiaux*, 2nd edition, Economica, Paris, 2002, p. 27-46.

[LAN 74] LANTNER R., *Théorie de la Dominance Économique*, Dunod, Paris, 1974.

[MAT 03] MATHIEN M., *Economie Générale des Médias*, Ellipses, Paris, 2003.

[MEI 05] MEIER W., "Média concentration governance: une nouvelle plate-forme pour débattre des risques?", *Réseaux*, vol. 23, no. 131, p. 19-52, 2005.

[MER 03] MERTENS S., LEFÈBVRE M., "Théorie économique et marchandisation des services marchands", *Non Marchand*, vol. 11, 2003, p. 11-27.

[MIC 02] MICHALET C.-A., *Qu'est-ce que la Mondialisation?*, La Découverte, Paris, 2002.

[MOR 05] MORISET Cl., MIÈGE B., "Les industries du contenu sur la scène médiatique", *Réseaux,* vol. 23, no. 131, p. 145-185, 2005.

[NEL 82] NELSON R., WINTER S., *An Evolutionary Theory of Economic Change*, Harvard University Press, Cambridge (MA), 1982.

[OFM 05] OBSERVATOIRE FRANÇAIS DES MEDIAS (OFM), *Sur la Concentration dans les Médias*, Liris Editions, Paris, 2005.

[PER 73] PERROUX F., *Pouvoir et Économie,* Laborde, Paris, 1973.

[RAL 00] RALLET A. "De la globalisation à la proximité géographique: pour un programme de recherche", in: J.-P. GILLY, A. TORRE (eds), *Dynamiques de Proximité*, L'Harmattan, Paris, 2000, p. 37-57.

[RAM 05] RAMONET I., "Médias concentrés", in: Observatoire Français des Médias (OFM), *Sur la Concentration dans les Médias*, Liris Editions, Paris, 2005, p. 15-18.

[SAK 02] SAKALAKI M., "Normes, conventions et reprétrie d'information", *Revue Internationale de Psychologie Sociale,* vol. 15, p. 117-146, 2002.

[SAK 05] SAKALAKI M., THÉPAUT Y., "La valeur de l'information. Evaluation des biens informationnels versus biens matériels", *Questions de Communication*, vol. 8, p. 355-365, 2005.

[SAK 07a] SAKALAKI M., KAZI S., "How much is information worth? The valuation of expert and non-expert informational goods compared to the valuation of material goods in lay economic thinking", *Journal of Information Science*, vol. 33, no. 6, p. 315-325, 2007.

[SAK 07b] SAKALAKI M., KAZI S., KARAMANOLI V., "Do individualists have a higher opportunistic propensity than collectivists?: Individualism and economic cooperation", *Revue Internationale de Psychologie Sociale*, vol. 20, p. 59-76, 2007.

[SAK 07c] SAKALAKI M., RICHARDSON C., THEPAUTY Y., "Machiavellianism and economic opportunism", *Journal of Applied Social Psychology*, vol. 37, p. 1181-1190, 2007.

[SAK 09] SAKALAKI M., KAZI S., "Valuing and representing information: The paradox of undervaluing information and overvaluing information producers", *Journal of Information Science*, vol. 35, no. 2, p. 153-164, 2009.

[SAL 94] SALANIÉ B., *Théorie des Contrats,* Economica, Paris, 1994.

[SEN 03] SEN A., *Un Nouveau Modèle Économique. Développement, Justice, Liberté,* 2nd edition, Odile Jacob, Paris, 2003.

[SHA 99] SHAPIRO C., VARIAN H., *Economie de l'Information*, 2nd edition, De Boeck University, Paris, Brussels, 1999.

[SIM 45] SIMON H.A., *Administrative Behavior. A Study of Decision-Making Processes in Administrative Organization*, The Free Press, New York, 1945.

[STIR 61] STIGLER G., "The economics of information", *Journal of Political Economy*, vol. 69, no. 3, p. 213-225, 1961.

[STIZ 02] STIGLITZ J.-E, "La connaissance comme bien public mondial", *Les biens publics mondiaux*, 2nd edition, Economica, Paris, 2002, p. 157-176.

[STIZ 05] STIGLITZ J.-E., "Gouvernement et transparence", *Le Droit d'Informer. Le Rôle des Médias dans le Développement Économique*, 2nd edition, De Boeck University, Brussels, 2005.

[THE 07] THÉPAUT Y., "Economie libérale et liberté d'expression dans le contexte de la révolution informationnelle", in: A. KIYINDOU, M. MATHIEN (eds), *Evolution de l'Économie Libérale et Liberté d'Expression,* Bruylant, Brussels, 2007, p. 27-58.

[THE 06] THÉPAUT Y., "Le concept d'information dans l'analyse économique contemporaine", Hermès, vol. 44, p. 1661-168, 2006.

[THE 02] THÉPAUT Y., *Pouvoir, Information, Economie*, Collection "Approfondissement de la Connaissance Economique", Economica, Paris, 2002.

[THE 02] THÉPAUT Y., LE GOFF R., "Services publics informationnels et collectivités territoriales: l'exemple manchois", in: G. HÉNAFF (ed), *Concurrence et Services Publics*, PUR, Rennes, 2002, p. 193-210.

[VOL 99] VOLLE M., *Economie des Nouvelles Technologies*, Economica, Paris, 1999.

[WIL 94] WILLIAMSON O., *Les Institutions de l'Économie*, InterEditions, Paris, (1st edition. 1985) 1994.

[WAT 04] WATTS D.J., "The "new" science of networks", *Annual Review of Sociology,* vol. 30, p. 243-270, 2004.

Chapter 11

Internet in the Public Library

11.1. Introduction

Think before going out. This cable operator's slogan, illustrated by photos of a surly librarian, invited us, the customer, to desert public libraries without regret: Actually, what's the use of leaving home when the modern Babel library is accessible from there?

That was in 2002. Six years later, the French have not deserted public libraries; visits, if not registration, are up [MAR 07]. All books are not (yet) digitized, the borrowing of printed documents remains the main reason for visiting, but not the only one. At the *Bibliothèque Publique d'Information* of the Pompidou Center in Paris, for example, nearly one in six users says he comes "to use the Internet" [CAM 07]. This practice, which has increased with the supply of public access computers in public libraries, raises questions: who are the users of this service? Why do they access the Internet in the library? Do they not have a computer at home or do they use a computer differently at the library? How is this practice combined with other uses of the library? And above all, how does it integrate itself, through combination or substitution, with other information and communication research practices?

We know that the Internet is the "medium for doing everything"; a mass medium and a vector of interpersonal communication [DON 07] at the same time. Due to this fact, the study of the Internet use raises methodological problems time and time again, as indicated by researchers. Whether it is a matter of consumption of cultural

---

Chapter written by Muriel AMAR, Agnès CAMUS-VIGUÉ, Christophe EVANS, and Françoise GAUDET.

products or consumption of communication, today we are seeing an "intertwining" of tools and uses, which prevents us from focusing on a unique object of study [SMO 07]. The complexity of new technologies which mix text, image and sound, and favor nomadism blur, for example, traditional boundaries between audiovisual culture and print culture, or between the "culture of going out" and the "culture of staying home" [DON 07]. From this point of view, the public library constitutes an interesting field of observation. In this public space, open to all, the diversity of the cultural supply (printed, audiovisual, digital, etc) and the ability to borrow or copy documents favors the multiplicity of practices. These possibilities give users the choice of "consuming" on the spot and/or at home. Furthermore, some libraries adopted the Internet very early, which affords a retrospective look at this practice.

11.2. A still inadequate national supply

Actually, two pioneer public libraries in France, – the city library of Issy-les-Moulineaux and the Bpi of the Pompidou Center – proposed public access to the Internet in their reading rooms in 1995 [CHA 97]. We will note that the precocious introduction of this new medium was not necessarily obvious in the library universe, where television and radio had made only timid appearances. This innovation was justified by the interest in the Internet as an information resource and by the will of librarians to "allow readers on the spot to question, not the available documents in the reading area, but the multiple sources of information and documents proposed on the Internet network" [BAU 96].

Three years later, according to the results of a survey launched by the directorate of Books and Reading of the Ministry of Culture and Communication (DLL), 137 city libraries – or 8.4% of all the public libraries in cities of more than 2,000 inhabitants – offered public access to the Internet [MAD 99]. Still modest figures compared to American libraries in the same era, but accompanied by almost unanimous agreement of the librarians on the use of this new service. Observers also noted that: "whereas today systematic discussions about Iinternet access in libraries remain, they focus only on the question of price, the control of uses, or the nature of complementary benefits offered. There seem to be unanimity on the relevance of the service itself" [POU 99].

The latest figures compiled by the DLL report 1,843 city libraries, or 65% of libraries listed, offering public access to the Internet in 2007 In 62.9% of the cases access is free but it is generally constrained. Users are often obliged to reserve a computer with Internet access for a limited time. Access to some features of the Internet, such as messaging or downloading, is frequently forbidden. A survey conducted recently in Brittany illustrates this reality well: although 78% of libraries of cities in this region with more than 10,000 inhabitants offered access in 2007, only 49% of them authorized messaging, 13% authorized chat, and 10% accepted downloading.

The example of the Bpi of the Pompidou Center confirms the existence of these constraints. After waiting in the line that forms daily at the doors of the "Beaubourg"[1], the visitor wishing to consult the Internet will be offered without delay the chance to visit many sites selected by the library on one of 164 multimedia work stations distributed in the reading areas. On the other hand, if he/she wants to surf in order to access information to his/her taste, he/she will have to enter another waiting line to reserve one of the 58 work stations dedicated to this service. He/she will therefore be able to navigate "freely" on the Internet for 40 minutes: we assume that he/she will be able to surf as he/she likes on the condition that he/she does not access sites blocked by the filtering software put in place by the library. Messaging, long forbidden, is now authorized, but downloading remains illegal. Despite these limitations, these 58 positions are permanently occupied.

In general, supply remains visibly inferior to demand, and the constraints imposed by librarians most often aim only to prevent some users from monopolizing a rare resource. We are not surprised in these conditions to note that, at the national level, the percentage of French people age 12 and over who admit to logging on to the Internet in the previous 12 months in a public place (cybercafé, library, post office, etc) reached a maximum of 12 or 13% of the population three years ago, whereas the rate of connection at home has not stopped increasing [BIG 08]. These average figures taken from the Crédoc (French Research Center for the Study and Observation of Living Conditions) *Conditions de vie et aspirations des Français* (*Ways of living and aspirations of the French*) survey, hide the important disparities according to age. It is mainly young people and qualified people who use public access: 25% of 18-24 year olds are connected in this way, and 25% of students. After 40 years of age, this percentage drops to 9%, and 3% after 59 year old.

Thanks to the observations of librarians and sociologists, we actually know that the Internet access is a service that is particularly prized by young users of public libraries (see for example [ZOT 06]). A recent Crédoc quantitative survey on the uses of French city libraries confirms it: although only 14% of users admit to having logged on to the Internet in a local library at least once, 43% of young users (between 15 and 24 years) are in this group [MAR 07]. The study shows that compared to the average French person, people who visit public libraries more often have a connection at home, which tends to invalidate the idea that domestic Internet access would systematically render library visit null and void. In reality, we observe here, once again, a phenomenon of accumulation of practices. Similarly, the *Conditions de vie et aspirations des Français* survey already cited indicates that

1. The nickname for the Center.

among the people who were logged on to the Internet in a public place in the last 12 months, 64% also logged on at home. Here again, the survey demonstrates a strong correlation of practices: "any type of connection leads to increased probability of also logging on in another way" [BIG 07].

Americans, for their part, have long considered that the services offered by their public libraries are mainly for disadvantaged people or those badly equipped at home. Today they notice that on either side of the digital divide – which unfortunately separates individuals with high speed connection from those with low speed connection or no connetion – everyone may turn to public libraries to become informed in his/her daily life and in particular to resolve problems of an administrative nature [EAST 07]. However, it is probable that American individuals do not go out for the same reasons, have recourse to the Internet on different occasions and do not use it in the same way.

The Bpi gives a good comprehensive view of this diversity of uses.

11.3. The Bpi: an observatory of expectations and uses

As particular as it is, this position of observation offers a very interesting framework for studying the question of Internet use in the public sphere. Actually, the Bpi is an encyclopedic library of national scale, open to everybody, but largely visited by students who represent nearly three-quarters of visitors. The image of modernity provided by this totally free establishment that exists within a national center of art and culture, the multitude of reasons for visit the Bpi and the slightly elevated average age of users – 26 years – make it a good place to analyze the Internet-public phenomenon. We would think that the emerging digital practices of the "philoneists" (lovers of innovations) may be well represented there.

In addition, this library since its creation has been accumulating observations and studies on the practices of its users. The Bpi actually has a studies and research department, which functions as a research cell and like an observatory of library publics at the same time[2]. Every three or five years, general use surveys are conducted on people using the library. While many targeted quantitative and qualitative studies (observations, semi-directive interviews, focus groups, etc) are

2. Outside of applied studies, targeted by the Bpi, the studies and research department leads more general and fundamental research on reading and cultural practices that are associated to it: it is interested, for example, in cultural uses of information and communication techniques and in the new modes of reading that emerge. Some of these studies are realized by the two sociologists belonging to the department. Others are conducted of by external research teams that join the framework of research programs that the studies and research department launches annually with the support of the DLL.

continuously conducted on such-and-such a type of use or user, the data presented here are taken from these different sources, and not from an *ad hoc* study on Internet use in library reading areas. Evidently we must use some methodological precautions if we are to put into perspective results stemming from protocols of diverse studies. Each of these studies has its biases, but also its specific mode of grasping the phenomenon. On the other hand, such studies offer comparisons in time that can turn out to be instructive in more than one way.

The data stemming from general surveys allow us – in principle – to follow the existence and progression of a practice such as logging on to the Internet in reading areas. Less than 5% of people questioned in 1997 did so *versus* 12.5% in 2006. This figure does not cover all Internet uses in the library, however. It only takes into consideration individuals who logged on with the help of Bpi computers, and not those who did it from a personal laptop via a Wi-Fi connection[3]. The questionnaire used in the Bpi has been made obsolete today by the emergence of a practice that has developed quickly enough: 12.5% of people questioned in 2006 came to the library with a laptop on the very day of the survey (three times more than in 2003) and two-thirds of this group admit to having used Wi-Fi during their visit[4]. The survey protocol used shows a form of institutional ethnocentrism: the evaluation being centered on the offer of the library, more than on the complete range of effective public uses. It found itself quickly exceeded by practices that hold as many bypasses of the supply than the interlacing of uses. We will came back to it soon.

Nevertheless we notice that the number of visitors who come to the library with the declared intention of using the Internet progresses steadily (4% of people questioned in 2000, 8% in 2003, and 10% in 2006). While not the major reason for the visit, it is common enough: 10% of the public, that is roughly 600 people per day. But only a minority – 1.5% of people questioned – had this sole intention in mind. Use of the Internet therefore essentially becomes another reason visitors come to the library, the first of which is to work on their own documents (one out of every two persons among those who admit coming to use the Internet) and to research a document or some information (also one out of every two persons). Furthermore, the differential between those who came to use the Internet via the Bpi work stations on the day of the survey and those who actually did so is 4.5 points (they consist of 8% in the first case and 12.5% in the second). These results imply that during their visit,

3. We asked the people whether they used the library's computers, and then, in the case of a positive response, whether or not they consulted the Internet.

4. We can see, significantly, that 20% of those who came with the plan to use the Bpi Internet admit having come with their personal computer on the same day.

some people use the Internet who did not plan to do so, or that using the Internet did not constitute in itself a reason for visiting among the people questioned[5].

We know that the Internet is a never ending source of enjoyment and wandering, but the reasons for visiting of those who we will call here, to simplify things, the "internet-plan" are definite. Three quarters of "Internet-plans" therefore came from a need to satisfy a school or professional demand. The remaining quarter have come to satisfy a practical need or a personal interest (against 12% only of the entire public on this point, i.e. 50% less). However, without being able to really extrapolate from these data for the time being, we can note that 31% of the "Internet-plan" admit to coming to the Bpi generally "for pleasure", against only 18% of the whole of the public.

Regarding personal equipment, 13% of the "Internet-plan" admit to having no access at all to a computer, compared to only 4.5% of all visitors, 62% of whom admit furthermore to having access to a computer at home, compared to 85.5% of the total population. Consequently we notice that a percentage of people who come to the Bpi to use the Internet do not have easy access to the Internet. It is evidently not a question here of attempting to make the numbers speak out of measure: these under-equipped people are in the minority, but they are despite everything tendentiously more represented among the "Internet-plan". On the other hand, and it is just as significant, 79% of the "Internet-plan" admit to surfing every day or almost every day on the Internet – wherever that may be – compared to 82% of the total population. This overcomes the fact that there is a bit of a gap on this point: it is mainly confirmed surfers and not occasional surfers or neophytes who use library Internet services. In 2009, the time has clearly gone when we would encounter people at the Bpi, as at the end of the 1990s, who were coming to try to surf on the Internet simply "to see".

Other descriptive data at our disposal for profiling the "Internet-plan" furthermore show that they represent relatively different characteristics compared to the total population of library users. Whereas the man-woman division among the "Internet plan" is close to that observed in reading areas (as many men as women in the first case, 48% of men *versus* 52% of women in the second), we will note that there are fewer students in the "Internet-plan" compared to the total population, and a greater number of working people, job seekers and retirees, (see Figure 11.1 below).

5. A differential of the same order was observed in the French National Library (BNF) in a general public survey carried out in 2005. Nineteen per cent of people questioned upon leaving the Haut-de-jardin level of the library said they had used the Internet on the day of the survey, whereas it was only a reason for visiting for 10% of people sampled.

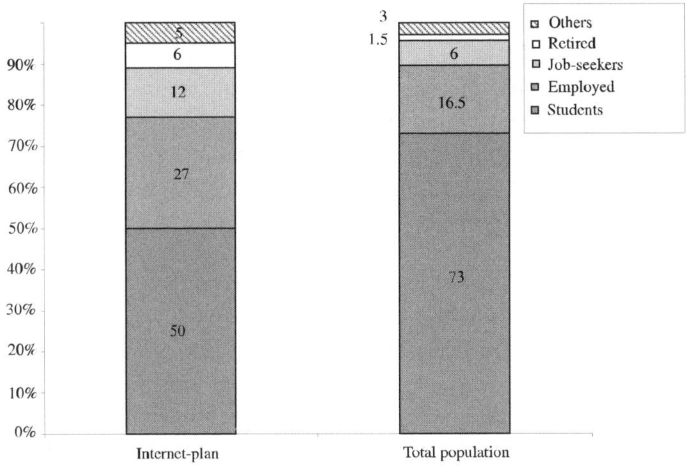

Figure 11.1. *Compared structure of the population of "internet-plan" and all Bpi (those visiting the library intending to surf the web on the left and all those who visited the library on the right)*

This distribution is a little more balanced. It has as a corollary, a higher average age (32 years). The "Internet-plan" individuals are older, for example, than users of books, who are on average 26 years old, which is the average age of all visitors. This counter-intuitive result apparently contradict observation data collected on other fields showing that those who are comfortable in the digital world are more likely to be young people. But we must not forget that the Bpi is massively frequented by young students who mainly use books, even in today's digital society.

These initial quantitative data taken from the general use survey are not sufficient. Consequently, it is convenient to complete them with other sources, quantitative and qualitative, notably to approach the question of types of use and their meaning. It is what we are going to attempt to do by examining some salient profiles. It is evidently not possible to cover the entire spectrum of user practices. The library, once again, offers the researcher a field for observations in which it is possible to study a multitude of practices without being limited to a specific domain: symbolic uses;practical uses of information and learning, cultural practices; diverse and varied communication practices (interpersonal or not, mediatized or not); and of course, concerning the internet, entertainment activities.

11.3.1. *Foreigners and the French*

Let us begin by examining a user profile that is well represented among Bpi surfers: people of non-French, or foreign, nationality. They represent 55% of the

"Internet-plan" whereas foreigners only count for 32% of the total population. Furthermore, we notice by comparing the profiles of people of foreign nationality who admit to coming to use the Internet with those of the French who come for the same reason, that the composition of the two groups is noticeably different (see Figure 11.2). It can be noted, for example, that among the French "Internet-plan", students are less represented, than among the foreign "Internet-plan". On this point, nationality is a significant line of divide.

This characteristic of Internet uses in the Bpi already struck us during a survey we carried out in 2004 on the basis of the study of log files collected on the "free Internet" work stations in the library [AMA 04][6]. Whereas Google was, unsurprisingly, the most consulted website in our sample, second place was occupied by a Russian language site, and fourth place by a Polish language site. In a more general way, the study of the language of sites consulted revealed that 61% of requests focused on non-francophone sites; a great linguistic variety characterized the consultations, with more than 20 different languages identified, among which English represented only 20% of sites accessed. Russian appeared in third position, and totaled 18% of sites listed. The study also revealed a clear distinction between the profiles of francophone and non-francophone consultations, as shown in Table 11.1.

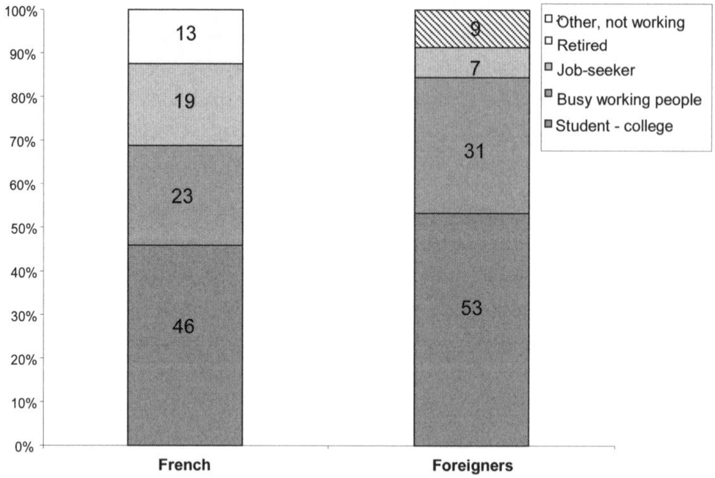

Figure 11.2. *'Internet plan" – French people compared to foreigners accessing the Internet at the library*

6. Study of connection data collected during the month of June 2004 on 50 "free Internet" work stations of the Bpi. See [AMA 04] for a description of the computer application used and precisions on the analysis corpus.

The categorization of a sample of sites consulted shows that sites grouped in the category "Practices" lead francophone consultations, undoubtedly because of the success of job-hunting sites (43% of consultations were in this category). On the other side, this category "Practices" is almost non-existent among the non-francophone consultations, while "Portals and search engines" category occupies a dominant position. Let us note that foreign news portals represent about a third of sites in this last category (therefore they are closer to the "News" category) and that games count for 93% of queries in the "Leisure" category.

The exploitation of statistical data therefore allows us to produce profiles of use. "French-speaking" profiles prefer access to exploitable offline intelligence (practical life) whereas non-French-speaking profiles are more centered on strictly online consumer services (such as games and news).

Francophone sites	**%**	**Non-francophone sites**	**%**
Practices	28.1	Portals and search engines	43.4
News	17	Leisure	22.4
E-commerce sites	16.1	News	14.9
Teaching	11.3	Dating	7.1
Portals and search engines	8.4	Documentaries	4.5
Web services	7.5	Web services	3
Documentaries	7.3	E-commerce sites	2.7
Dating	3	Teaching	1.3
Leisure	1.3	Practices	

Table 11.1. *Francophone and non-francophone consultations in number of queries (other than Google)*

These particularities of linguistic communities who frequent the library are expressed as much in Internet use as in that of other services offered by the library, such as world television stations, foreign press or self-training areas. We can conclude that being foreign or not being a French speaker influences uses more heavily than being an Internet user in the Bpi. The same observation can be made for job-seekers.

11.3.2. *Job-seekers*

The study of log files of "free Internet" work stations shows, as we have seen, the interest of francophone Internet users in job search sites. Searches for jobs represent almost half of the connections grouped in the category "Practices". Thus we count in our survey 10,832 queries made on the ANPE site – the first French job information site consulted. In total, other job search sites had more than 6,000 queries. Let us note that job seekers make use of all available means: this type of query is also frequent on multimedia work stations giving access to digital resources and sites catalogued by the Bpi (15.3% of all queries).

Data collected thanks to detailed interviews, individual or collective, allow us to go beyond these traces of use and observe the documentary journeys of people looking for work[7]. Peter or Paula, for example, come to the Bpi once or twice a week, stay less than two hours and only consult magazines and the Internet. This type of journey can encompass other resources, such as those found in the self-training area.

Whereas Internet use is indeed indispensible for answering job ads today, the Internet is also used to go beyond this, into the territory of training and improving people's standard of work. In this case, visit to sites offering training programs is compulsory. Therefore, Tom, a 30-year-old forklift truck operator in search of work came to consult the Internet in the Bpi because he was seeking to be admitted to a workshop organized by AFPA (the French National Association for the Vocational Training of Adults):

> "It's not a good thing when you don't have a computer, you have to get on the Internet. I'm going to ask for Internet access to be able to go… actually, in the AFPA website. To see, yes, what they suggest as training. To see the level… the entry conditions too. Because I think it's not everybody who, who goes there".

This young unemployed man echoes deep changes that have been affecting our society since the 1990s. An entire part of the social game unfortunately happens on the Internet. Today, to find a job or a training course becomes more difficult without a connection to the Internet. Outside of the fact that the net gives access to job ads or training offers, the Internet is a way of quickly responding to these advertisements. But there again, the technical resource can become an obstacle when it is imposed as a norm on the job market. This is emphasized by this same user:

---

7. Data collected in focus groups held at the Bpi in November 2007 [CAM 07] and from the study on the self-training area of the Bpi. [CAM 06].

"I found an ad, they were looking for someone to install medical material, prepare orders, train, etc, well that's not a problem, driver's license for more than two years, ok, oral and written standard French, it's not a problem… so 'If you are interested in these offers, e-mail…' so I have to send my CV and a covering letter to the e-mail address… There it is, no telephone… anyway it's something that's not normal. It's that if you don't have a computer, you can't work, roughly speaking."

Here, the library effectively gives solutions. It facilitates access to the Internet, which is indispensible, and by doing this provides the chance to remain in a professional circuit. It completes the ANPE offer, and allows the users regularly practice using computer tools.

Genevieve, a commercial assistant who is looking for a job, therefore get used to coming to the self-training area of the Bpi to use educational software for office suite and language learning. She does not have a computer at home and she feels the need to practice what she has learned through the workshops. During her visit, she can therefore improve her skills, access different job ads, answer them by e-mail, and prepare herself for interviews at the same time:

"that boosted me to come yesterday. It gave me courage. I came yesterday, I worked on PowerPoint and after I checked the job ads ", she said.

11.3.3. *Practices in which the Internet interferes*

Internet use at the Bpi, far from being isolated from that of other information media available in the library, on the contrary seems to support others uses by bringing in with it all the advantage of a comprehensive medium. Let us note, for example, that some users take an Internet access ticket the time they arrive, without any definite plan and without being sure of using it, but in case they might "feel the need" [CAM 07]. On the contrary, Internet consultation sometimes happens during the library visit without there being prior intention.

The Internet is, in these cases, viewed as an available object, made accessible in the same way as books, newspapers and compact discs; it is expected in a public place designated for information and culture. Among people who admit to having used the Internet from Bpi computers, a little more than half also admit to having used books during their visit (as was the case of 59% of all users) [CAM 07]. If they consulted fewer books than average library users, these web users posted scores a little higher than the average on the other media (see Figure 11.3).

Consequently, for a good number of users, the widened supply of Internet in the library goes well with the offer that the library makes. Simply put, the logic of one and the other accumulates. Regular users can often be heard saying "Everything is in the Bpi"; in the same way, "everything is on the Internet". In any case, it is a similar encyclopedic model, as noticed by Bruno Maresca:

> "the encyclopedic model of the Internet and that of the multimedia library are fundamentally of the same nature. The scale of the first is less vast than it seems, to the extent that the very great majority of Internet users only explore national pages on the web. The supply of the second is potentially much larger than what its shelves in free access suggest, to the extent that multimedia libraries supply the public with connections to databases opening to numerous fields of learning" [MAR 07].

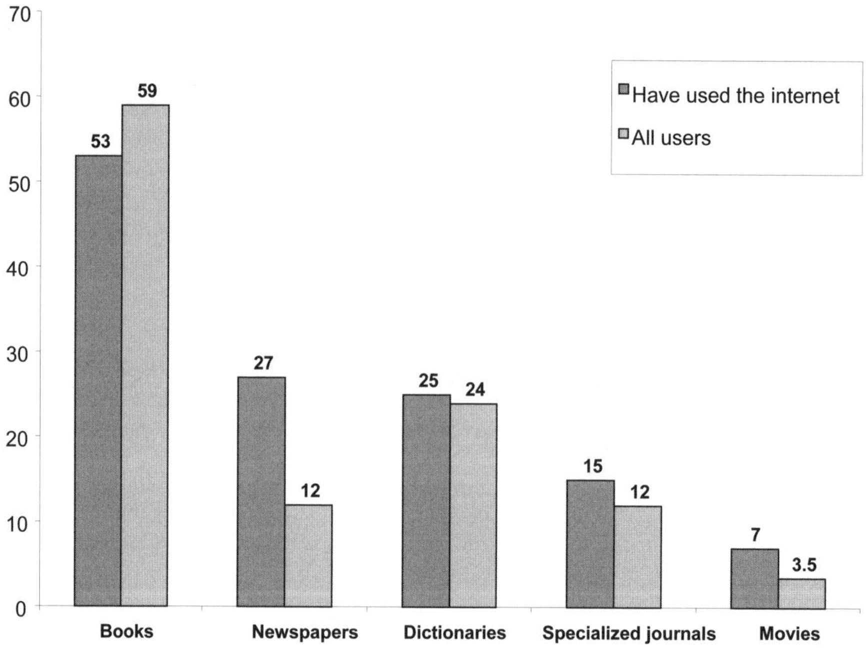

Figure 11.3. *Consultation of different types of documents in the Bpi on the day of the survey*

The visit to the library is therefore justified by the availability of a range of collections and services in the same place that permit each person to use this or that medium according to his/her needs. Free access to expensive databases or websites is an important advantage over connection at home even if, unfortunately, users often don't see the difference between free web and expensive web. Therefore, in the Bpi, the two kinds of offer, accessible via the same interface and presenting the same appearance of free access, are often considered on the same front – uniformity of modes of access contributing to this phenomenon becoming commonplace. Some users are nevertheless sensitive to the tagging of the web carried out by the library, as well as the financial investment, by the way of subscriptions made by the establishment:

> "Although in Beaubourg, it is ready. The Sudoc, Universalis encyclopedias, you go on the web and you get immediately... in Beaubourg, the terminals are already all programmed. And the work stations in the newspapers area, it is the same. They have subscriptions that are not necessarily on personal computers. It seems to me. [At one's home] one cannot, it is long to find. While you have SUDOC immediately. You already have it pre-programmed, Universalis encyclopedia, they are subscribed so they already have it. So it is ok..."[8]

But this "virtuous" use of the Internet, according to the policy of the institution, is not shared by everybody in Bpi areas. As in the BNF, non-documentary uses of the Internet are not rare – far from it [PED 01]. The connecting data of "free Internet" work stations, as we have seen, confirm what a simple observation allows us to see: the work stations are used as well for practical reasons (access to the ANPE, to commercial sites, etc.) as for entertainment, for example to access messaging and visit dating sites. These practices are not easily discussed in interview situations, but nothing prevents these users from stigmatizing others, which gave rise to a slightly lively exchange during a focus group we organized in 2006:

> " – To pick up again on the Internet, I (...) use a little, but I also go behind to see... I am doing voyeurism; I look at what others are doing. I am a little fed up of seeing 'you are beautiful my dear, I would like to communicate with you' messages. That has a gift for getting on my nerves.
>
> – Even if it is a private correspondence, I do not see any necessity at all to have a negative look on mails that are nobody's business. How can that get on your nerves? I do not see the inconvenience that that poses for you. Regarding availability of work stations, maybe, but regarding mails content, I do not see it at all...
>
> – Although there are some who are going to wait and who are going to be stopped in their searches...

8. Testimony collected in a focus group organized by the Bpi studies and research service in 2006, see [CAM 07].

– Ok, but it is not the content of the mails that should be a problem for you…

– No, it is simply because of the others who are waiting.”

11.4. Private in public and *vice versa*

What the first speaker is deploring is the privatization of a public work station for personal use, which he considers a diversion. This point of view is sometimes shared by librarians, faintly wanting their establishment to be transformed into a cybercafé. These librarians quickly find themselves overwhelmed by the reality of the uses, when it is not by the imperatives, even by the philosophy of the technique: Internet use does not let itself be compartmentalized so easily.

Here again, the Bpi offers us a good example of evolution of supply policy under the combined effect of pressure from the public (which did not understand the banning of messaging) and technical constraints (which, in reality, did not allow curbing all possibilities of access to messaging). Also and above all it shows the impossibility of dividing uses of the Internet between those librarians consider legitimate within the establishment and others being *a priori* a matter of private life. Internet “media for doing everything”, actually lends itself to all sorts of practices and the use of e-mail can turn out to be indispensible for seeing through projects encouraged by the library. Upon reflection, librarians for example found it illogical to forbid the sending of CVs by e-mail from work stations that are furthermore defined for giving access to job search sites. The removing of the ban authorizes an entire variety of uses, which can be in relation to traditional library missions or not. Besides, it is probable that this diversity of practices is often made by the same individuals, each one being free to share connection time given to him/her between documentary use of the web (in the wide sense of the term), and private correspondence or fun activity.

Everything ends up being mixed up: games, work; inside, outside; private, public; etc. What many researchers have already noticed in the tertiary sector in terms of porosity between the world of work (office, company) and the private universe (at home, for oneself), is thus verified on the field of libraries, whatever their type. The introduction of the Internet in the library contributes even more easily to blurring the boundaries between home and public areas, as the library is a familiar space, where one voluntarily goes with peers, where one stays on, one installs oneself, one has one’s habits [EVA 00]. Public institutions perceived by their users as a “second home” are rare. The provision of an interpersonal communication tool in public libraries can only reinforce this feeling of appropriation.

11.4.1. *Using the Internet in public*

However, everything is not "as it is at home" at the library. Using the Internet there is a practice that presents characteristics that can be perceived by users as advantages or inconveniences, and that depend greatly on the context of use. The first and most evident, which we just had a glimpse of, is the lack of intimacy. This is true for any activity carried out in the library, including for reading, but sociologists have long collected its veracity and its impact concerning the use of screens. Joëlle Le Marec, for example, by observing the consultation of catalogs on line at the Bpi, noted that this public dimension was nothing trivial and could even have effects on information research [LEM 90]. She cites the case of a user who launches research on the subject "sexology" and who, feeling observed by those who follow him in the waiting line, abandons his research.

The screen is a place where you post something about yourself openly and publicly whether it is to exchange, to value a skill, or on the contrary to censor yourself. There is an effect of demonstration on the screen. Some offenders at the Bpi find this out at their expense when they are denounced by other users, who are shocked to see them visit forbidden websites. But the presence of others does not only create inconveniences. Jean-François Barbier-Bouvet, in his work *Publics à l'Oeuvre* [BAR 86] stresses that, contrary to print, screens are the right support for sociability and sharing; he observes, for example, how much more than in other Bpi areas, multimedia areas are places where users abandon their anonymity, by commenting out loud on images that appear on the screens.

That is because of the form of the screen – a vertical, illuminated form accessible to all – and because of the cultural proximity that most individuals entertain today with this familiar device. The works of Dominique Boullier and Franck Ghitalla [OUT 03] are based on practices observed in the Bpi and the Cyber-base of the *Cité des Sciences*. These show that Internet use in public is the opportunity for individuals to exchange informal learning. The use of the technical object, as we know, often goes together with incidents that can be experienced badly if they are confronted in isolation. That incites individuals to implement a practice that authors call "social navigation": discussion and sharing in so far as use of the Internet brings difficulties.

This practice is confirmed by number of observations, in the Bpi and elsewhere. During an exchange between a librarian and a young person who was not succeeding in using the Wi-Fi, for example, we saw an older user spontaneously intervene to offer his help. After having explained to the young man that he had to go on the Bpi website to choose a password, the man began to manipulate the computer, searching for the network assistant. He examined the toolbar, looked at the control panel and identified the problem: "there is no Wi-Fi on your laptop". The young man, disappointed – he just bought the device – understands that he also needs to buy a Wi-Fi card. The experienced user immediately adopted the *tu*[9] form to speak to him. It can be understood as a sign of recognition sent to a person who is part of the same community, that of Internet users. Patrice Flichy showed how much the community ideal showed what he called "Internet spirit" [FLI 01]; the observation reported here indicates that the reference to this community link is operational in the library and is thus a new way to be there in public and by yourself at the same time.

In these public places, "social navigation" is practiced not only by users, but also, of course, by librarians. Dominique Boullier and Franck Ghitalla suggest the need for a training to the basis of the Internet. Our observations confirm this training is still quite often necessary – more than we believe. Some libraries set up real training sessions. As for the Bpi, it stopped providing this service and the training dispensed by librarians is often in the margin, for example, on the occasion of a request for information at the information desk. The survey conducted in Brittany in 2007, already cited, draws the same conclusion, indicating that a third of libraries surveyed offer a training to the Internet, but that this training is most often carried out an individual basis and upon demand. These libraries prefer to offer advice as and when needed rather than offer a service according to modalities of training defined *a priori*.

The American survey already cited indicates that the aid provided by staff is a service appreciated by some user groups, in particular the elderly. It notes furthermore that people who benefitted from this assistance have a better success rate in the search for information [EAS 07].

11.4.2. *A familiar space in the library: finding your Internet*

With the introduction of the Wi-Fi network in the library, to which our young unlucky user attempted in vain to connect to, the owners of laptops can escape other constraints, linked this time to the use of a collective tool. However, for a number of visitors, using a public work station a is not a matter of a constraint, but an advantage, the equipment being provided on a free or low-cost scale, and the library being in charge of maintaining the computers and other equipment in good working order: "it is practical, sometimes this does not work at home. That happens to me (...) but I know that when it does not work at home, I run to the library, it works"[10].

---

9. *The subject pronoun* tu, *meaning "you" is used to address friends and family and is the informal form, as opposed to* vous, *which is used with people in authority and is more formal.*

10. Testimony collected in a focus group organized by the studies and research service of the Bpi in 2006, see [CAM 07].

However, the use of a public work station is not without its disadvantages. From his/her first visit, the novice user will first discover a foreign interface, and have to find his/her bearings, before beginning to navigate. After which, he/she will have to abide by the standard definitions of this collective tool. It may be difficult or indeed impossible to adjust the consultation screen to his/her liking, to open an excessive number of windows, to find his/her bookmarks or collect new ones. It is also impossible to take digital notes or store documents consulted in order to be able to find them during another visit.

These obligatory constraints being a matter of a public good do not belong to digital technology: the library's rule also forbids annotating books or cutting up newspapers to reorganize the information in the form of a press file. But maybe they are more disturbing in this particular case. This is what Dominique Boullier and Franck Ghitalla suggest in the study cited above, by comparing results obtained on domestic environments and public spaces [OUT 03]. The authors insist on the "plasticity" of digital universes:

> "the technical framework of the digital document is actually everything as much given than constructed by the user and it is not only a matter of 'reading comfort': everyone adjusts (or can adjust) the screen resolution, choose to exploit one or more windows, modify the size of the document or only some parts of it… to tell the truth, there rarely exists a common phenomenal version of the same document from one PC to another, and it is the reason why developers also make their products under 'minimal versions' on the web knowing that they will be modified by users. But it is also the reason why activity models are so pregnant in the digital universe, maybe much more than with print. From there, a good part of difficulties encountered on public station with 'curbed' work stations and software."

Certainly, connecting to the Internet allows everybody at any moment and from anywhere to find a familiar virtual space – favorite websites, e-mails and address book, personal spaces, documents stored in Google docs, etc – once the user has tamed the new working environment. But it seems that that is no longer enough. The growth of new technologies is accompanied by demands for more and more personalized services. After access to messaging, Bpi users did not delay in requesting the implementation of the Wi-Fi network.

The possibility of connecting freely to Wi-Fi actually contributes to causing other material and symbolic barriers to fall. It modifies the institutional environment considerably. Coming with their own laptop allows users to free themselves from traditional supports, which are sheets of paper, exercise books and pens (a word processor is used to take notes and write). If this nomad tool (laptop) allows them to access software that facilitates the emancipation and the escaping of the context proposed and imposed by the institution (they listen to music with headphones plugged into a laptop – while working or not – they play off-line games, etc.), connection to the Wi-Fi network allows them to step over other boundaries.

In the first case, they are importing supports and practices that come from the private sphere into the public institution; we need to take this into consideration given the rapidity with which these practices develop. But it is not exactly new to bring crosswords, your own newspaper or your walkman with you to the library, which are along the same principle.

In the second case, bypassing traditional institutional barriers seems to be of another nature: the private sphere and public sphere are interlaced and in some cases undifferentiated as users are never cut from their network(s) and from what happens outside the library (via e-mail, chat, instant messaging); to a certain extent they make barriers fall.

When we walk through the library, we can therefore observe more and more people who work alone or in groups and who above all permanently "play on several tables": multiple windowing or reducing the taskbars of some applications on their personal computers allowing them to be joined by e-mail at all times or to join the exterior.

The superiority of the laptop is that, unlike the iPod, Blackberry or mobile phone, it more easily suggests serious and laborious activities and that it is *a priori* quieter. That is why laptops have so easily conquered the protected territory of libraries, with the complicity of librarians.

Today, it is difficult to imagine that those who go out systematically with their laptop could or should do without it. The addiction resembles that to the mobile phone; we understand better why, when it is announced that the Wi-Fi is not working in the Bpi for technical reasons, some leave the waiting line in a rage after sometimes having waited a very long time. Public libraries today are put in a hierarchy according to the quality of their access to the Internet via cable or Wi-Fi, in addition to their collections and traditional services: people visit the library and spend time because the digital connection is good.

11.4.3. *Between domestic space and the library: optimizing tasks and time management*

The Internet therefore offers users the opportunity to engage in online activity in different places that range from the private space at home to the public station in the library. Users seize it to adjust what Dominique Bouiller and Franck Ghitalla call their "information production chain" [OUT 03].

This personalized chain is shared not only in space, but also in time. Information research carried out in the library is no longer limited by the schedule of the institution, but is given rhythm by the constraints of individuals' use of time. Operations are put on hold in order to be dealt with at a more appropriate time, thanks, for example, to the sending of links to the home. Observations in the library allow us to see that such uses keep growing, and can now be met in the same way that demands to record or transfer data collected in the library can now be met by using transportable USB keys or e-mailing information home.

According to Dominique Boullier and Franck Ghitalla, the different temporalities (individual, institutional, collective) are complementary. Collective and individual memories form an original layout, a new space/time:

> "Between the Cyberbase, its workplace and the domestic computer, it is an entire system of connections that was implemented through the use of e-mail. Following their experience, our observed therefore seem to live on the web like in their offices or their apartments, creating a vast network of material complementarities where individual memories are written." [11]

Qualitative surveys had already shown users anxious to save time, forcing these individuals to best manage this coming and going between their home and the library. Catherine, for example, insists on the fact that she goes to Bpi with "a voluntarily constrained time budget"[12]. Therefore, she explains, her selection of documents will be more efficient.

In this same logic that favors selection over exploration, she only uses the sectors of the library that are familiar to her. This limited journey, which leaves from a known space, is also observable in online practices: the study on the uses of "free Internet" work stations in the Bpi shows that 8 out of 10 sessions begin by direct access to a particular site, while the recourse to search engines or directories only intervene during the session [AMA 04].

Users therefore consult, in priority, a known site or one that was recommended to them and then eventually broaden their searches. Whereas the limited duration of library sessions probably encourages Internet users to make their queries as "profitable" as possible, this constraint is not defining. Recent queries on web use at home show that the journey of marked up itineraries is not specific to Internet use in

11. [OUT 03], p. 80.
12. Bpi Focus group 2006.

the library: in their homes people would tend in 2006, even more than in 2002, to use routine sites[13].

Our own observations confirm the satisfaction that users take from the use of these devices. Time can be streched almost infinitely, to profit from the temporalities of the private sphere. From the institution's point of view, the question of the complementarities is posed differently. We are witnessing an increase in adaptation demands from institutional time to the individual time of users.

During the survey carried out on the Bpi website, for example, people questioned complained about the fact that access to the catalog is not possible, for technical reasons, during some hours in the middle of the night [MAR 04]. From then on, it really becomes legitimate to wonder whether the dynamics of Internet technology will have effects, in the near future, on the mode of organization of the library.

11.5. Conclusion

In 2006, the Crédoc survey on French city libraries created surprise by pointing out that not only was library use not weakening but that the majority of their users were friends of the Internet [MAR 07]. The following year, a report of the Pew Internet and American Life Project ended in similar conclusions [EAS 07].

Therefore the Internet has not killed the library. On the contrary, never has the legitimate library and the digital bazaar gone together better, to the point where expectations may cause confusion: users expect a "search engine" from the library so they can search all of the collections, and they expect that the information identified on the Internet benefits from an almost institutional validity.

False twins more than brothers at loggerheads, the library and the Internet do have similar publics and similar practices. As we have seen, online behaviors are inscribed in the logic of "pre-digital" practices and Internet users are more inclined than others to go to the library. We can quote again Olivier Donnat's observations, that the Internet compared to other medias (notably television) illustrates this paradox of being very largely used at home while remaining linked to a "going out culture".

---

13. According to the work conducted by Thomas Beauvisage, routine Internet sites occupied in 2001-2002 a quarter of the navigation time, compared to a third in 2006. This evolution occurred notably to the detriment of transient sites which do occupied no more than 16% of web use time in 2006 compared to 25% in 2002 [BEA 07].

In a more global way, the domestic/public, exterior/interior relationship is carried out in an unusual way with the Internet. In the same way that the Internet and the library illustrate a certain encyclopedic model differently, we can put forward the hypothesis that the Internet and the library embody diversely a modality of cooperation.

> "Unlike 'strong' cooperations, which are based on a preexisting community of values of intentions, weak cooperations are characterized by 'opportunistic' training of links and collectives that do not presuppose in advance collective 'community' intentionality or belonging" [CAR 08].

This analysis that Dominique Cardon develops by examining forms of communication on Web 2.0 platforms [AGU 07] puts into perspective the originality of the articulation between individualism and solidarity induced by technical devices and the necessity to maintain a quite common dynamic at the same time.

How do we characterize and live in this public space that is the library today, although this institution is no longer only apprehended across traditional spatial or cultural categories (displays, collections) but as a meshing of real and virtual places (sites, links, etc.)? We are witnessing a blurring of frontiers and probably the disappearance of some locations, but also the making of new cognitive paths. In this information landscape, new rules are to be invented between professionals and users.

11.6. Bibliography

[AMA 04] AMAR M, BEGUET B., *Les Consultations 'Libres' d'Internet à la Bpi: Étude exploratoire*, Bpi, 2004. http://site.bpi.fr/modules/resources/download/default/Professionnels/Documents/Etudes%20et%20recherche/Internet_libre.pdf, accessed October 26, 2009

[AGU 07] AGUITON C., CARDON D., "The strength of weak cooperation: an attempt to understand the meaning of Web2.0", *Communications & Strategies*, vol. 65, p. 51-65, 2007.

[BAU 96] BAUDE D., "Internet à la bibliothèque publique d'information", *Bulletin des bibliothèques de France*, vol. 41, no. 1, p. 57-60, 1996. Available at: http://bbf.enssib.fr/consulter/bbf-1996-01-0056-007 accessed October 26, 2009.

[BEA 07] BEAUVISAGE T., "Les usages routiniers de l'informatique à domicile", *Réseaux*, vol. 145-146, p. 217-247, 2007.

[BIG 08] BIGOT R., CROUTTE P., "La diffusion des technologies de l'information dans la société Française", *Crédoc*, novembre 2008. http://www.cgti.org/rapports/rapports-2008/DTIC-2008-Etude-complete.pdf, accessed October 5, 2009.

[CAM 06] CAMUS-VIGUE A. "L'autoformation à la Bpi: autonomie et autodidaxie dans une bibliothèque en libre accès", in: *Bibliothèques et Autoformation: la Formation tout au long de la Vie, quels Rôles pour les Bibliothèques à l'Heure du Multimédia*, Bpi-Center Pompidou, Paris, 2006, p. 137-255.

[CAM 07] CAMUS-VIGUE A., EVANS C., "*Les publics de la Bpi: Enquête Générale de Fréquentation*", Bpi, 2006.

[CAR 08] CARDON D., CREPEL M., HATT B., PISSARD N., PRIEUR C., *10 Propriétés de la Force des Coopérations Faibles*, InternetActu, 2008. Available at: http://www.internetactu.net/2008/02/08/10-proprietes-de-la-force-des-cooperations-faible/, accessed October 26, 2009.

[CHA 97] CHAZAUD-TISSOT A.-S., "Usages d'internet à la bibliothèque publique d'information", *Bulletin des bibliothèques de France*, vol. 42, no. 3, p. 34-40, 1997. Available at: http://bbf.enssib.fr/consulter/bbf-1997-03-0034-006, accessed October 26, 2009.

[DON 07] DONNAT O., "Pratiques culturelles et usages d'Internet", *Culture: Études*, Département des Études de la Prospective et des Statistiques, November 2007. Available at: http://www.culture.gouv.fr/deps, accessed October 5, 2009.

[EAS 07] ESTABROOK L., WITT E., RAINIE L., "Information searches that solve problems: how people use the internet, libraries, and government agencies when they need help", Pew Internet & American life project, 2007. Available at: http://www.pewinternet .org/PPF/r/231/report_display.asp, accessed October 5, 2009.

[EVA 00] EVANS C., CAMUS-VIGUE A., and CRETIN J.-M., *Les habitués – le microcosme d'une grande bibliothèque*, Studies and Research Department, Bpi-Center Georges Pompidou, Paris, 2000.

[FLI 01] FLICHY P., *L'Imaginaire d'Internet*, La Découverte, Paris, 2001.

[LEM 90] LE MAREC J., *Dialogue ou Labyrinthe? La Consultation des Catalogues informatisés par les usagers*, Studies and Research Department, Bpi-Center Georges Pompidou, Paris, 1990.

[MAD 99] MADDALONI M.-C., "L'information numérique dans les bibliothèques municipales: état des lieux", *Bulletin des Bibliothèques de France*, vol. 44, no. 4, p. 66-69, 1999. Available at: http://bbf.enssib.fr/consulter/bbf-1999-04-0066-009, accessed October 26, 2009.

[MAR 04] MARESCA B. and MARTIN O., *Perception et Pistes d'Optimisation pour le site Web de la Bpi*, www.bpi.fr, 2004.

[MAR 07] MARESCA B., *Les Bibliothèques Municipales en France après le Tournant Internet,* Studies and Research Department, Bpi-Center Georges Pompidou, Paris, 2007.

[OUT 03] GHITALLA F., BOULLIER D., GHOUSKOU-GIANNAKOU P. *et al.*, *L'Outre Lecture: Manipuler, (s')approprier, Interpréter le web*, Studies and Research Department, Bpi-Center Georges Pompidou, 2003.

[PED 01] PEDLER E., ZERBIB O., *Les Nouvelles Technologies à l'Épreuve des Bibliothèques*, Studies and Research Department, Bpi-Center Georges Pompidou, Paris, 2001. Further details available at: http://editionsdelabibliotheque.fr/livre/index.cfm?GCOI=84240100845420&fa=preview, accessed October 5, 2009.

[POU 99] POUTS-LAJUS S. and THIEVANT S., "Observation d'Internet dans différents lieux d'accès publics", *Bulletin des Bibliothèques de France,* vol. 44, no. 5, p. 30-34, 1999. Available at: http://bbf.enssib.fr/consulter/bbf-1999-05-0030-004 accessed October 26, 2009.

[SMO 07] SMOREDA Z., BEAUVISAGE T., DE BAILLIENCOURT T., ASSADI H., "Saisir les pratiques dans leur globalité", *Réseaux*, vol. 145-146, p. 19-43, 2007.

[ZOT 06] ZOTIAN E., "Modes d'usage et d'appropriation: l'exemple des enfants de Belsunce à la bibliothèque de l'Alcazar", *Bulletin des Bibliothèques de France*, vol. 51, no. 6, p.68-75, 2006. Available at: http://bbf.enssib.fr/consulter/bbf-2006-06-0068-013 accessed October 26, 2009.

Chapter 12

Electronic Editing for Mobile Devices: Original Audiovisual Contents on Mobile, Socio-technical and Socio-economic Conditions of their Emergence

12.1. Introduction

Whereas the number of subscribers was nearly 59 million in June 2009 (or a penetration rate of 91.8%), mobile television services, several technical difficulties of which have been recently smoothed away, are still in emergence and moderated use phase.

The (IDATE[1]) data in 2006 reported that 18% of users are interested in video and 15% in television on mobile phone, with a certain craze in generation Y 2.0, or the digital generation. Even though, thanks to the development of smartphones, television on mobile phones is available to an increasing number of users, it is still being held up by the delay in the deployment of the DVB-H network.

PMT makes it possible to receive television services broadcast on mobile phone terminals with a reduced size video screen or to receive them on larger size screens.

Chapter written by Bruno HÉNOCQUE.

1. IDATE is one of Europe's foremost market analysis and consulting firms.

A semantic difference needs to be made between mobile television, of the iPod type, and television on mobile phones. Is this PMT service therefore a major innovation comparable to the transistor for the radio? What is the intensity of this deconstruction-reconstruction phase of television media? Several technical, social and cultural dynamics converge and favor its growth, despite difficulties in terms of economic viability. Techniques, first and foremost, have improved. There has been an increase in the number of digitized signs transmitted by the microwave channel, the reduction of the entropy linked to the digital compression and restitution of a quality video image opens perspectives to contours that are still badly defined on television on mobile. Social and cultural dynamics, have changed due to the emergence of a generation born between 1976 and 1995, video lovers and those equipped with a very intense display culture.

In this context, the interrelations between producers, distributors, components manufacturers and mobile Internet users are still largely being built. Actually we must consider the emergence of new participants who come to add inactive content to these products by using large historical television companies.

Surely it is still a matter of niche content, in specific formats, produced by partner companies of operators and large audiovisual companies? This cohabitation does not challenge the primacy of big chains and operators.

It actually matters for editors and also for the operators, some of whom also get involved in content, to respond to the increasing demand from their subscribers and to bring out new margins. Furthermore, the added value is less and less in the network and more and more in content that is incessantly renewed. A program that can be streamed and is accessible on mobile phones depreciates in value very quickly and can rapidly be pirated.

It will be enough from now on to distinguish three audiovisual contents on mobile:

– Flow programs (news channels, series, enjoyment, etc) conceived for the big screen then declines on mobile phones or is adapted to the terminal, as was the case of LCI mobile. The programs of big audiovisual companies are largely dominant on mobiles. Digital terrestrial TV made its entrance recently on this medium.

– A video niche in original formats conceived by new participants in content editing for mobile telephony. This evolution was difficult to imagine before 2005. It is a matter of these new participants responding to the diversity of situations of use, at home certainly but also for a significant part in a displacement situation. Their production drains from the new audience and constitutes a promotion channel for operators, artists and editors.

– Unpublished videocasts shared on sites by a young public in search of a designer freedom. Partnerships have emerged between operators and editors of amateur content in the last few years. They allow us to access hundreds of thousands of videos free of charge on dedicated sites.

In this emerging context, dominant players hide behind their logic.

Therefore, to increase the security of digital video broadcasting to a handheld device (DVB-H) content, operators would like to impose the SIM card, however DVB-H, which is a system for digital distribution for mobile devices, can also be received on portable TV, camcorder and camera. This position explains in part the backward steps taken by this technology in France. It will also be enough to consider the impact of positioning of economic stakeholders and European political instances on the choice of DVB-H system.

We must also consider, however, the temporary technological steps forward taken by the mobile phone companies Orange (a subsidiary of France Telecom, Orange has 182 million customers throughout the world) and SFR (a subsidiary of Vivendi Universal) on *Bouygues Télécom* thanks to the adoption of 3G and 3G+, third-generation technology norms that allow us to pass in terms of debit from 250 kbit/s to some megabits/s. To that is added a disparate geographical cover – 60% of the population being covered by 3G and 20% by 3G+.

Beyond politico-economic choices and territorial disparities, the main thing the analysis focuses on is the emergence of videos in unedited formats whose strategic agreements are studied by the operators and the amateur video creators who can thus end up being integrated in video catalogs for mobile.

The first point dealt with will focus on the concept of television on mobile devices in terms of capacity of the channel and viewing screen. The difficulties focus on the heterogeneity of transmission speeds and very little on the screen area of mobile devices, a constraint that is quickly surpassed by young mobile Internet users in particular.

The following point concerns the strategies of participants, the partnerships between editors and transporters around audiovisual formats that are emerging. Issues of economic viability still remain uncertain in the face of content distributed by large traditional television chains.

The third point will focus on the original content produced by editors specializing in television on mobile devices and on their interrelations with the designers of amateur videocasts distributed afterwards free of charge on dedicated sites. These sites are supported by television channels such as *Arte* or *M6* and equipment producers such as Samsung within the context of *festival pocket films* (promoter: SFR). Other festivals supported by operators, equipment producers, television channels and editors have been developed, such as the *disposable film festival* in the USA or the *Festival Vivo Arte Mov* in Brazil

12.2. On the capacity of the channel and the quality of reception

12.2.1. *Channel capacity and quantity of information transmitted*

In a few years, technical progress has progressively ironed out the limitations in terms of media coverage and channel capacity that transmits the signal, which is limited to a certain power [SHA 46]. It has however beem found that these progresses are unequally distributed across the territory. According to Catherine Le Drogo [LED 07], in 2007 3G covered 60% of the population, 3G+ 20%, and in turn DVB-H must cover 30%.

As a matter of interest, remote transmission of images animated in synchronism with sounds, in broadcasting or in streaming, supposes a conversion into digitized and compressed electronic signals, then restitution on the screen and as a function of physiological properties of the eye of a color video image adding red, green, blue. The passband necessary for a television signal is linked to the millions of points (pixels) that make up the image on the screen in a second. The luminance determines the contours of forms visualized and the chrominance gives color to the forms of the image [BAT 02].

At this stage, we must point out two facts:

– a rate[2] that is too weak creates bad quality images for cross-fade streaming. Actually streaming associates compressed streams of image files, sound tracks distributed live or on-demand and texts;

– compression leads to a loss of quality, the entropy being notably important for animated images.

With an increase in rate by 3G[3] and an improvement of resolution, the number of images per second went from a maximum of 15 to 25.

2. Rate: speed of execution or reception of digital data by a channel expressed in bits per second.

3. 3G (third generation): this mobile telephony technology norm allows rates of 2 mbits/s, which is more than five times the rate obtained with Edge. It is supported by the Universal Mobile Telecommunications System (UMTS) norm.

However, these technological advances, under the pressure of consumer waiting, by far exceed the hexagonal frontiers and depend on European political and economic logic, with representations and multiple efforts to gain influence between firms on the performances of other competing technologies. The system of digital terrestrial broadcasting destined for a DVB-H 4 mobile terminal is supported by the Brussels Commission, after having been the object of multiple tests coordinated in France by French television companies TDF, TPS and Canal Plus. The results of tests of systems in competition with each other can be found in the publications of the European Audiovisual Observatory at Brussels [OBS 05].

The complementarity of 3G, 3G+[4] and DVB-H[5], coming soon to France, allow us an improved access to all the content for about one year, in a ubiquitous context. The DVB-H relay will bring a higher flowrate and a better transmission quality.

3G+, which is supported by a broadcast[6] technology, increases the rate in considerable proportions, which goes from 250 kbits/s[7] to 7 megabits/s[8].

3G+ has been available on terminals for three years and constitutes a strategic technology for mobile phone company Orange, as for SFR. The opening of a 3G+ network, which will then enable customers to watch television on their mobile phones, for Bouygues Telecom is imminent. Bouygues Telecom opened a 3G+ network in 2009 and has retaken parts of thr market with its astonishing quadruple play: 2h mobile calls, unlimited fixed telephone, unlimited television and unlimited Internet for less than 45 Euros per month.

Therefore, the increase in rates of 100 kbits/s to 250 kbits/s, and finally to 7 mbits/s, and the fluidity of the movement by the passage from 15 to 25 images/second characterizes the development of high-speed then very high-speed

4. 3G+ (or 3.5G): very high-speed mobile based on the HSDPA system (High-Speed Downlink Packet Access) of data transmission expressed in a million bits per second.

5. DVB-H,is literally a portable digital video distributor. DVB-H is a digital terrestrial broadcasting service destined to be received via mobile terminal. This system is supported by European instances.

6. Broadcast: transmission procedure which consists of distributing a similar package of data to all potential receivers, i.e. a limited quantity of programs for an unlimited number of clients. This is the system that is normally used for the distribution of radio, television or the encoded version of a live event.

7. kbit/s: a bit is the abbreviation of binary digit. It is a matter of a binary element (0 or 1). A bit/s is the unit of measurement of the rate of information flow emitted or received in a second. The coding is presented in the form of a binary suit [SHA 49]. A kbit/s represents 1,000 bits per second.

8. Megabit/s: a megabit is a unit of measurement worth a million bits.

mobile. The venture proposed is the creation of longer videos with shorter delays for downloading and better quality images for small screens in broadcast mode. This evolution of rate, for the telecommunication part of the mobile television service, was marked by different steps, largely distributed in the wider public press: General Packet Radio Service [9], Edge[10], 3G and 3G+ and the DVB-H network, already used in parts of Europe and Asia.

A DVB-H terminal is a 3G, 3G+, and even Edge tool at the same time. It enables the television service on mobile using each one of these telecommunication technologies, which assures the transport of information (bearers).

In a mobility context, the television service on mobile device software (which manages the type of connection used without the intervention of the user) selects *ad hoc* technology as a function of the quality of the reception and geographic cover. The interoperability of networks allows messages to circulate without cutting out. The quality is evidently debased, because of a lower rate, if it is a matter of Edge technology.

For distribution in the Metro train system, mobile television uses a radiant cable deployed in all the tunnels. Tests, carried out mainly on DVB-H technology by consortiums of television companies, radio chains, technical distribution service providers and mobile telephony operators were judged to be conclusive that the DVB-H relay worked well.

This diffusion and compression technology was tested in 2005-2006 [OBS 05] in frequency bands of radio terrestrial broadcasting. The DVB-H norm has also been used in Italy and Germany for almost four years now.

Dwelling a bit on these recent technical progresses is justified by the stakes of this transmission, which frees us more and more from space-time constraints. The putting in perspective of Claude Baltz brings us back to the important thing: "we are immerged in space" [BAL 07]. The questions of transmission constitute an "ontological necessity" as they modify our relationship with time and space. The capacities of transmission, with fiber optic, which has increased one thousand times in 50 years, has opened up economic perspectives to transporters who can invest in contraction of space-time for each user at the same time. This has a long history in telecommunications, which provide distance vision apparatus that go back up to the telegraph and the telectroscope. Cyberspace is progressively deployed in all places

9. General Packet Radio System: A radio system of communication by packages of 170 kbits/s.
10. Edge: the Edge (Enhanced Data rates for GSM Evolution) standard is an evolution of the GSM norm allowing GSM rates to be multiplied by three, or 384 kbits/s.

and in an instant, with, however, delays in terms of geographical cover. An improved transmission is the door of access to "an immense act of collective synchronous intelligence" [LEV 98] which converges in the moment.

The challenge of a cyberspace is less and less caused by transmission constraints and is actually "the multiplication of its communities, the interlaced bushing of its pieces" [LEV 98] in order to give artistic, informative or community density at the time given to us.

The video-on-mobile device comes to contribute in its turn to the construction of this cyberspace, with content that is not only that of cultural industries but also content that is produced by fans of the medium. The creators often produce humorous echoes of current events. They seek to create a convenience, a complicity with the receiver whose pleasure is to find the trace of the situation of reference in the humorous statement.

These few considerations regarding access to news, culture or entertainment content leads us to consider the crucial question of the reception screen.

12.2.2. *Screen ergonomics*

The mobile screen acquires its patents of nobility little by little, as shown by the 4 Screens European Festival which discerns gold screens for mobile devices and the Internet, just like for television and cinema. The screen of the mobile device is inscribed in a network of screens, a continuity of images of better quality since the launch of 3G and 3G+. The mobile internet user therefore goes from image to image, framework to framework, plan to plan [AMI 91], from short story to short story. It is situated in particular in a multi-supports logic of diffusion, allowing a continuum of the home to public or private transport and places of work or pleasure.

As a function of situational constraints, it accesses images by television set, computer or mobile phone. The capacities of mobile phones have become identical to PCs! Furthermore, the maintenance of a flow of images in a situation of mobility and in a situation of sedentary nature touches on the use of small screens considered as floating receivers.

Whereas components manufacturers experimented a few years ago on the market for terminals of variable sizes, the demand led to a preference of screen areas on smartphones of about 9 cm, while allowing a good visibility of images on screen. The "contract" of visibility goes back to the expectations of the user of any terminal in terms of monochrome signal and chrominance signal. A satisfactory visibility "contract" includes several parameters:

– light and colors;

– screen surface;

– illusion of depth;

– fluidity of movement;

– added to sound quality.

In this domain, progress on mobile devices is considerable, considering the recent increase in phone networks.

A comfort of optimal viewing would undoubtedly imply a surface of 11 inches, the equivalent of half an A4 page, therefore a pliable screen without us being able to see the bend in a viewing situation. But the rise in tests organized by operators indicate that mobile Internet users in a very large majority are not unhappy with the small size of screens, in the framework of audiovisual diffusion.

In this context, parameters that enter in the visual exploration must remain present in the mind in order to reduce cognitive cost.

The size of the object is preponderant. The more it is reduced, the greater the quality of the lighting and contrasts between visual elements and the funds must be.

The distance of average reading depends on the object. If the distance of reading is 40 cm, characters must not be less than 2 mm [GAI 97]. It is convenient if need be to reduce the distance between the eye and the screen. For an observation at 5 m, the minimal height should be 22 mm.

The size of the object image on the retina and the distance from the optical center to the retina are also to be considered.

The visual axis is just as essential. Visual acuity falls to the extent that the observer moves away from the axis. This visual field includes a central zone of 2° to 4° angles, called the foveolar field [GAI 97].

The influence of these parameters on viewing must not cause us to forget other criteria that come from the color code, choice of clearly identifiable symbols and more globally of plans adapted to the size of the screen. All these considerations enter into the reduction of cognitive cost.

Even if young people integrated the practice of small screens in their daily life and the passage of one digital screen to another in a few clicks (and with an often enviable dexterity!), many older subscribers however remain doubtful faced with the size of the image on their screen, with diagonals of only 60 mm.

This size brings us back to that of windows, 4 cm x 6 cm, accessible on the web in 1998, in the framework of broadcasting television programs through streaming. The reduced size of images and characters can actually make up a true visual handicap. With regard to this, the size of screens on smartphones has offered for more than a year a much better viewing comfort for watching television on a mobile phone.

In use of a mobile device at home, a connection on a television set – such as is practiced for a digital photographic apparatus – should be able to better bring comfort of vision [SAB 07].

It is probable that in the near future screens that are more comfortable for a video or television service will exist and will be commercialized, without compromising the compactness of the terminal.

This global improvement of transmission and reception conditions supports an original production of video programs, the contours of which it is convenient to specify here.

12.3. Emergence of an original production for PMT

12.3.1. *Index Multimedia, first European publisher of original content*

Information must be understood as “a measure of the freedom of choice we have when we select a message” [SHA 49]. Therefore, Warren Weaver [SHA 49] explains, “there is more information if we operate a choice among a totality of fifty standard messages than if free choice is only made among a totality of twenty-five”.

Hyper choice on a mobile device, in any place and at any time, leads to asking ourselves questions before programming and indexation choice.

To understand how categories of video programs conceived for mobile devices are articulated, a putting in perspective of this activity is necessary.

Index Multimedia, the first publisher of mobile television programs in Europe, gives us the opportunity to do so as a producer of 5,000 audiovisual programs per month. The video catalog is rich, with two million titles. This multimedia publisher also broadcasts 35 channels per day. The company distributes its programs for specialty channels (humor, personal interest, youth, cartoons, cinema). In addition it produces live television in the most demanded registers and genres: information, sports, music, live concerts, youth, and humor in collaboration with the artistic world.

These other partners consist of almost 60 telephony operators. Large mobile phone companies such as SFR, Orange, Vodafone, Telefonica and T-Mobile are involved in these partnerships.

One of the key factors of success is the production of original and attractive formats of about three minutes duration, or times that correspond well to the opportunities of use of the mobile device (a few minutes, a total of 10 minutes or more). Consultations with Orange, according to Catherine Le Drogo who carried out marketing for mobile television are therefore less than five minutes in 93% of cases, of which 25% for live television use, 41% of video on demand and 34% for mixed use.

The second activity of importance concerns video games in Java and interactive past times adapted to the mobile phone. The Java games catalog is at the top of European operators, with an exclusive commercial agreement with Vivendi Universal for mobile games, and with Manta (the first mobile portal dedicated to video games). This cultural industry, more and more situated as an institution in the culture and arts domain, develops its own concepts.

Its ideological content forms the object of controversy when thematics are prints of "militarized masculinity" [GEN 08]. This video game production, whereas it does not enter directly into our problematic, amplifies the video creation and live television phenomenon and enters in the search of a viable economic model. The perspectives it offers attract the interests of powerful economic stakeholders: the mobile virtual network operator Neuf Cegetel, which was repurchased by the operator SFR, for example, was launched at the beginning of March 2008 to distribute video games for 15-25 year olds.

Index Multimedia creates a lot of program content in the studio and cutting room, in the first place if the piece does not exist. The company ensures further the direction of programs, the definition of needs from studies on users, the program schedule and the editorial target.

In Index Multimedia's[11] programming strategy, an important place is given to genres that are a big success with mobile Internet users. These are in fact that are not represented in traditional audiovisual programs. They are in fact mini audio sketches, minicasts or mini video sketches.

The dominant genres are:

– 20 minute cartoons;

---

11. This firm is held by the Japanese company Index Corporation, global leader in mobile video content.

– 13 to 20-minute long series;

– sex appeal;

– the live show, like comedy or the theatre. Several comedies are, however, adapted to these short series (for example Franck Dubosc, Real Leforestier, etc.), to the reserve that almost these formats seem more adapted for DVDs with big audiences and applause from the public. The other break is that the live show is, for these recognized comedians, more lucrative than the recording of videos for mobile.

Multimedia Index in addition broadcasts the cartoon channel and comedy channel – proof of its strength in this genre. The famous series *Seinfeld* is accessible on portable device in streaming or in video (for a duration of mini sketches of five to six minutes) and because they are from mainstream television and have a big fan base are likely to be a huge success.

Humor goes back to the sensitive or taboo themes that exist in personal or private life, and finally exposes even themes that concern the intimacy of private life in public [CHA 06]. In a tradition that goes back to Raymond Queneau with *Zazie dans le Métro* (*Zazie in the Subway*), the young consumer accompanies his/her supports with these sketches that turn look down upon adults attitudes in metro.

Therefore he elaborates his relationship to the world across comical enunciation situations constructed on a triadic relation including the speaker, the receiver and the target, understood as "that about which the comedic act is exercised" [CAH 06].

The effects go from connivance to cynicism by touching on complicity, criticism or derision.

Whereas humor brings success, live show audiences remain for the time being limited, for questions of screen format. The laughing festival in Nantes was retransmitted via streaming in mid-2007 and received a reduced audience of just 750 connections on SFR. Michel Polnareff, a French singer who was popular in the mid-1960s to early 1980s had hardly any more connections (1,100). It is truly a matter of a niche distribution.

The lengths of connection for these programs go from 20 to 30 minutes, and are therefore longer than the funny videos of a few minutes that encounter much more success for mobile Internet users. This success is for reasons that hold, that include the cost of the transfer and undoubtedly also the (dis)comfort of viewing for more than several minutes and limited opportunities of use. The series that are conceived in this way for the large television set (of, for example, half-hour programs) must often be cut in a mobility context (to, say 10 minutes), which brings frustration.

What is left is a size challenge: the definition, still fragile in an emerging sector, of an economic model paying correctly as a function of investments and the creation of values for each author. The publishers of cultural content, submitted to the object of profitability or cost reduction, must constitute attractive and original catalogs, as they are submitted to public attention-capturing requirements with whose values, norms and behaviors they must integrate perfectly [MIE 90].

The rise of multimedia publishers carrying out lots of marketing studies allows us in this framework to orientate the search for new scenarios.

An entire production economy is progressively put in place, by articulating authors' activities and different transporters. These original audiovisual contents emerge very slowly. Canadian author Marshall MacLuhan explained in the past that the contents of new media is often traditional media such as traditional channels (TF1, M6) or paid channels such as Canal+. In the beginning emergent media produces little original audiovisual contents [BOU 08].

12.3.2. *The modes of cooperation between publishers, operators and subscribers*

A company like Index Multimedia is a partner of TV channels and mobile telephony operators.

The distribution agreements ensured by Index Multimedia are situated at different levels, synergies and alliances. They are not able to be explained by the only economic rationality or by "techno-determinism" [MIE 06].

Between the publisher and the conveyers there exist three complex modes of cooperation that are carried out on several levels:

– the company allows only video for an operator like Bouygues Telecoms, which has its high-speed i-mode portal;

– the company enables mobile portals like Virgin mobile (which bought tele2 mobile), to manage the technical aspects and for reading at the same time (business to business);

– its main activity is to gather content. In this configuration, the publisher ensures the commercial management of the operator (business to customer). This mode of cooperation represents 70% of the sales figures of a company like Index Multimedia.

Subscription to services managed by the operator seems to constitute the best model as it is more advantageous than payment for the act of streaming. For the syndicates of industries, information and communication technology and associated services (TICS Alliance), only a model based on subscription payments is viable, considering the investments agreed to by conveyers and producers [ALL 05]. A part of the subscription cost is then recouped by the operator and given to the editors.

The advantage of the subscription is an unlimited access for a price that ranges from about 9 euros (about $14.00) to 29 euros (about $42.00).

More than 85% of telephone subscribers pay or would pay 5 euros (about $7) for television on a mobile device and 78% would pay $10 euros. The decrease in numbers willing to pay higher sums of money is steep: 58% would pay 15 euros/month (about $21.00), 45% would pay 20 euros/month (about $29.00). The percentages then plummet: only 20% of subscribers would pay 25 euros/month (about $37.00) and finally about 10% would go up to 30 euros/month (about $44.00) [ALL 05].

To stimulate subscriptions, the mediators (producers, directors, authors) get close to an event-driven model. Therefore, the principle of free preview video clips that have the objective of stimulating the desire to buy the DVD, allows the operator to gain audience numbers and the artist to gain publicity. Furthermore, the organization of mobile film festivals also contributes to this policy of publicity.

In order to construct a viable economic model, it is sufficient in addition to develop several different formats for advertising spots (ringtones, logos, gags, animated logos, competitions, games) of a duration of 20 to 30 seconds. The essential point for the consumer is that the advertising spot is broadcast during the time it takes to download the video.

To increase their visibility, programs are associated with different co-texts, to begin with the electronic program guide (EPG), a powerful information tool, with classing of programs by genre. To the extent that the size of catalogues increases, search engines of content similar to those of the web are used. The production of information is not identical from one operator to the other.

For SFR, it is also a matter of suggesting a presentation of programs in the form of a textual contextualization of images.

This co-text fills a metalinguistic function through the linguistic qualification of stories, places and actors. This denomination allows us to reduce the uncertainty regarding the content. It cannot be reduced as in other spheres of activity, like the logistics and transport, to abbreviations that reduce redundancy and therefore allow us to transmit a maximum of information in a minimum of signs. The harbor logistical activity therefore depends on a lexical of 200 abbreviations that covers the entire foreseeable operation [HEN 04]. Such is not the case of renewed content everyday.

Therefore, the profusion of content obligates us to reinforce content visibility on the screen and to distinguish two large production categories: multi-support and original content.

12.4. From multi-support content to original content

12.4.1. *Multi-support content*

In France, 22 million individuals listen to or view a media content outside its original support, of which already 31% of young people between 16 and 21 years old already consult web content on their mobile phones. The information is notably transferred by repetitions of images and stories. The history of media teaches us that emerging supports proceed first by imitation (among the symbolic examples, the first direct to French television in 1950 was a piece by Marivaux retransmitted in French comedy) before original content emerges. Videos in streaming however are object of an adaptation on mobile phone. Formats are notably shorter.

Users are going to watch on mobile phones what they heard on the radio or already saw on the television set or even read in the free morning or evening paper. Large television groups clearly occupy a dominant position and take back their programs on mobiles by adapting the content.

The richness of the work of Laurence Balkia-Tabary [BAL 06] is in suggesting a typology of repetitions of images of a channel or from one support to the other:

– intra-sequential repetition = the taking back of images from the same television;

– thematic multi-sequential repetition – the taking back of images of other programs with another thematic, for example the gaffes on a channel;

– auto-promotional repetition;

– commented repetition of images of programs in other programs.

These repetitions assume a recontextualization of image-sources and of media-sources. The images are not discovered but recognized. They assume themselves, "pass one on the other" [AMI 91]. Several image categories are therefore taken back from one channel to the other. Mobile Internet users are going to be able to increase the information revealed in the morning. The media supports interlaced therefore enter into information search strategies [FIG 07].

12.4.2. *Unpublished formats between clips and short films*

The past "communication contract" between the subscriber and the publisher has been specific to the mobile, not only because of identities and subscribers' roles but also from their very structured production by the media and the media genre. Two types of format on mobile phones are being developed. What we mean here is that we must expect a way to structure programs to adapt them to the mobile in terms of duration, plans and sequences.

François Jost [JOS 06] therefore distinguishes the formats of supply and flow of programs. The supply programs list all the "constraints" that weigh on the conception of the scenario: length of episodes, character of characters, types of possible histories.

For flow programs, the format goes back to the rules of setting and situations. It is a fundamental point, which is evolutionary over the weeks the programs are broadcast, as a function of the measures of audience.

Flow format completely innovates the 52 episodes of a 60 to 90 seconds of daily life that have been broadcast on Orange since the 2 January 2008.

Another unpublished fact for a funny series: the logic of inflection is no longer exclusively television set-Internet-mobile, as the 52 episodes conceived for the mobile are also suggested for Canal+ TV (Canal+ Sports also has sports programs for the mobile). In this case there is a new opportunity to adapt the constraints of communication support.

Furthermore, there exists an expectation on the part of the mobile Internet users *vis-à-vis* sporting niches such as football or baseball. These niches are retransmissions in exclusivity, and are destined to reach small segments of clientele. Not all of the sports that are little carried in the media on television are concerned, however, because of screen size constraints. A small screen size is not compatible with large screen shots representing the player in his/her environment, such as a baseball or football field. The location of a ball on a small screen is not easy. Other shots seem better adapted, for example locking onto the head view (with perception of the emotion on a face), the big close-ups (a part of the face), the big shots (from high over head), close pans (bust of character), average shots (character locked, conversation shots) and American shots (three-quarters of the character).

For these formats, between videos and short films, the small screen therefore seems little adapted for sports that unfold on large stages outdoors whereas a basketball championship could be adapted for mobile on the other hand.

The multiplication of information viewing moments or videos favors solitary breakaways at home, although the family television set is most often watched in group. The subscriptions for television on mobile lead to a relative individualization of practices. "This tendency will go on reinforcing itself" with the emergence of new media broadcast by cultural industries or with the development of personal subscriptions, already noted Bernard Miege, almost 20 years ago [MIE 90]. The term "autonomization" appeared in the 1960s [DUM 63] in the framework of the emergence of a social time linked to the reduction of schedule charges at work. For so many, this autonomization and its individual practices also aim at the exchange and sharing across the still-recent concept of videocasts for mobile.

12.5. Mobile screen culture of young people

12.5.1. *Screen culture of the Y generation*

Mobile Internet users very quickly took over the opportunities opened by the viewing, conception, housing and referencing tools to create and share videocasts and videoblogs. The phenomenon made common on the net, has extended to the mobile phone through the bias of a mobilcast service or for smartphone, by syndication thanks to a PC feed (RSS) towards the mobile.

By screen culture, we understand [PAS 99]:

> "an informal training of codes of technique that relies on a know-how, empirical knowledge and mental representations at the same time."

Televisual reception in particular develops competences in the knowledge of image language, in the decoding of audiovisual syntax, which allows for example the anticipation on the unfolding of the scenario. This screen culture is currently manifested by a strong desire concerning consumption of video content on mobile phones in particular, in what is often referred to as generation Y [HUN 06].

This generation Y (or Y 2.0) includes individuals born between 1976 and 1994. They are characterized by a great ability for network and team games and a screen culture developed from the age of four by video games, then the mobile phone from six years old and blogs from eight years old. This generation fully took over nomad technology. These individuals balance the traditional values by their open minds with a need for deep renewing of methods of management.

If the development of video on mobile has been quick in France. It does not achieve anything like the uses in South Korea, where mobile Internet users devote 60 minutes per day on television on mobile [LED 07].

12.5.2. *Practices of consultation in a mobile situation*

The mobility and availability of the terminal encourages the consultation of videos while traveling. According to the statistics of the operator Orange [LED 07], between 20 and 30% of consultations take place while traveling. The positioning of the television on mobile device is affirmed as television elect at home or in displacement.

Times such services are most frequently accessed are 10:00, 12:00, 17:00 and the off-peak times of classical television, which corresponds to the segmentation of a school day and to periods of travel. The places preferred, according to several recent surveys, are waiting rooms, public transport and the work place, in addition to the home. The mobile Internet user is therefore constantly linked by a breadcrumb trail to live television. The alienation is not experienced as a time and space cut from the visibility of the television set. But these data do not allow us to understand the choices and practices of mobile Internet users, or make ethnographic observations *in situ*. Benoit Cuny (Multimedia Index) therefore observed that we hardly see television use on mobile devices in the street. Julien Figeac [FIG 07] carried out 42 interviews *in situ*, in the face of each media support, on the emerging practices of subscribers of the operator Orange displacing itself in the Paris and Toulousse agglomerations.

As a result, if individuals wish to develop uses that conform to their aspirations by using mobile Internet during transport situations, they also have to put up with the constraints of neighboring passengers.

In this regard, the seated position, despite the sound that is propagated in transport in common, seems to be favorable to the standing position of the television spectator in front of his or her receiver [FIG 07].

Therefore, if the time of transport is be favorable to viewing because of a demand for continuity of programs, a move from the big screen towards the small portable screen, the interpenetration of the public sphere and the private sphere obliges us to permanently put up with the constraints of neighbors.

12.5.3. *Self-produced partners of publishing*

Self-produced content (often self-programmed) constitutes one of the most spectacular emerging practices of MPT with live television, video-on-demand and specific content [LED 07]. This new content contributes to the astonishing diversification of sharing possibilities that has recently become available on the mobile device. It is convenient here to define the mobile television podcast, which is at the crossroads of three strong generation demands among 18-25 year olds: the Internet, mobile and iPod. The podcast comes from the contraction of iPod and broadcasting. It is a matter of a hybrid service (a mixture of television for distribution and iPod video for viewing) currently tested across EPOC, an open platform, the creation of which we still find follows the economic model.

With this concept, the mobile phone podcast becomes a sort of multimedia jukebox capable of permanently downloading video and audio programs, which can be viewed at any time. In push-to-store mode, the content is literally pushed in the memory of the terminal.

Amateur producers therefore conceive, in this enlarged web associating hereafter Internet and mobile, self-produced videos that they can if need be send to the editors, in the framework of copyright and Creative Commons notably, with respect to conditions of citation (ownership rights, indication of the source of the author). French television channels like TFI, LCI, Direct8 and CanalJ quickly seized this new format of broadcasting, and since this time journalists have been creating their own videocasts and videoblogs.

One of the key questions is that of modalities of a cooperation between these videocast creators and multimedia publishers. Actually it is necessary to write the script, record it, ensure the assembly, house it, and reference it on portals. Benoit Cuny, director of Multimedia Index content, prefers to bank on a partnership by considering that these self-produced videos can be integrated in catalogs of the enterprise that is positioned as content aggregator. This integration is not the object of a compensation. This partnership "drains the audience". Multimedia Index is therefore more and more frequently solicited by young directors. These contributors then have their content published on dedicated sites, therefore benefiting from an opening and a viewing on mobile. This content has been accessible exclusively since summer 2007 when Dailymotion and entered a partnership with the operator. Thousands of videos, the ergonomics of which was adapted to the size of the screen of mobile devices, are available on 3G and 3G+ networks. This type of service is available from a free, downloadable application. The cost of data transport remains with the client, which is reduced by subscriptions and is partly financed by advertising. According to Income consulting, the market for publicity on mobiles (mpublicity) will thus have increased by 45% in 2009.

12.6. Conclusion

The quality of the signal received, and in particular the absence of noise, reveals at one extreme a set of industrial and political choices and at another that of the quality of the images. The technical obstacles are progressively being ironed out, the signal conveyed in transit from the transmitter to the receiver without the latter having to worry about network changes, because of their interoperability. It is the television service software that manages successive connections. However, an inequality of access to the most advanced digital technology remains. This inequality can arouse incomprehension for mobile Internet users who have a heterogeneous quality of reception.

Digital processing allows the mobile device to be inscribed in a network of screens through which the mobile Internet user conserves a permanent link with information understood as a measure of the freedom of choice we have when we select a message. One of the aims of the improvement of the capacity of the channel and screen ergonomics is to liberate itself from the constraints of space and time, because of the availability of content. It also aims to allow access to a wider choice of services that are not exclusively resumed at the taking back of images from the big television set. To the original audiovisual content stemming from young, specialized companies are added amateur videos accessible on dedicated sites in a framework of exclusive partnership between some operators and publishers of the shared video service. Videos are open to discovery and enable us to put an end to the looped images broadcast by the channels.

In any state of case, the rise in television services on mobile devices is part of a larger phenomenon of deconstruction-reconstruction of the televisual space, already transformed in depth by video on demand. For many, the desire for video and television on mobile devices should be eased in the months and years to come. The debate and surveys about eventual harmful effects, on younger users in particular, of electromagnetic waves transmitted by 3G+ mobile devices, mainly during telephone conversations, has only just begun.

Thanks in particular to:

- Benoît Cuny, content manager, Index Multimedia;
- Julien Génétine, product manager, Samsung Electronics France;
- The Institute of Economic and Social Research on Telecommunications.

12.7. Bibliography

[ALL 05] ALLIANCE TICS, Union des syndicats des industries, des technologies de l'information, de la communication et des services associées, *Enjeux de l'Introduction de la Télévision Mobile en France*, Paris La Défense, December 2005.

[AMI 91] AMIEL V., "Chroniques de l'écran qui passe (Sur une tendance contemporaine à la superposition des images)", in: P. CHAMBAT, P. LÉVY (eds), *Les Nouveaux Outils du Savoir*, Descartes Publishing, Paris, 1991, p. 177-184.

[BAL 06] BALKIA-TABARY L., "Transferts d'images à la télévision. Dynamiques répétitives et formes de réception", *Communication et Langages*, vol. 149, p. 15-27, September 2006.

[BAL 07] BALTZ C., "Tous shannoniens?", *Racines Oubliées des Sciences de la Communication*, vol 48, p. 91, Hermès, Paris, 2007.

[BAT 02] BATTU D., *Télécommunications, Principes, Infrastructures et Services,* Dunod/01 Informatique, Paris, 2002.

[CHA 06] CHAREAUDEAU P., "Des catégories pour l'humour"*, Humour et Médias, Définition, Genres et Culture, Questions de Communication*, University of Nancy Press, Nancy, 2006, p. 7-17.

[DUM 62] DUMAZEDIER J., *Vers une Société du Loisir*, Le Seuil, Paris, 1963.

[ECR 07] ECRAN TOTAL*, Un Français sur trois Pratique la Convergence*, vol. 681, Paris, 2007, p. 1.

[FIG 07] FIGEAC J., "La configuration des pratiques d'information selon la logique des situations", SociéTIC, document coordinated by: P. FLICHY, F. MOATTY (eds), *Réseaux*, vol. 25, no. 143, p. 19-44, 2007.

[GAI 97] GAILLARD J.P., *Psychologie de l'Homme au Travail. Les Relations Homme-machine*, Dunod, Paris, 1997.

[GEN 08] GENVO S., "Histoire et culture des jeux vidéo", in: S. GENVO (ed.), *Les jeux Vidéo, un bien Culturel?, MediaMorphoses*, vol. 22, Ina-Armand Colin, Paris, p. 21, 2008.

[HEN 04] HÉNOCQUE B., "Les messages électroniques des intranets d'entreprise: médiations techniques et médiations socio-culturelles", in: F. MOURLHON-DALLIES, F. RAKOTONOELINA, S. REBOUL-TOURÉ (eds), *Les Discours de l'Internet: Nouveaux Corpus, Nouveaux Modèles?, Les Carnets du Cediscor 8,* Presses de la Sorbonne Nouvelle, Paris, 2004, p. 165-176.

[HUN 06] HUNTLEY R., *The World According to Y: Inside the New Adult Generation*, Crows Nest, Allen and Unwin, Montreal, 2006.

[JOS 06] JOST F., *Comprendre la Télévision*, Armand Colin, Paris, 2006.

[LED 07] LE DROGO C., "TV mobile, la renaissance ou le néo-classique de la télé?", *Bulletin de l'IREST*, vol. 103, p. 219-223, 2007.

[LEV 98] LÉVY P., "Le mouvement social de la cyberculture", *Cyberculture, Rapport au Conseil de l'Europe*, Odile Jacob, Paris, 1998. Available at: http://www.archipress .org/levy/cyberculture/biblio.htm, accessed October 5, 2009.

[MIE 90] MIÈGE B., “La consommation culturelle: déplacement vers les pratiques privatives”, *La Société Conquise par la Communication*, PUG, Grenoble, p. 22-29, 1990.

[MIE 06] MIÈGE B., “Billet irrévérencieux sur l'économique et le communicationnel”, in: J. FOURCHY, P. FROISSARD (eds), *Economie et Communication*, *Réseaux*, vol. 44, p. 153-156, 2006.

[OBS 05] OBSERVATOIRE EUROPÉEN DE L’AUDIOVISUEL, MULTIMEDIA ET NOUVELLES TECHNOLOGIES, *Yearbook*, Annual Volume 4, Conseil de l’Europe, 2005.

[PAS 99] PASQUIER D., JOUET J. (eds), *Les Jeunes et l'Écran*, *Réseaux*, vol. 17, no. 92-93, 1999.

[SAB 07] SABATHÉ F., “Télévision mobile améliorée. TV Mobile, la Renaissance ou le Néo-Classique de la Télé?”, *Bulletin de l'IREST*, vol. 103, p. 218, 2007.

[SHA 49] SHANNON C.E., WAEVER W., *Théorie Mathématique de la Communication*, University of Illinios, 1949, Classic Collection of Human Sciences, CEPL, Paris Retz, 1975.

List of Authors

Muriel AMAR
Urfist de Paris
Ecole nationale des Chartes
France

Agnès CAMUS-VIGUÉ
Bpi – Centre Georges Pompidou
Paris
France

Stéphane CHAUDIRON
University of Lille 3
France

Viviane COUZINET
LERASS
University of Toulouse 3

Amos DAVID
LORIA
University of Nancy 2
France

Christophe EVANS
Bpi – Centre Georges Pompidou
Paris
France

Françoise GAUDET
Bpi – Centre Georges Pompidou
Paris
France

Luc GRIVEL
University of Paris 1
France

Bruno HÉNOCQUE
University of Le Havre
France

Madjid IHADJADENE
University of Paris 10
France

Sylvie LELEU-MERVIEL
University of Valenciennes and Hainaut-Cambrésis
France

Jean-Paul METZGER
ENSSIB
Villeurbanne
France

Fabrice PAPY
Document numérique & Usages
University of Paris 8
France

Sophie PÈNE
René Descartes University
Paris
France

Alexandre SERRES
University of Upper Brittany
Rennes
France

Brigitte SIMONNOT
Paul Verlaine University
Metz
France

Yves THÉPAUT
University of Rennes 2
University of Paris 1
France

Philippe USEILLE
University of Valenciennes and Hainaut-Cambrésis
France

Index

U, V, Y